The Yellow Sparrow

The Yellow Sparrow

Memoir of a Transgender Woman

Santa Khurai

Translated from the Manipuri by
Rubani Yumkhaibam

SPEAKING
TIGER

SPEAKING TIGER BOOKS LLP
125A, Ground Floor, Shahpur Jat, near Asiad Village,
New Delhi 110049

First published in Manipuri as *Sendrang Hangampan*
First published in English by Speaking Tiger in 2023

Copyright © Santa Khurai 2023

ISBN: 978-93-5447-415-6
eISBN: 978-93-5447-407-1

10 9 8 7 6 5 4 3 2 1

*This book is dedicated to the
transgender community of Manipur*

Contents

Author's Note   *ix*

Prologue   1

The Yellow Sparrow   5

Epilogue   258

Acknowledgements   295

Author's Note

This memoir is based on various events, trials and tribulations I have faced in the past many years. In writing this memoir I have not borrowed style and content from the writings of other authors. Rather, I have chronicled the events of my life in the simplest manner. Looking back at the events recorded here, I realised that Manipuri society has changed in many ways, and along with these changes, the conditions of Nupi Maanbis or transgender women, as they would be known in English, in this region has also changed. Remembering attitudes and social conditions of the past gives new impetus to the present, and most importantly, a new hope.

From my younger years till the present, I have had to face events of a different nature and magnitude. Disappointment, despair, lies, mockery, disrespect have been a constant part of my life. But I carried on living and tried to paint a happy face through it all. At the same time, I was aware that I could never live the happy life that men and women around me lived. Now, I reckon such obstacles were crucial moments of learning and resilience.

My father constantly expressed his displeasure at my

feminine nature, while my mother felt humiliated in front of neighbours, relatives and friends. None of the hardships the three of us experienced were our fault, each of us was right in our own way.

There were countless differences between my life and experience as a woman and society's conception of a woman. This gap led people to condemn and isolate me, they could not accept me as part of their society. I have chronicled the pain and suffering I felt in the wake of such an indifferent gaze and hatred all about me. Since I was considered a person who was 'different' from others, not many people were interested in listening to my problems and frustrations. This suppressed pain and anger led to a feeling of relief and bliss the moment I started reliving those moments and writing this memoir. The feeling of lightness was akin to what one experiences when sharing one's burdens with friends.

I have many happy memories too from my adolescent years, mostly the jokes and conversations I had with my Nupi Maanbi friends. For the longest time, I have been desirous of sharing these stories with the world. It has been my conviction that others will also feel the charm and warmth of these stories and anecdotes. But I could not share my treasured moments with others in earlier days, I was branded a 'homo' and I laboured under the fear that people would mock me rather than laugh with me. The only humble satisfaction was to record all those events in my personal diary, and thus relive those moments of happiness and friendship.

Once day, after a bitter disagreement with my father, I wrote a narrative poem called 'The Yellow Sparrow'. My mother tried to mediate between the two of us, but she could never stand up for me strongly enough owing to the social mileu that was purely hostile towards me. It was also true that my mother was completely alone in her efforts to defend me, this was her lonely suffering.

Re-reading the poem brought back images of the mango tree in our courtyard. The day after the quarrel, I came out and sat despondently under the tree. My mother was sitting in the portico, with tears in her eyes. She murmured something inaudible to me. A few sparrows were eating the rice in a *phoura* placed in one corner of the courtyard. With the hem of her shawl, my mother scared the sparrows away. All except one sparrow flew away. I went near this odd sparrow and found that one of its wings was broken, hanging loose by its side. The sight of this helpless sparrow saddened me. I picked it up and put it in an earthen pot which I hung by a thread from one of the branches of the mango tree. Ruminating about the sparrow who was 'different' and could not fly with the rest of the flock, made me draw a parallel with my own condition. This particular incident, which followed the quarrel with my father, and my mother's distress, inspired my poem, 'The Yellow Sparrow'.

Prologue

In the eaves of a thatched house
There was a nest of sparrows
The straw of the roof kept the nest warm.
When the rays of the morning sun
Shone through the thatch,
The sparrows chirped merrily,
Welcoming the new day.

Among the sparrows, there was a mother sparrow
And one hatchling
Every day, the mother sparrow
Would pluck out the feathers
From her child's tender body with her sharp beak.
The innocent young sparrow cried out
Each time her beak pierced him
But he did not know why
His mother was causing him so much pain.

Like other sparrows, he wanted to fly out of the nest
To seek food and play with his friends
But the mother forbade him from playing
In the company of others
And his featherless body left him handicapped
He could not fly.

Each time the baby sparrow
Looked into his mother's eyes
He saw her anxious heart filled with fear
And helplessness
She would be calm only when he was beside her.
The young sparrow never asked the reason
For her inexpressible pain
And the mother kept her worries buried.

His heart was filled with disappointment
As he saw other birds flying in their colourful flocks
His head was filled with countless queries
Why?
What defect of nature or accident
Has caged me inside the nest?
Why does my mother spread her wings over me
And keep me unseen and unheard from the world
Outside this nest?

With each new day
The mother plucked more feathers
1, 10, 20....
Until she finally reached the corner
Of the young sparrow's eyes.
Unable to bear the pain,
The young sparrow finally voiced its protest.

But the apprehensive mother
Plucked more feathers
Thus new conflicts were born
Between the mother and the child
And grew intense, like a blazing wild fire.
One day
Through tears, the mother said:
You are different from the other sparrows,
Your innocent body is spewing a host of
Yellow feathers, incessantly, alarmingly.
Your yellow feathers are spreading
All over your body till the corner of your eyes.
I have lost the courage to pluck your feathers anymore.
Unlike any other sparrow, you are born with yellow feathers
My worries have come to nothing
They will ostracise you from the rest of the flock,
You will live friendless and lonely for the rest of your life.

Thus the mother wept as she related her sorrow
From that day onwards
The young sparrow came to know himself
Burdened with the tragedy of uniqueness,
He lived his life—lonely and isolated.

But the shining yellow hue of his feathers
Could not be kept hidden
As time went by.
He gazed at his own feathers
That Mother Nature had made unique.
The golden hue of the yellow feathers
Reflected clean and bright
Though drenched by the cold winter rain.

The yellow sparrow fell in love
With his own molten loveliness,
The yellow feathers that were shunned by the world
Golden and glorious
A breath of joy escaped from his beak,
And he broke into a happy song
My feathers are the Yellow Gold,
I am the Yellow Sparrow
Whoever saw him called 'the Yellow Sparrow',
The colour yellow became his identity.

The Yellow Sparrow

My memory goes back to the summer of 1989. It was the beginning of May; I must have been about sixteen years old at the time.

The high school examinations had finally come to an end. Suddenly I had plenty of leisure time—no books, no studies, no school. I waited lackadaisically for the results, I was not too concerned about what the outcome would be. On one of those days, I decided to pay a visit to Ebok, my maternal grandmother. The occasion was the yearly *chaklon katpa*, the ritual meal offered to the deity of the clan. As far as I can remember now, it was my first visit to Ebok's house. I still have a vivid memory of the house—it was situated at the entrance of the Kongpal neighbourhood. The first thing one saw was the imposing *sangoi*, an outhouse with a roof of aluminium sheets, that stood majestically in the spacious courtyard. The courtyard was surrounded on three sides by living quarters that also had aluminium roofs. The eastern side of the house was flanked by a thick cordon of giant reeds and Indian cedars, and to the south of the *sangoi*, there grew a big *chorphon*, a Ceylon olive tree. A small lane ran outside the compound wall beyond which lay the Kongba river. As I recollect it, the basin of the Kongba river was very narrow. I did not see children playing along its basin, which struck me as unusual; river basins were usually the playground for children those days. Only a few babul and ficus trees stood timid and deserted on the bare banks of the river.

All the men present at the *chaklon katpa* ceremony wore *pheijoms,* a dhoti-like piece of clothing. Amidst this uniformity, two men stood out. While all the menfolk wore the *pheijom* in the traditional manner, these two had worn it in the lungi style, that is, the hem of the *pheijom* almost reached their ankles. They had also covered their heads with white *enaphis,* the shawl worn by Meitei women on religious occasions, leaving only their faces bare. They appeared quite extraordinary to me, and I was filled with curiosity about them. In the course of the day, I came to know their names—Romen and Manimohon. After everyone else had gone inside, they continued to linger at the gate of the house. It was evident to me that they were waiting for someone important to appear. Both men were deep in conversation, oblivious to their surroundings. After a while, a man arrived on a bicycle. He wore a pair of dhoti pants and had a sling bag strung across one shoulder. The two men must have been waiting for this newcomer. They greeted him with affectionate banter and then accompanied him in the direction of the house. The newcomer had a slim, oval face, a thin layer of powder on his cheeks and a light hue of crimson on his lips. Later, I got to know that the newcomer's name was Denao. A modest patch of skin glimpsed through the open collar of his shirt revealed a fair complexion. After parking the bicycle at the corner of the *sangoi,* Denao and his friends disappeared into a room.

The ritual meal was ready, all the guests at the ceremony had taken their seats. But the trio who had aroused my curiosity was not to be seen in that august crowd. They were huddled together in a room, engaged in some private conversation. A middle-aged woman stood at the door of the room and called out in a peevish tone, 'You, homos, come out now. Everyone is ready for the meal. What mischief are you hatching in the room?' (In those days, in Manipuri society, 'homo' was the term used for all effeminate men and boys—anyone whose mannerisms were like a woman's, or even men who were controlled by their wives.)

A voice from inside the room called out, 'Be patient, we are coming.'

The woman replied, 'You have all sorts of replies. Does anybody understand you? It is useless talking with you.'

Another from the group replied, 'Memcha, you are pure annoyance. Aren't you the one pointlessly replying? We said that we were coming.'

When they finally came out of the room, Denao had changed into a *pheijom*, which he wore in the same manner as his two friends. It was evident that even when they wore *pheijoms*, they adapted that article of male clothing to suit their peculiar style. They sat in a row along the wall of the *sangoi*, and I sat down in the row in front. While they ate, they continued to talk in muted voices. Every now and again, they would glance at the immediate surroundings, make a mysterious gesture followed by a subtle nudge at each other and covert chuckles. It appeared as though they had some secret knowledge of their milieu. To me, their gestures suggested a spirit of mirth and gaiety.

An elderly woman sitting behind them chastised them, 'Why are you giggling?'

One among the trio impudently replied, 'Well, you are old and look like a tattered wicker basket. You surely would not understand why I laughed!' Those who heard the rejoinder broke into loud laughter. The elderly woman had no choice but to laugh. 'Nobody can compete against a homo's rebuttals,' she said.

Whatever I heard and saw that day—the group of three men uniquely dressed and addressed as 'homo', the candid exchange of light yet bold banter between them and elder women—was very new to me. It was true that some people did call me 'homo' at school, but the word was never mentioned in my domestic environment. Hearing it used so casually by everyone at the *chaklon katpa* venue filled me with both fear and an indescribable nervousness. 'Homo' was a derogatory term, associated with all kinds of obnoxious characters, like men whose behaviour, physical features and character was deviant from the conventional idea of manliness or masculinity. Whenever anyone called me by that term, it made me feel angry and ashamed.

After the meal, all the guests left one by one. Ema, my mother, Eche, my elder sister, and I stayed a while longer on Ebok's insistence. Meanwhile, standing on the edge of the *mangol* (roofed verandah), Eney, my aunt, called out to someone: 'Nupi, nupi.' In a short while, a girl my Eche's age or a little older, chewing *kwa,* a paan of beetle leaves and areca nuts, nonchalantly walked towards Eney. The girl asked, 'Why are you shouting my name? Do you know the tone of your voice makes you sound like a crow?'

Eney sighed, 'My children have no manners.' After this brief exchange I came to know that the girl was Eney's daughter. The girl asked, 'Ema, who is going to clean the *korfus?*' She was referring to the traditional aluminium vessels used for cooking food.

Eney replied, 'You can request Romen and Denao to clean the *korfus.*'

The girl shot back, 'You can ask them yourself. I do not want to talk with homos.'

Eney enquired, 'Where are they? Have they left?'

The girl replied, 'They must be in their room, talking about men, as usual.'

Eney scolded her daughter again, 'Shut up now.'

After this sharp exchange between mother and daughter, the girl returned to her room. At that moment a realisation materialised in my mind—Romen is also a homo, like I am. However, I could not understand what 'talking about men' meant. What were they talking about? I was curious. All these questions reminded me of Marjing, a boy I was once attracted to. What were my feelings about him? What was that attraction about? I could not give a name to my feelings for him. Regardless of all the unanswerable questions and emotions, the strong attraction towards Marjing lived on in my mind for a long time.

Denao and Manimohon had changed into pants, while Romen wore a *haophi*, a traditional woollen shawl, in the style of a *phanek* or sarong, and a top that had a boat neck, like the ones women wore. Cleaning the *korfus* was a tiresome task nobody was willing to perform that day, but the three men agreed without complaint. They picked up the *korfus* one by one and headed towards the Kongba river. Maintaining a safe distance, I followed them to the river, the only place where they could clean the humungous *korfus*. Without attracting their attention, I took up a position as close to them as possible, pretending to be an ordinary stranger playing at the riverside. To complete this impression, I picked up a stick and began to poke around in the tufts of grass on the river bank.

They did not seem tired. They talked and laughed as they worked, and their laughter appeared to feed them with new energy. My curiosity about them growing like an organism inside me; I wanted to be a part of the conversations that had kept them in such good spirits throughout the morning. However, there were a few barriers—I was a stranger to them; moreover, they were much older than me. There did not seem to be any ground on which I could start a conversation with them. My desire to be a part of their world was simultaneously overshadowed by the fear that my parents would reprimand me for my association with them.

All these anxieties and problems could not kill the newfound longing to be included in their world. I wanted to be like them in every manner, as though a mysterious bond had tied me to them. But that day, the best I could do was to position myself at the periphery of their world. Their intimate conversations, which I longed to hear, could not reach me from that distance. Nevertheless, my effort was not without a humble reward—I could overhear them when they raised their voices to engage in a light banter with a few married women working on the other side of the river.

One of the women asked: 'Why are you made to clean dirty *korfus*? Your soft hands will get chapped. All those eligible young men might find chapped hands unattractive.'

One of the homos replied: 'Actually, we are under training for the tough routine that will inevitably follow marriage.'

The woman asked: 'Good, then where are those men who will marry you?'

One of them replied: 'Mine is from Wangkhei.'

Another replied: 'I do not have a man. But I know how to compensate for the lack of a husband in my life. I will procure a huge, white marble block from somewhere, and place a *kundo pareng* on it, so that I don't remain a spinster all my life. You see, that is also a valid marriage.' A *kundo pareng* was a wreath of non-scented jasmine flowers used in the Meitei marriage ceremony.

Everyone on both sides of the river seemed to enjoy the banter. The trio continued cleaning the *korfus*, while the women looked on. After a short silence, one of them looked up in the direction of the bridge nearby and exclaimed aloud, 'Tamo Element, buy us *kwa*.'

As I looked in the same direction, I saw a well-dressed man in his thirties. He was Element, his receding hairline was easily recognisable. I knew him to be a well-educated man from our neighbourhood, the kind of person who read international magazines; from these magazines, he must have understood a bit about homos. He was very friendly towards them and somehow always treated them like women.

Element turned his head in no particular direction, 'Who spoke to me just now?'

Pointing at Romen, one of the trio replied: 'This beauty, the one as charming as a plump pomelo fruit.'

Element said, 'Fine, come along.'

The group took a break from *korfu* cleaning to join Element at a nearby paan-dukan, a small shop that sold betel leaves and other eatables on the roadside. I also followed them. Standing at the far corner of the lane that ran alongside the paan-dukan, I observed them. It was not an effective hideout but I still did not have the confidence to go near them. Denao and Manimohon went inside the paan-dukan, while Romen and Element stayed outside, absorbed in their conversation. It must have been a very interesting discussion. I was so engrossed in watching them that I didn't hear a man shouting from behind me, 'Watch out!' The loud interruption attracted the attention of Element, Romen, Denao, Manimohon, and possibly everyone else in the vicinity, but I only cared about these four. At that moment, my existence was revealed to them.

Denao was the first to comment. 'Romen, isn't this the child who sat beside us at the meal?' In the seconds that followed, I saw Romen's countenance clearly for the first time. His features were distinct—he looked like a young Meitei girl, he had a chubby, round face, and slightly long, silky hair.

Romen replied: 'Oh! This is Eche Sanahanbi's son.' Then addressing me, he said 'What are you doing there? Come here.' His words gave me a sudden feeling of triumph. I might not have known of his existence before that day, but he was not a stranger to mine. This momentarily made me feel a little more confident about myself. I was aware of my diffident personality. I was shyer than most people my age. This was manifested in my initial reluctance to approach them even when they were encouraging me to do so.

Fortunately, Romen's insistence finally gave me the courage to go up to them. But the moment I drew near, I was overcome with bashfulness again. I was certain that everyone present at the scene had their eyes fixed on me. I was also burdened by the fear that Ema and Eche would catch me in the act of talking with people whom everyone called homo. I knew I was one of them. Indeed, this awareness must have driven my desire to be with them. Amid this newly awakened awareness, I asked myself—Why did this inexplicable vacillating feeling cripple me at the thought of being close to them? Another unsettling question arose in my mind—why were they different and tabooed? As I confronted these questions in my mind, the answers came in a rush—the conflicting emotions stemmed from my fear of being discovered, from the fear of being seen as 'homo' in my neighbourhood and family, from the fear of being seen with homos. Ultimately, it was the probability of alienation from normal society that bound me in a snarl of constraints. After all, 'homo' meant a world of abject humiliation that stripped one of respect, love, and humanity in society.

I wanted to ask: Homo, who are you? How did you begin your journey? What are your faults? What makes you abominable in the eyes of the world? Everyone looks upon you as a showpiece, a circus item. Many exploit and throw you away without the slightest remorse. Is this how you play your part in this world? You seem to float incessantly on the turbulent waves of the river that doesn't have a bank or an ocean to flow into.

Turning to Denao, Romen said, 'Be nice to this boy. Buy him any snacks of his choice.' Denao beckoned to me to come to him.

Most teenagers my age had their own friends with whom they socialised, went to the cinema and local concerts and so on, quite independently of their parents. But, due to a lack of exposure to those outside my immediate family and neighbourhood, a certain level of naivety informed my interactions with people. My lack of social skills was apparent from the way I talked and behaved. But that day, despite my inherent awkwardness, I responded to Denao's invitation.

'Give me another *kwa*,' Denao told the shopkeepr. The *kwa* was meant for me.

Romen interrupted him, 'Are you out of your mind? The boy is only a child. How do you think he will eat *kwa*?'

'You think this is a little child!' Denao responded.

Their dispute over my status—a child or a boy or a teenager—was embarrassing for me. Something told me at that moment that I was not a child anymore, rather I was old enough to show maturity and confidence, and to eat *kwa*, perhaps. However, Romen's objection seemed to have changed Denao's mind. 'Well, boy, do you want to eat biscuits?' he asked.

Again, my shyness made me mute, while Denao persisted with another alternative, 'Do you want toffees?'

'I am fine, I do not want to eat anything,' I politely replied.

Denao did not give up. 'You can have NP chewing gums, the ones that have a green covering.' He continued his chatter, 'Where are you from, child?'

I replied, 'I am from Khurai Lamlong.'

Next he asked me, 'What is your name?'

I replied, 'Abothey, I am also called Santa.'

Denao said, 'Ebecha, I see something of importance here. This child's voice is distinctly different, this means something. Isn't it so?' Ebecha was another name for Romen. I came to realise later that these people have affectionate feminine names for each other.

Romen replied pensively, 'It's true, his mother is worried, and she talks a lot about him. He is studying at Don Bosco, a very bright student.'

Denao exclaimed, 'Oh! This is the one you talked about.'

Romen concurred, 'Yes, this is the one.'

Hearing Romen talk about me with such familiarity created so many questions in my mind. I had always believed that Ema did not know about my true identity which was hidden in the deepest recesses of my being. However, Romen's knowledge of me, which he had learned from Ema, contradicted my presumption about her ignorance. Also, the fact that Ema talked to Romen about me was beyond my imagination. So I was not, after all, a total stranger to Romen, although he was a sort of mystery to me. I also realised that they were talking about me like I was a homo. It was a moment that would have an impact on me for the rest of my life. Through this conversation, listening to Romen and Denao, I confirmed to myself that I was a homo. Their conversation lifted my spirit, as though I was allowed to feel emotions denied to me for the longest time.

Finally, I said, 'Da Romen, I will go now.'

Denao interrupted me, 'No, don't call her Da, call her Eche.'*

Denao's bold demand that I should call Romen 'Eche', sister, made me laugh. The sound of my own laughter surprised me, I had never laughed so uninhibitedly before. Perhaps a new energy was born in that gathering of people who were so different from others.

After that brief and heady interaction, I returned to Ebok's house. Perhaps they were still talking about me long after I had left. On my part I could not stop thinking about Romen—his soft complexion, the arch of his eyebrows that rivalled the curve of a *hangen,* the slender, curved frame of the traditional Manipuri fishing net. Romen was a unique, beautiful homo.

At the end of that day of so many different experiences and emotions, I reached home. However, the events of the day continued to live in my consciousness and became a source of daydreaming. Fear of my family's disapproval could not stop me from desiring the company of the trio that had impressed me so deeply. In the midst of my turbulent dreams, the tag of homo weighed down heavily on my troubled conscience. My mind felt restive and wandered away to imagining events that had not happened yet—even if I became their friend by a benevolent stroke of fate, what would I talk about with them? What would be the

---

*The dichotomy in the use of the pronoun 'he' for feminine males or transgender women, is because the Manipuri langauge is a gender neutral language; the same term is used for both genders who are identified as men or women through their given names. For the purposes of this book, the pronoun 'he' has been used for feminine males. Santa herself began using the pronoun 'she' for herself much later (*see* Epilogue).

subject of our conversations? What if my neighbours came to know about my friendship with Romen and his friends? I ruminated on the repercussions of the friendship, without finding any solace for my fears and apprehensions.

The next day I waited for an opportunity to visit Ebok's house, the only place where I could meet Romen. Leaving the house would definitely attract the attention of both family members and elders in the neighbourhood. Somebody might see me leaving and report it to my parents. But I could not give up the hope of meeting Romen, and waited for an opportune moment. The moment indeed arrived around 11 a.m, when the neighbourhood looked deserted. It was usually the time of the day when the elders retired for a brief siesta. I took advantage of this moment to slink out of the house, and headed towards Kongpal on my bicycle. It was also very important that there was nobody at Ebok's house at that time. But the moment I walked inside the gate, Eney, my aunt, greeted me. She was surprised to see me, but thought that I must have come on an errand from Ema. To avoid any questions about my presence there, I instead asked if Ebok was at home.

My enquiry about Ebok was merely a cover-up for my secret plan to meet Romen. I knew very well that Ebok's daily routine centered around the Lamlong Keithel market. Every morning she went to the market to sell vegetables; oftentimes, she visited us on her way home. According to this predictable routine, it was futile to come looking for Ebok at this time of the day. Moreover, I was also aware of the risk involved in my venture—if Ebok came to know about my visit to her house, she would certainly tell Ema. I was treading a perilous path.

So, Eney's reply did not surprise me, 'Ebok is not at home now. She has gone to the market early in the morning.

She will come back only in the late afternoon. Did your mother send you for something?'

I replied, 'No. I have come to pick *chorphons*, from the olive tree.'

She exclaimed, 'You have come to pick *chorphons*! You could have asked your Ebok, and she would get them for you tomorrow. Did you tell your mother that you would be coming here?' She was intrigued that I was not at school at that time of the day. 'Didn't you go to school today?'

I replied, 'Eney, I told Ema. We don't go to school these days, the final exams just got over.'

It was a big *chorphon* tree. Eney could not reach the branches even with a long bamboo stick. She called out to Romen to come and pick the fruit for me. 'Amujao, Romen! Help Sanahanbi's son, he wants to pick *chorphons*.' In truth, who cared about *chorphons*! My only goal was to meet Romen. So, when Eney asked Romen to help me, she unknowingly helped me fulfill my goal.

Amujao, Romen's younger brother, was the first to come out of the house, but he was not the one I wanted. I was wishing for Romen to appear on the scene. In the next moment, almost like a miracle, Romen suddenly appeared from the back of the house, along with another person. Romen was wearing a lungi, his head was covered with a scarf. There were knitting needles in his hands that indicated that he had been knitting.

Romen exclaimed, 'Oh! You are here?'

I replied, 'I have come to pick *chorphons*.'

Romen took the bamboo stick from Eney's hands and struck at one heavy branch of the tree. Amujao and I collected the *chorphons* as they fell to the ground. Romen said that I would need a polythene bag to carry the fruit. He invited me to come and sit in his room for a while.

It was a bright, hot day and it would be nice to rest in the room before I returned. He introduced me to the new person, Borajao, who was also a homo. Romen called him Bobo. Borajao, who was my age, was very masculine, which made him look very different from Romen with his beautiful features.

From that day on, I regularly visited Romen's house, that is to say, Ebok's house—Romen was her grandson, and he and his father, Ebok's eldest son, and his mother, my Eney, all lived together. Inspite of this relationship, visiting him was not an easy task. I was always under strict surveillance, as my parents didn't want me to associate with girls or homos. And Romen was known to everyone in the Khurai area as a homo, he was very open about his feminine nature. So I had to plan things carefully. Ebok left her house to go to the market at around 10 a.m. and returned at 2 p.m. During this time, my siblings would go the neighbours' homes to play with their friends, eat their mid-day meal and so. It was only during these hours that I could slip out and meet Romen.

Gradually the gulf between Romen and myself that I had imagined to be unbreachable, seemed to be getting narrower. His friends also extended great kindness and affection towards me. They told me stories of their male lovers, and the subsequent pain and heartbreak they had endured. These stories introduced me to the inner world of homos, mainly their feminine nature, simplicity, resilience, and the close and loving relationship they shared amongst each other. I started identifying my emotions with theirs. Moreover, was I not one of them? They did not understand English well, so once in a while they asked me to translate the love notes written in greeting cards that their lovers sent them. And, thus, I became their translator. On one occasion, they asked me to read the messages written at the end of a love letter from one of the male lovers—*You are my sweetheart, love never ends, love is the language of the unspeakable heart.* They did not know what these sweet words meant, but they were not content with not knowing. Such was their spirit. I was glad to be of use to them, it made me closer to their world. They often complained that they could not get married to their male lovers. Despite their deep desire to be in a loving conjugal relationship with men, the latter often discarded them.

Gradually, the world of homos started revealing itself to me. They did not want to be a part of the common crowd. They existed as a closed community within which they shared their lives and communicated exclusively with each other. Their constant refrain was, 'We homos know that our lives are difficult, but we cannot shed off our identity.' Their perspective on life educated me on the biases from which they suffered. One aspect of their candid acceptance of life was never-ending humour. Life's defeats and trials did not deter them from dreaming and living. One amongst them would say, 'We homos are fragrant *chinichampra,* yang yang vines; drones cannot desire us, we bloom in the passionate longing of wasps.' Another one would say, 'The jasmine flower is exquisite, but cannot be offered to the gods. But again, a marriage cannot be consecrated without the wreath of jasmine flowers. We are beautiful and precious, though we are unacceptable in our own homes.'

I thought of Romen, who would often cry when his family members used harsh terms while quarelling—words like '*Ngamark shamarak* (in between fish and animal)', 'sissy', 'homo, you better die'. But it was also true that they would not stay angry for long, somehow, all the siblings would once again eat meals together, and if Romen was upset, one of the family members would console him and try to make him understand why they were rude to him. Though they did not like his feminity and openness about his true nature, he was always considered a member of Ebok's family. It was the same for most homos in Manipur, but it is also true that most of the love and gentle concern came from the women in the family—our mothers and sisters—not the men. It was a period of vital importance in my life, it seemed that the seeds of the future were sown in those moments. Till my last breath, I will never forget those days. One by one, the number of my homo friends increased. They affectionately called me Santa.

It was spring, the season of Lai Haraoba (a festival dedicated to Unmang Lai, the pantheon of deities of the Meitei indigenous Sanamahi religion). One noon, a beautiful young homo called Maibi Macha visited Romen while I was sitting at the latter's house. He wore an olive-coloured shirt and a pair of grey pants. Maibi Macha had a comely bearing. He was known among Romen's friends as Sonam. He was from Lamlong, Lainingthou Leirak. As soon as Maibi Macha came to know that I was also from Lamlong, he said that we could go to Lai Haraoba at the Puthiba ground together. Romen casually asked, 'Is Khamba Maibi coming?'

Maibi Macha replied, 'Yes.' Observing me intently, Maibi Macha said that Khamba Maibi's facial features were similar to mine. Romen also looked at me and concurred with Maibi Macha, 'Yes, exactly. They look like siblings.' I had also heard about Khamba Maibi, he was a popular maibi, that is, a medium or shaman, but I had never seen him in person. It was also true that in the past, my neighbours looked forward to watching Khamba Maibi in any event of Lai Haraoba in our locality.

The wait for examination results continued. The abundance of free time came with the temptation to go out in the company of friends, which meant venturing into newer activities. Maibi Macha's suggestion that we should go together to Lai Haraoba was very attractive. We decided to meet at the Puthiba Lai Haraoba ground. Maibi Macha and I had become friends, but I never told him the exact location of my house. If Maibi Macha were to ever visit my house, my family would surely discover my homo identity, and I would be confronted with umpteen questions from Baba and Ema.

Ema and Baba never allowed us siblings to stay outside the house after dark. Regardless of this unwritten family rule, I agreed to meet Maibi Macha at Puthiba that same evening. The only problem was that I would not be allowed to leave the house alone, so I insisted that Eche should take me to Puthiba ground. Ema said that we would be going to Puthiba the following evening when the Henjunaha dance drama in which my sister was participating, would be performed. But I could not delay my outing by a second, let alone an evening. The second-best alternative was to request Nando, our neighbour, to take me to the Puthiba ground. Ema agreed to this. She also gave me five rupees, a fair amount of money, to buy a snack of roasted sunflower seeds. Nando was a year or so senior to me, and so he was in charge of me for the evening.

To reach the Puthiba Lai Haraoba ground, we had to pass through the dreaded Chandam neighbourhood. Usually, I did not have the courage to venture into Chandam after dark. Due to the complete absence of public facilities in our villages, such as street lighting, the neighbourhood was ominously dark after nightfall. The thick bamboo groves flanking both sides of the Chandam lane had a ghostly look. Halfway into the Chandam lane, one came across a huge mango tree that looked supernaturally imposing. The mango tree grew within the boundary of Ngangkham Ebok's homestead that lay on one side of the Chandam lane. The outer branches of the tree stretched across the lane. At the foot of the mango tree could be seen a pile of dried paddy husk that did not seem to deplete all through the year. The sheer dimensions of the tree were enough to strike fear in the hearts of onlookers. During the daytime, the tree's imposing character gave the Chandam lane the face of a desolate landscape, opaque and invincible. Our elders said that at high noon and midnight, evil spirits haunted the vicinity of the mango tree. It was also said that Ngangkham Ebok's daughter and her lover took their own lives by taking poison at the foot of the tree. The young lovers could not unite in marriage owing to the taboo of *yek-salai,* that is, the exogamous clans of the Meitei kinship. It was also said that during the daytime the bamboo trees on either side of the lane wilted and spread their branches across the ground and any innocent person stepping over the seemingly ordinary, drooping foliage would be killed by a blow of the possessed bamboo plants that would suddenly stand upright. My Pupu (grandfather) warned us that if we ever come across any wilted bamboo plants or cedar reeds, we must avoid stepping over them. He said that the evil spirit that possessed these plants was called Haigatlang.

That night no amount of mortal fear could overcome my desire to reach the Puthiba ground; my desperation overshadowed all the stories and beliefs that I had heard about the workings of the evil spirits who shared the world of human beings. The sounds and scenes of Lai Haraoba filled my ears and imagination with excitement and the thought of impending freedom weakend the impact of all the legends of the Chandam neighbourhood. I broke into a happy ditty until Nando admonished me, 'Santa, stay quiet. We are approaching the mango tree.' Suddenly, I was afraid. It seemed that all our cognitive faculties were numbed, we were not able to walk past the dreaded mango tree. Nando counselled that we must pee and fling the urine upwards towards the sky to ward off the spirits, only then would we be able to escape the horror of the moment in which we were frozen. However, I found it embarrassing to pee in his presence, or anybody's presence. I could never do it. I asked him to share his urine with me. My bizarre suggestion elicited a sharp rebuke from Nando, 'You miserable child, how hopelessly bashful you are! Are you a sissy?' I replied, 'You are also afraid.' Nando started peeing and asked me to collect some of his urine in the cup of my palm, which I did. After donating his urine to me, he collected some more in the cup of his palm. The little ritual of warding off the powerful spirits that haunted the spot consisted of throwing the urine into the air above our heads with a chant, 'I can defeat you'. After performing this act which symbolised the overpowering of the spirits, we ran towards the end of the Chandam lane, with our eyes closed. When we opened our eyes we had already reached the end of the lane. This was how we crossed the dreaded Chandam lane that night.

Nando met a few of his friends at the venue. I was not interested in socialising with his group. After looking around for Maibi Macha, I finally saw him standing under a berry tree, which was also the entry point for the men coming to watch the ritual proceedings of the Lai Haraoba. I tried to think of an excuse to disengage myself from Nando and to explore the place with Maibi Macha, just the two of us as planned. However, with Ema's strict instructions in mind, Nando had resolved to be my guardian for the entire time

I was at the Lai Haraoba. Wherever I went, Nando would follow me, unless I could think of a good reason for him to leave me alone. I told Nando that I wanted to pee.

Nando said, 'All right, I will come with you.'

I said, 'It is embarrassing for me.'

Nando replied, 'What exactly is embarrassing about it? We are boys.'

I insisted that I would go alone, which irked Nando. 'This boy is annoying. I cannot even enjoy my time here. Go to Konsam Ibomcha's house and relieve yourself.' This was the opportunity I had been waiting for. Ibomcha and I went to his house that was at a little distance towards the east of the Lai Haraoba ground. To make my excuse believable, I went inside the toilet and pretended to be peeing.

Ibomcha was notorious for pulling mischievous pranks on his friends, and that night, he lived up to his reputation. When I came out of the toilet and was looking for a way to escape from the house without being seen, he sprinkled water on me. It gave me a shock, and for a second, my heart stopped beating.

Not far from Ibomcha's house, there was a low trench. A thick growth of wild cedar bushes formed a hedge on either side of this trench. The trench was divided into two halves by a narrow lane, used by people coming to and from the Lai Haraoba ground. While I was crossing this lane, still trying to recover from the momentary shock of Ibomcha's prank, my left leg slid into the sludge in the trench. I could not bear the feel of the filthy sludge, but the pond at the Puthiba ground was the nearest place where I could wash my leg. While washing myself in the pond, I reflected that it was an unnecessary effort, I could have just wiped off the mud with leaves or something. Meanwhile, an elderly maiba came out of the small *laishang* or shrine by the pond and ordered Ibomcha, who had been standing there and watching me trying to wash my leg, to fetch something. Maibas are male priests and traditional healers; women could not become maibas. I could not hear clearly what thing they were talking about. Ibomcha asked me to accompany him, but seeing me still struggling at cleaning my leg, he advised me to stay where I was and wait for him until he returned. The elderly maiba stayed behind too. This was my chance. I did not wait for Ibomcha, instead I took the small route at the back of the *laishang* and finally reached the place where Maibi Macha was impatiently waiting for me. As soon as we met, he complained, 'I have been waiting for you for many hours. If I was pregnant, I would have delivered the baby, too, it was as long as that.' I told him that we should not mingle in the crowd because anyone could see us. We shifted to another spot towards the farther corner of the *laishang*. From that spot nobody could detect us but we could observe many people including the maibis. The maibis wore heavy make-up and full-blown sunflowers as *samjirei nachom* (a small bunch of flowers worn in the hair or the ear). They wore a white full-sleeved blouse and white full-length *potloi*, the traditional bridal costume of a Meitei bride, over which they wore a *sharong*, a piece of multi-coloured cloth worn around the waist.

I said to Maibi Macha, 'I think the *potloi* must be heavy.'

Maibi Macha replied, 'Ebema, they are used to wearing *potloi* and so they probably do not find it heavy.' Then pointing his index finger, indicating one of the maibis in the distance, he said, 'Do you see that maibi? That is Khamba Maibi, the most talented of all the maibis.'

'Why the name Khamba?' I enquired. 'Isn't that a man's name?'

Maibi Macha replied, 'Because a maibi laba is a male, Khamba is a male.'

Until that time I was under the impression that only women could be maibis. I was also very scared of maibis. After seeing Khamba Maibi, I came to know that men could also be maibis. But even after Maibi Macha said that the maibi we were talking about was a male, it was hard for me to believe that this was a fact.

The *laibou* ceremony had begun. Khamba Maibi turned his face to the man who was beating the *pung*—drum— and gracefully danced to the rhythmic beat. The skill and grace with which he danced enthralled the onlookers. The male maibis reminded me of the old Hindi film heroines, their make-up and dancing was identical. I had watched a few Hindi films that were regularly screened at the big *shumang* or courtyard of Thoidingjam Leikai. These screenings were organised by Tamo Ibotombi, who used to work at the Usha Cinema. I knew the names of a few heroines in those films. They looked alike to me, all of them wore very dark eye make-up and fancy coiffures. Sundari Pawan, the heroine of *Anurag,* automatically came to my mind. Halfway through the *jagoi*—the traditional Manipuri dance—Nando unexpectedly arrived at the spot where we were and said that Baba had come to take me home. Jolted out of my musings by this interruption, I did not have the wit to even say farewell to Maibi Macha. I left immediately. This must surely have annoyed my new friend.

The next morning, a few women from the neighbourhood came to our house to weave clothes on Ema's *darum*, the tool used to organise the threads before putting them on the loom. I was sitting on a *phak*—a mat made of dried water rush leaves—in a corner of the verandah, anxiously waiting for Eche to leave the house, so that I could use her eyeliner pencil. Yes, I had a new desire to wear some make-up.

Sitting where I was, I could overhear the conversation between Ema and her friends. One woman asked Ema, 'Echowbi, were you there at Puthiba last night?'

Ema replied, 'No. Their Baba was very upset that I allowed Ebungo to go. But I heard that Ibotombi Maibi did not come.' Ebungo was my pet name which my parents and elders in the neighbourhood sometimes used.

The woman replied, 'No, he did not. People say that he is sick.'

Ema said, 'It is always so charming to see Khamba and Ibotombi dancing together.'

'Yes,' agreed the woman. 'This time only Khamba presided over *laibow*. The other maibis are newcomers.'

Ema said, 'We will go tonight.'

Hearing Ema's plan, I felt a rush of excitement. Immediately, I began to hatch a new plan to meet Maibi Macha.

According to Ema's plan, we ate very early that evening. Carrying a wicker stool each, Ebok, Ema and a few other elderly women from the neighbourhood headed towards the Puthiba ground. Eche had left earlier as she had to rehearse for the Lai Haraoba *jagoi*. The rehearsal was at Enaocha's place, and Eche would also need more time to put on make-up and wear the traditional dress for the *jagoi*. At the venue that night, boys my age were sitting on the side designated for men. However, Ema made me sit beside her throughout the time we were there.

As we watched the *jagoi*, we could hear a few people talking about Sama Maibi, who was performing the maibi *jagoi* at the ground that evening. Our neighbour, Ebok Ebema, joined the conversation, although she was not addressing anybody in particular, 'Sama is now young and beautiful. But after a few years, age will take away her beauty.'

Ema replied, 'Indeed, maibis appear more beautiful in their youth. I still remember Khamba Maibi and Ibotombi Maibi at Nongmaleima looked more beautiful in their younger days.'

Sama Maibi was tall, her eye make-up and eyebrows were very distinctive. While performing the traditional *jagoi*, she moved in all four directions of the *laibung*, the sacred performing ground for Lai Haraoba rituals, a skill she executed with ease and grace. Sometimes, she distributed the offerings of fruit made to the deities by the worshippers. After a few days, Puthiba Lai Haraoba concluded.

$$\equiv\equiv\equiv$$

The examination results were declared. I had cleared all the papers, and got admission in Manipur Baptist Convention School, at Chingmeirong. In those days, buses were the main mode of transport. I had to take the local bus to reach school, the bus fare was ten rupees. My visits to Kongpal were also becoming more frequent. On many days, immediately after getting home from school, I changed out of my uniform and rode to Kongpal on my Hercules bicycle. My destination at Kongpal was the bank of the Kongba river, in front of the Nongmaleima Laishang. I was always joined by my homo friends at this spot. They were particularly appreciative of my expertise in reading and translating 'Blue Jeans', a popular romance series in English, which had pictures, like in a comic book. Despite the fact that none of them had formal schooling, they had strong ideas and impressions about many things.

Romen wrote beautiful love letters to his lover. Initially, I could not appreciate the beauty of his words. However, as I grew older, his letters started unravelling their depth, he must have felt emotions of pain, longing and love very deeply. One day I told Romen about Marjing. After listening to my story intently, Romen said, 'Listen, a homo's love never bears fruit. It is like straining the fine grains of sand in a sieve. Though the heart refuses not to love, do not believe in a man's love. They will exploit us, manipulate us, and then ultimately marry a woman.' I did not doubt that his counsel was a wise and well thought-out one, but I was not worried by the idea of the futility of a homo's love. I did not pursue the matter further.

One day, towards the beginning of winter, I visited Romen. When he heard that I had come, he came out of his room and greeted me and then he took me to his room. I could see that he was worried and upset. He said, 'Ebungo, we have to visit Surjit now.'

I asked, 'Who is Surjit?'

Romen replied, 'He is from Heikru Makhong. He is my lover.'

I said, 'How will we go? It will be dark soon.'

Romen said, 'No, it will not take long. I only have to meet him briefly.'

I protested, 'Da Romen, I cannot reach home after dark. How will I accompany you? I will be late.'

Romen said, 'I do not want to ask other friends. But if you cannot accompany me, it is fine.' I could see the anxiety and sadness reflected in his face and felt bad. After thinking it over for a while, I said, 'Fine, let us go.'

But now Romen said, 'If you return home late, your mother will surely scold you. So, you should go home now.'

I reassured Romen with these words, 'My family had hinted that they would allow me a little freedom after high school. Now is the time. Let us go, just let us not be late.'

Romen finally yielded to my insistence. I parked my

bicycle at his house. We were going on his father's Luna.
Since it was the end of autumn, a light fog had begun to
gather in the evenings. Romen gave me a *haophi* to keep
myself warm. Romen drove the Luna and I sat on the
backseat. I was, however, beset by anxieties. My family
and neighbours might see me in the company of Romen
while riding past Lamlong. But I did not tell Romen about
my worries. As soon as we reached the Lamlong Bazar, I
covered my head with the *haophi,* to avoid being seen by
my neighbours. I uncovered my head only when we reached
Heikru Makhong, it was my first visit to that place so no
one would recognise me. Romen parked the Luna at the
corner of the small bazar.

Not far away from where we had parked the Luna,
there was a small ground that was overshadowed by a big
banyan tree. There was something ominous about the place,
something hauntingly emotional about it. The banyan tree
made the place more gloomy. (It has been many years, but
I still have vivid memories of the place, and whenever I
visit Heikru Makhong, I am reminded of Romen. The place
has become very crowded and busy now, its landscape has
changed. It does not have any trace of the desolation of
the past.)

We walked to a paan dukan that was owned by a local
woman. The woman was very busy and did not notice
Romen and me approaching her shop counter. Romen and
the woman exchanged a few greetings. The woman asked,
'How are you, Romen? I'm seeing you after a long time.
Have you parted ways with him?'

Romen replied, 'Have you seen him lately?'

The woman replied, 'I saw him a while before. Probably
he is at home now.'

Romen said, 'What do we do now? Can you send
somebody to give him a message to come here?'

The woman replied, 'There is nobody around. Even my children are studying now.'

Romen said, 'No problem, Eche. I will stay here, let's see if he is still around.' The woman said something and then carried on with her work. We remained standing at the paan dukan, waiting for someone to appear on the scene. While we were waiting thus, Romen directed my attention to a small group of people. 'Ebungo, do you see three men walking there?' Indeed, I could make out three shadowy figures walking a short distance from where we were standing. I replied, 'Yes.'

Romen said, 'The tall one in the middle looks like him, I am hoping it is him.' I did not reply but Romen continued talking to himself. The small bazar became darker as the evening advanced. A thick fog had already overwhelmed the silver sheet of the moonlight. Three persons were walking towards us, but it was difficult to see their faces clearly in the fog. Romen nudged at me, which meant that one of them was indeed Surjit.

I said, 'Why don't you call him? He could not have seen you in dark.'

Romen said, 'Stay calm. He will come here.' Romen's voice sounded different this time, different from the tone in which he had spoken before. Meanwhile my tension was growing as the hours advanced. Thinking about my bicycle that I had left at Romen's place made me even more anxious. As predicted by Romen, Surjit indeed came and stood beside us.

Surjit asked, 'How long have you been here?'

Romen replied, 'It has been only a while. I thought you did not see me.'

Surjit said, 'I saw you.'

Romen asked in reply, 'Then where did you go?'

Surjit replied, 'I did not want to meet you while my friends were around. So, I thought I would leave my friends elsewhere and then meet you.'

This time Romen said in a slightly peevish tone, 'What are you thinking?'

Surjit replied, 'What did I do? Are you starting to argue, again?'

Romen insisted, 'No, tell me the truth?'

Surjit said, 'Let's go and sit somewhere else. It is not polite to let anyone overhear us.'

We left the paan dukan and stood under the large banyan tree.

Romen said, 'I understand the game you are playing with me.'

Surjit said again, 'What have I done?'

Romen asked, 'Why are you hiding the fact that you have a woman? Why can you not tell me the truth?'

Surjit said defensively, 'Who told you that? If you believe in whatever others say, how can we be together?'

Romen said, 'I know everything, Surjit. My conviction is not based on what others say. I can interpret your attitude well enough.'

Surjit replied, 'Yes, you are right. My ex-girlfriend and I are together again.'

Romen asked, 'What about me?' Surjit did not answer his question. Both of them remained silent for some time.

Then Surjit asked, 'Who is this child?' He was talking about me.

Romen replied in a broken voice, 'Why are you keeping this a secret from me, Surjit? You know the feelings I have for you, your betrayal will not bring you any happiness in the future.'

Surjit replied, 'Ebecha, I love you. But our relationship is futile.'

Romen asked, 'Didn't you know that before?'

Overcome by pain and anger, Romen slapped Surjit on the face. He did not stop there, he tore at the latter's shirt, several buttons fell on the ground. After this helpless response to Surjit's betrayal, Romen fumbled on the ground and started weeping. Seeing his distress hurt me deeply. I realised at that moment the truth of what he had told me, that homos couldn't have a fruitful relationship with men.

A callous Surjit did not even attempt to console Romen. He only asked Romen to stop crying, lest somebody should hear the weeping. His indifferent attempt at silencing Romen showed his true colours. What a cold-hearted man he was! Meanwhile, a man passing by called out, 'Surjit, what are you doing there?'

Surjit replied, 'Nothing, I am just standing here.'

The man said, 'Let's go.'

Surjit replied, 'Go ahead, I will join you in a short while.' As soon as the man left, Romen stood up. 'How can you can do this?' he asked Surjit.

Surjit asked, 'What?'

Romen asked again, 'How can you part ways with me now?'

Evading Romen's desperate pleas, Surjit replied nonchalantly, 'Let me not hear you talk any more about these futile things. It is getting late. Besides, you have brought along this child. Let us meet some other time.'

Romen's weeping had become more distraught. He said, 'Are you in a hurry to leave? Well, then, go if you wish to. Do not hope that you will see me again.' With a new determination, Romen wiped his tears. He clasped my wrist and said, 'Ebungo, let's go.'

While Romen was kick-starting the Luna, I closely observed Surjit's face—there was no hint of unhappiness or remorse after such an intensely ugly confrontation. Romen's pain and anger did not seem to elicit any sympathy from him. He was unyielding. Had he loved Romen, even by the slightest degree, he would have surely consoled him. Moreover, Romen was like a woman, and had Surjit reflected over this a little bit, he would not have left him alone at that time of the night, in tears, in the cold and fog.

If a human being being truly loved something, she or he would hold onto it under any circumstances. No amount of dirt and filth would diminish the love and respect for that thing. She or he would rescue it from all the dangers and hatred of the world. No amount of impurity could make it ugly and unloved. However, many are willing to throw away things the moment they cannot find any more charms in them. Human beings are diverse. I did not know what kind of human being Surjit was.

If a man betrays a woman, society considers it a very grave matter. In many cases, such circumstances lead to *Keina Katpa*—the tradition by which a man and woman are forced to get married if they are found meeting in isolation, or if a married woman is having an affair with another man (this form of marriage is completely opposite to the traditonal form, here the two persons are forced to become a couple at the spot where they are caught by other people). This is the norm in our society. That day Romen was no different from a woman who was discarded after a betrayal. However, Romen's heartbroken complaints and the callous response of his lover were not heard by anyone. Romen's story was to be witnessed only by the mute, defenceless greenery and darkness of the immediate surroundings. I was nobody to even raise my objections to the heartless Surjit. Romen could not recount the injustice and pain he was going through to anyone in our society.

Was he not a human being? Yes, he was, and that was the reason why pain and betrayal hurt him. What was his fault? Was it because he did not conduct himself like a man despite being born as a male, or because he was in love with another man? In this unfortunate relationship, it could not only be Romen who was in love. Our elders have a saying that one hand alone cannot clap, and so Surjit too must take his share of responsibility for this relationship.

Romen's pain injected a new sorrow in me, I could feel tears in my eyes. Throughout the long ride from Heikru Makhong to Kongpal, Romen wept incessantly. His tears made me forget my anxiety about the reaction that would follow my arrival home that night. Rather, his pain filled me with a new courage. As he wept, he kept talking to himself, sometimes he interrupted himself and asked me a question or two, 'Ebungo, do you think he does not love me? Do you think he will not come back to me? But I know he loves me. How will I find the answer?'

He continued, 'I was the one who helped him during his hard times. His stepmother never showed him any affection. I will not help him anymore. Let him come to me in times of need. I should ask him to return the pants I gifted him, and then I will burn them right in front of him.' His anger was confronting him with all sorts of imaginary fears and unanswerable questions. In this desperate abyss of love and longing for Surjit, he had only himself to answer his insecurities. 'It is my fault, being born a homo is our fault. Don't even think of falling in love with men. Their mission is to exploit us.' Then he turned towards me even as he rode and said, 'There is not a single man that would be willing to stand up for homos.'

He was too lost in his world to be aware that we had reached Lamlong. I informed him that we had reached the gate of my house. 'Da Romen, you can stop here for a while,' I said.

He asked, 'Why? Are you not coming to my house to take your bicycle?'

I replied, 'It is very late now. I will get my bicycle tomorrow.'

Romen said, 'That is right, it is late. What will you say to your family?'

I said, 'It will be fine. I will explain it to Ema.'

He left and I walked inside the gate of our house. Barely had I climbed up the steps of the *mangol*, when Ema, who was standing in the verandah, probably waiting for me, said, 'Your Baba is very angry. Don't you know that the Army has rounded up the entire Lamlong to arrest *naharol*? There is a possibility of a combing operation, not even a single soul is on the street now. Where have you been?' Her scolding diverted my thoughts from Romen's distress to the Army's operations to hunt down *naharols*, the local term for insurgents. The presence of the Indian Army in our neighbourhoods had become a normal part of our life. This momentary distraction was ended by Baba who started lashing at my legs with a *thongak chei*—the iron rod used to secure the door. 'Do not give him food. He will always be a failure.' Pronouncing these bitter words, he went inside the house.

I also went inside. It seemed that I had fallen out of everyone's favour; my sisters went about doing their chores without uttering a single word. Baba's extreme reaction to my coming home late was inexplicable. In my neighbourhood, many boys my age were still outside, watching films in the cinema halls at that time of the night. I believed I was educated enough to look after myself. Baba's violent beatings and unpleasant verbal abuse was slowly shaping a divide between him and me. Where was the affection that was supposed to bond father and son? His worries about my safety were the natural consequence of his fatherhood, but he could have given me a chance to explain why I had reached home late. That night was the first time I told a lie to Ema—I told my family that I had gone to Kongpal to enquire about coaching classes. But my bicycle tyre developed a puncture at Netaji Ground. That was where I met Romen, and he and I decided to keep my bicycle for the night at his place. While I was coming back on foot, I lost my way. Fortunately, I met an elderly man who helped me reach home safely. My narration of the events of the day had no connection to the reality, and in years to come I was conditioned to constantly tell lies to save myself. I was born in freedom, but my family's harsh treatment compelled me to suppress and hide the person I was, the real I.

That night fond memories of childhood visited me. I distinctly remembered moments of freedom enjoyed in my primary school years. Freedom faded away as my conflict with my family became a daily affair. Once Ema quarrelled with Thanda, a girl in our neighbourhood, over occupying a space on the banks of the Imphal river. The quarrel was provoked by Thanda impudently calling me a homo. In her struggle to make me more masculine, Ema discouraged me from having girls as my friends. She even hid the *phadis* or rags from me out of fear that I would wear them as *phaneks*.

Often, I went to Eche Manitombi's house. I borrowed two *phadis* from her, wore one around my body in the manner of a *phanek* and the other on my head like a wig and pretended that it was my long hair. Sitting at her loom, Manitombi would jocularly ask me to do the Twist, which was a popular dance then. I was Manitombi's 'happy company'. She had a child with a married man from the neighbourhood. She did not have any friends around the place, her mother never allowed her to go out of the house. Eche Manitombi's only occupation was to weave on her loom. Once I danced under the big *chorphon* tree in their *shumang*. I also sang the song, *'Taningdy okchare laonamba kahoimu-o'*. In the meanwhile songs could be heard playing on megaphones in preparation for the *Thabal Chongba* at Chandam Lampak. This was the traditional dance which is performed at the Yaoshang festival in the month of March. Men and women join hands and dance in an open field with lights and music. Eche Manitombi said, 'Abothey, smile while dancing. If you smile, you will look more beautiful than a film heroine.' She never stopped me in anything I did. She often said, 'You are very talented. Learn dancing or singing.' But our little routine was short-lived. Nganhkam Ebok had already warned Ema against my song and dance performances at Manitombi's house and soon my visits came to an end.

I also remembered an event from my days in Class V. Oja Ebomcha, who was a founder member of the local club, told Ema that I could participate in a programme at Khurai Social Youth Club at Lamlong. The occasion was the club's Foundation Day. I got the second prize for reciting a poem. That day, a feminine-looking boy sang the song *'Ngaikhigdara laklaroidra mabu'* by Yangnu Golmei. His looks and talent deeply impressed me. Another participant performed a monologue called 'Welcome Devi *bu unnarubada'*. Both the performers got prizes. As a child

I was very close to the club members, Eche and I use to sing with Oja Ebomcha. Some of the other members like Ta Rajen, Ta Eanaotomba, Tachou Somarendro and Yambung Tikensana told me many stories. One day a few boys called me homo while I was coming back from school. I reported this to Ta Somarendro when he visited us in the evening. He consoled me and said that he would talk to the boys and warn them not to bother me again. It made me feel good that he supported me. Those were very happy days in my life.

Everything changed with time. Yambung Tikensana's father died following a police beating. After the tragic death of his father, Yambung left Manipur to study for his Master's degree. The club members also dispersed and disappeared to different locations after the Indian Army hunted them down on the charge of being members of banned insurgency groups. Nobody commemorated the Foundation Day of the club anymore. The building of the KSYC club was replaced by many small shops in the coming years. As I relived the distant memories, I was sure that my old friends would have helped me and showed me affection in my present condition.

The following day, I told Ema the truth about the bicycle, that I had left it at Romen's house. She was very saddened by this disclosure of my association with Romen. But the things that where happening in my life were beyond her control. I think she understood this and so she did not chastise me. That day Ema and I went to Kongpal to bring home my bicycle. Ema did not tell Baba about my budding association with Romen or the visit to Ebok's house to retrieve my bicycle.

Eney greeted us and told us that Ebok had gone to the river to wash vegetables. We went to the riverside and found Ebok by the water. After exchanging some small talk, Ema said, 'Ebungo left his bicycle with Romen yesterday, we've come to take it back.' After washing the vegetables that would be taken to the market later that day, the three of us returned to Ebok's house. The atmosphere was ripe for a conversation, and so we sat together in Ebok's room. Eney also joined us. Eney wanted us to have our morning meal with them, but Ema declined. 'Eney, some other day. Today I have to return home. My children will not be able to manage the household chores in my absence. I only came for the bicycle. Their Baba will be very angry if he comes to know that the bicycle was left here. It is very difficult to manage growing children.'

Eney said, 'Indeed. See, I have gone through difficult years in bringing up my nine children. Now they are able to stand on their own feet. But what about Romen! I'll not be able to die peacefully. It worries me so much to think about the future of this son of mine.'

Ema said, 'I can understand your worries. Is Romen going to be like this forever?'

Eney said, 'I don't know what will happen. Since his childhood, he has never thought of himself as a boy. His brothers and father beat him a lot, but even the constant beatings cannot change his ways. But he is the only one of my children with whom I can discuss my worries and hardships.'

Then Ema asked, 'Eney, does Ebungo come here very often?'

Eney replied, 'Yes, I see him frequently these days. Romen says Ebungo has a very good nature and is also good in studies. He is very fond of Ebungo. Why are you asking? What happened?'

Ema replied, 'Nothing happened. Just asking. This year he is spending a lot of time outside the home. His Baba is blaming me for this. His school session has just started. Ebungo never says that he comes here. He must inform me.'

Eney left the room after a while. I could see anger and disappointment reflected in Ema's face. Tears filled her eyes. I wanted to see Romen but sensing her discomfort I dropped the idea. It was Ebok's turn to question me, 'Ebungo, why do you visit Romen so often? He is not a good person. Are you going to ruin your life in his company? If I find you visiting Romen again, I will tell your Baba. Romen and his friends meet here every day. They wear *phanek*-like dresses and waste away their time doing nothing well. Even women do not behave like this.'After a while, Eney's daughter also came to talk with Ema. She also had a few complaints to make to Ema against me. 'He comes here every day to meet Romen. I have wanted to tell you about this. Ebungo is going to be spoiled, Eche.'

Everyone who came to see Ema told her not to let me be seen in the company of Romen, they warned that I would be ruined. Only Eney showed any affection towards Romen and spoke of him with loving words. I failed to understand why these people distrusted Romen. He was not a drunkard, he did not stay out of the house the whole night. He did not indulge in any of the wayward behaviour that the youth those days were guilty of. In fact, he was engaged in productive activities such as knitting and weaving to earn a decent income; he did not gossip and speak ill of others. He was constantly giving me good counsel, like, 'Even if you are homo, consider your education very seriously.' It was very strange that they would dissuade me from meeting Romen. Why did his own family treat him so harshly? How would the rest of the world treat him then? His beauty and goodness were opaque to the world surrounding him.

However, from that day on I stopped going to Kongpal.

I was the first person in the entire neighbourhood to pass the matriculation examination in the first attempt, with a very good score. Baba did not show any happiness or pride in my little accomplishment. In contrast, he was visibly happy with the results of his other children. Undoubtedly, they were very close to him; for me, it was only Ema. Whatever affection I had in my life at that time I got from her. Any paternal interaction between Baba and me was non-existent. In truth, I was not the man people wanted me to be—I stayed inside the house all the time, either studying or lost in my thoughts. I was not willing to induct myself into the hall of masculinity subscribed to by Baba and society. To conform to society's expectations, at the cost of banishing my own self and the desire ingrained in my blood, was a form of slavery to me. I would rather dream of being an impoverished woman who wore a piece of jewellery made of alloy and then looked at her reflection in the mirror, than a rich man walking in the street in golden boots. Baba had no reason to feel pride in whatever I was, I was already a failure in his eyes.

From Class XI onwards, I started openly wearing feminine clothing. I was seventeen years old and I had passed the tenth standard with high marks. This gave me the courage to ignore what people, including my parents, talked about me. I felt I was mature enough to do as I wished. Besides, in those days, most people could not pass the matric exam in the first attempt—even my eldest sister had appeared for it five times. My success in studies was also my strength because it was always associated with my identity—whenever people said my name, they would always add 'even though Santa is a homo, he is brilliant in studies, one should admire him for that.' So my educational background also acted as a shield and boosted my confidence to live the way I wanted to, as a woman, which had been my dream ever since I began to understand the world around me.

I usually sat on the side of the girls in the classroom. Sometimes, one of the boys would write me a love letter and pass it to me. I had three very dear friends—Aruna, Chanu and Sonia. We visited each other's houses. These new friends were a part of my life's changing directions. Other than these three girls, most people in the school did not want to be friends with me, rather they derided me. One day when I had skipped school, the three of them came to my house. I was very happy to see them, Ema was also very welcoming towards the girls. She was happy to know that they were my classmates. I was surprised to see them back from school so early. They said that our Vice Principal, who was also our maths teacher, had granted the students a half-day, to encourage the Class XII students to prepare for the final examinations. 'I knew that would happen, so I didn't come today,' I said.

Sonia chirped, 'Ebema! We missed you today. Without you, it was very quiet.'

Chanu said, 'Santa, Rajen Sir explained the salt analysis, but it is still not clear to me. Give me your practical notebook.' I asked them about Ratan, a classmate of ours.

Chanu teased, 'Ebema, you appear to be very interested in him.' Then Aruna also contributed her bit, 'I wish you togetherness in life. Why don't you two elope before you finish Class XII?' I protested, 'Oh no, it is not like that.'

We were having fun, talking, laughing and teasing one another. I did not see Baba entering the room. All of a sudden his words thundered out at us, 'It is getting late. Go home now.' Everything happened so fast, the sound of our laughter suddenly disappeared. Baba's rude interruption shamed me in front of my friends. They were intelligent girls and could sense my embarrassment. I should have said or done something to rescue my friends from that tense atmosphere, but I myself was a pitiful creature in that household. But what about my friends? What was their fault? Despite knowing that I was a homo, they dearly loved and respected me. Baba's behaviour was an insult to them. It was possible that Baba was well-meaning from his own perspective, but he did not seem to understand that feelings and sentiments could be expressed in less harsh ways. Words could convey love in the same manner that they could create hatred.

Aruna was quick-witted enough to salvage the situation. 'Santa, we should go now, we are getting late for coaching class.' Nervous and ashamed, I tried to protest, 'Stay for a while.' But Sonia said, 'Let's meet at school tomorrow.'

Thus, I was utterly humiliated in front of my friends. My insistence that they should stay was a fake request, I secretly wished them to leave as soon as possible. Another fear struck me, the fear of losing the friendship, trust and affection of those who loved me and had accepted me. Would Baba's disrespect affect my friendship with Sonia, Aruna and Chanu? Finally, I accompanied them outside the gate. At the gate, some boys that I had not seen before teased us, 'Sarat, your friends are very pretty.' (Sarat was my given name, which I later officially changed to Santa.) This uncouth behaviour further embarrassed me.

That afternoon I complained to Ema about Baba's rude

behaviour. Ema supported me. She too was angered by what had happened and went immediately to talk to him. 'Why did you act like that in front of his friends?' she asked him. Baba sneered, 'Friends? He is a boy, he should have male friends. Why is he laughing and chatting with girls? Is he a girl?'

Ema said, 'Your thoughts are very negative. You cannot be friends with anybody.'

As their argument continued, I started crying. Suddenly I felt very sad—was I adopted? Was it better to die? Should I run away somewhere? It was evident that Baba hardly shared a good relationship with me, but I still had respect and concern for him. The unworthy incident that day, in front of my friends, changed my attitude towards him for all time to come. I began looking upon him as a cruel man who did not deserve respect and affection.

In those years, many boys my age in my neighbourhood took drugs. Drug addiction was becoming a widespread social problem among the youth. It was a grave fear in the minds of parents. I was one of the rare boys who was still unclaimed by drug addiction. Baba must have surely seen this with his own eyes, it was clear that I was not causing him any problem. It was also heard around that time that many young men collected money from people in the neighbourhood in the guise of *naharols*. Manipur commandos frequented our streets to identify and punish the culprits. But I was not amongst them—I did not even eat *kwa,* and never failed in exams. Then why did Baba reject me in that cruel manner? In the streets, I was greeted with the insulting word, 'Homo'. They did not just say

homo, insults and humiliations were added to hurt me
further—'You homo, black sheep', 'homo, why don't you
die?', 'homo *thigunlao* (asshole)'. They even said that homos
were born to burden the earth, and it would be much wiser
for parents to kill off homo children when the time was
right, the sooner the better. These words were not coming
only from young people who could say anything in youthful
insolence and ignorance, even middle-aged people said the
same things to us. The mature and the immature seemed to
have become united on this issue! Sometimes they blamed
our parents for letting us become homos, as though being
a homo was a choice one could make.

Wherever I went, society's disparaging mockery haunted
me—'homo' followed me everywhere. Where should I go
to hide from the rage of hatred and humiliation? I started
hating myself, I started challenging society. The more I saw
the differences in Baba's affection for my siblings and for
me, the more rebellious I became. My fearless determination
to wear make-up and women's clothing were the gifts of this
phase of my life. I became emboldened hourly as I walked
this path each day. Time went by and in the year 1991 I
wrote the final examinations for Class XII. This was an
important landmark in the road towards freedom, sorrow,
and the unknown. I finally grew up.

It was the summer vacation once again. The long hot days
could only bring boredom if one chose to stay at home.
I often visited Maibi Macha to escape from the ennui. In
his company, I was introduced to a few other homos in
Khurai—Ronu, Bob, Mohonsingh, and Poison (most trans
people took on different names, and that was his chosen

name). Among these friends, Mohonsingh was the only one older than Maibi Macha and me. How had I not known about these people before—they were my neighbours after all! I visited them almost every day. After eating the morning meal I would go and join them. My family did not have a clue about my new company.

On one such visit, Poison asked me to accompany him to a poultry farm at Porompat, to buy chicks. It was drizzling, so we took a rickshaw from Poison's house. On reaching the poultry farm, we were told that there were no chicks in stock at that time. We would have to wait for the fresh stock to arrive. This interval gave me the chance I had been waiting for to test my family's attitude towards homos. As part of the litmus test, I told Poison that we should utilise the time to go to my house, eat a meal, and then come back to the poultry farm. The point was to ascertain if my family would completely reject someone like Poison! Unaware of my intention or even if he had known, he might not have protested, he agreed. First, we went to his house in a rickshaw to leave his umbrella, then both of us walked to my house. The light rain had stopped by then. On reaching the gate of my house, I saw Baba sitting in the *mangol*, reclining on the portico. I could feel a shiver down my legs. I asked Poison to wait for me outside the gate.

Poison said in surprise, 'What? You said that we would be eating together!'

I said, 'I think the meal is not ready yet.'

'But it is already noon!' Poison protested.

Hesitantly, I took him inside my house. I could not think of any other excuse to make him wait outside the gate. As we walked past him, Baba gave us a cold stare. That hostile expression was not unusual for Baba, where I was concerned. Poison and I went to the kitchen. While we were eating, Poison noticed my mood and asked, 'Why are you eating so fast, you are going to choke to death.' Trying to hide my tension, I replied, 'It is said that if you eat fast, followed by regular sips of water, you get full sooner.' I don't know about Poison, but I did not enjoy that hasty meal. I did not even have the courage to go outside to wash my hands. So, we cleaned our hands with a glass of water on the very plates on which we ate. My only concern at that time was to leave the house as soon as possible.

As I was trying to escape from the house, Baba addressed me, 'Where are you going? I asked you to trim the hedge at the back.' It was then that I remembered the task he had given me a few days before. I had evaded the task till then as it would mean working with him; being around Baba was uncomfortable for many reasons, apart from his habitually strict countenance. On hearing Baba's loud injunction, Poison had hurriedly walked away towards the gate, without looking back. When Poison and I finally managed to leave the house, he said, 'Don't ever invite me to your house again. Your father looks very disagreeable.'

I replied, 'Don't worry so much. It is not what you are thinking, he just looks serious and scary.'

Poison spread the news of the day's ugly encounter with Baba to every friend in our circle. This was enough to prevent them from visiting my house, even upon my insistence. They would refuse, saying, 'We are afraid of your Baba.' The situation at Poison's house was not much better. We could visit his house without inviting venomous stares or harsh words but that was where it ended—we could not talk and laugh the way we usually did, we were always conscious of the presence of the others in the household.

There was a small *sangtap*—an outhouse usually attached to a house—in front of Poison's house, and beside the *sangtap* was a small pond. This outhouse was the den where Poison's younger sister, Momoni, kept her loom. We often sat on the bench of Momoni's loom. This was a good spot from where we could get a panoramic view of the street that led to Porompat. We would sit on the bench and gossip about the people on the street. Our gossip sessions ranged from a discussion about our future, our longing for lovers, make-up and cosmetics, and films. A young homo called Khoidong, from Poison's neighbourhood, would often join us.

Young Khoidong always had a scarf slung over his shoulder. He had a quirky manner of talking that was very amusing. We always made him recite the Shumang Leela dialogues that were regularly played on the radio those days. (Shumang Leelas were plays that were performed in the open courtyard). One day while reciting a Shumang Leela dialogue, he said *'punsisida'*—life—in place of *'ahingsida'*—night: *'Eteimagi Ramesh michik miraokhol tadraba punsisida*—Brother-in-law, Ramesh, in this still life.' This error completely changed the meaning of the line and made us roll in laughter.

On many evenings, we pooled in whatever money we had to buy *singju* and *bora*—local snacks—from Koknganbi's *potpham,* a makeshift stall for selling eatables, at the Lamlong Keithel, the local market. I was always a fast eater. To honour this ability, my friends gave me the title, 'tractor'. Poison, Ronu and Bob could contribute more money than I could. For me, contributing five rupees daily was an impossibility. The money came from Ema who procured it from Baba, by quoting a good reason like buying books or stationery items. But nobody needed to buy books and stationery every day. There were limits to my fabrications too!

The Lamlong Keithel at Khurai looked very different in those days from what it gradually transformed into in the years to come. There were ramshackle stalls where people sat and sold various items. The women who sold vegetables returned home early, while the ones who sold fish continued even after dark. The only system of lighting in the market was a dim *podon* (lamp). Around the time the vegetable women left, we gathered at the market. Every evening, we reached the same place at the same time, none of us had to wait for the other. It was as though our movements were perfectly synchronized.

When the weather was pleasant, my friends and I went to Khuman, to sit on the bank of the Imphal river. Usually we walked through the 2nd Manipuri Rifles compound, which was the easiest and shortest route to get to Khuman. From the conversations we overheard, it was evident that the compound was open till late at night for film screenings. It was said that around that time, a cinema ticket at 2nd Manipuri Rifles cost 50 paise, but later on, the price was increased to two rupees.

Our conversations predominantly centred around our desire to be women. Bob told us an interesting story about the James Bond film, *The Spy Who Loved Me* that was showing at Imphal Talkies. He said that the heroine was previously a man who became a woman after surgery. Bob's revelation filled me with a desperation to watch the movie. The problem was that I had never seen a movie in a cinema hall before. Besides, Baba worked at a workshop at Majorkhul during the day, and if he saw me around Imphal Talkies, it would be the end of me. In those days, Imphal Talkies was notorious for showing B-grade films.

Bob's stories about American films led me to a reverie about America. America must be a very liberal place. I dreamt of leaving Manipur for America on a ship, to work hard, settle down and earn lots of money. With the money, I would change myself into a woman and become famous. This reverie was interrupted by the thought that if I left home without telling my family, it would really worry Ema and Baba. But they would surely come to know about my accomplishments once I had achieved fame and fortune, and this would be the occasion for a family reconciliation. A beautiful dream of freedom and success! I was too much of a dreamer to be able to foresee the reality that would unfold in the years to come!

It was not just me, Bob galvanised everyone's curiosity with that casual revelation about the James Bond heroine. Poison started firing away questions—How did the heroine look? What kind of dresses did she wear? Bob replied theatrically, 'The heroine is out of this world, her figure is similar to Santa's, she has burgundy hair, she wore a swimsuit and smooched James Bond. This is the most amazing part, you cannot figure out that she was previously a man.' We discussed how the actor could have changed into a woman. More enquiries ensued—How did the actor get the skin of a woman? Could she get pregnant? How was the breast enlargement achieved? Bob replied—'It is America! A servant in America is far more advanced than an officer in Manipur.' I also added my bit of information, 'Forget everything! The penis can be removed, and the vagina can be constructed by trans-grafting skin from another part of the body. I am wondering how breasts can be enlarged.'

Poison replied, 'I heard there is a certain drug for that. I heard Erai, who runs a hotel at Moreh Bazar, has very big breasts.'

Ronu joined in, 'I heard that in earlier times Meitei women used *laphu tongga*, the stem of the banana tree, to enlarge breasts.'

I asked, 'Is that really so?'

Bob said, laughing, 'You all are crazy. Leave it. Your breasts will be ripped apart.' But Ronu's words made me wonder and I could not rest until I knew if what he said was true. I decided at that moment that I would experiment with *laphu tongga*.

The next day around noon, just before bathing, I plucked a few stems of *laphu tongga*. If I sat by the pond, people would notice me. So I went to sit by the trench that lay between our *sangoi* and Thoidingjam Daddy's *yennakha* (backyard). I carried a bucket, some rags, and soap to the place. Cautiously, I took out the *laphu tongga* from the bucket, squeezed out a few drops of juice and started rubbing the juice on my chest. Since the *laphu tongga* was not juicy enough, I folded it in my palm and rubbed it directly on my chest. While I was struggling in this manner, my second eldest sister caught me unawares. She must have come to visit the toilet. '*Haima*! Ebungo, what are you doing?' There was an expression of disbelief on her face, my actions must have been totally incomprehensible to her. I had no time to hide the *laphu tongga* or what I was doing. The only answer I could come up with was, 'I am just exfoliating my skin.'

'Your skin will be bruised,' she exclaimed and saying this she took the *phadi* from me, rubbed soap into it and rubbed my neck, back and chest. 'This is how you do it, your skin looks brighter now.' My panic subsided only after she left. I drew a sigh of relief that I had managed to cover up my outlandish attempt to achieve well-formed breasts.

After bathing, I was very anxious to see if the *laphu tongga* juice had had any effect. I needed a mirror in which I could see myself from head to toe, but the mirror that was fixed at the corner of the *mangol* was only large enough to show my head and neck. Ours was a very big family, and so the mirror had to be in the *mangol* for everyone's use. It would be extremely stupid of me to remove my shirt to check the effect of my experiment with *laphu tongga*, and besides, the mirror was not wide enough to reflect my image. I ran my hands over my chest and felt that it was a bit enlarged, in addition to a sensation of itchiness. Ronu was telling me the truth!

From the next day onward, I plucked many more *laphu tongga*, squeezed out the juice and stored it in a bowl. Every night after everyone was asleep, I massaged my chest with it. I had only used the juice for a few days, but in my imagination, I was already beautiful and busty enough to work in American films.

One day, while clearing the ground beside the pond, Baba saw the banana plants that had been stripped of several layers of their stems. He started questioning who had stripped the *laphu tongga* in this manner. In the Meitei tradition, *laphu tongga* had to be plucked on auspicious days of the month. Baba was upset to see the denuded banana plants. Ema said she did not know who did it. While Baba continued to complain about what had been done to the banana plants, I had an equally disturbing concern— he may come across the squeezed out *laphu tongga* stems that littered the ground at Thoidingjam Daddy's *yennakha*. I lost no time in collecting the sapless *laphu tongga* in a sack and, hoisting it onto my bicycle, I rode off towards the bank of the Imphal river. My secret was dumped on the bank of the river.

Even after repeating the same process every day for several days, I did not get the breasts I desired. The initial excitement dwindled into frustration. My friends also didn't know anything about my secret experiment. My plan was to continue using the juice until my chest was visibly enlarged, I had wanted to surprise them with the results.

One day we went to the Khuman Lampak ground. On our way there, we were discussing radio dramas when I suddenly blurted out the whole story. My narration of the *laphu tongga* experiment sent them into peals of hysterical laughter. Poison jocularly said that it would be better if I shot myself in my chest with *bullet kapi* and the blisters formed from the wound would look like breasts. His outrageous suggestion was greeted with more laughter. Bob said, 'Nupi (girl), forget all this. We must go to Moreh.' There was a sense of urgency and excitement in his voice. Since Bob was already acquainted with Erai, he would easily find accommodation at Moreh. Poison, Ronu and I advised him that he should visit Moreh to buy the medicine that Erai had used for all of us. We would pay him back the money later.

After this, they resumed their discussion about radio dramas. From what they said, most of these dramas centred around the themes of love and separation. Bob had learnt many dialogues from these dramas. He could quote these dialogues line by line in the exact tempo and mode of the original delivery by the artists, it was as though he was reading out poems.

I contributed my share in this exchange. I had carried the 'Blue Jeans' romance series with me. I translated the dialogues written in English. Surely, I must have made a lot of mistakes while translating the dialogues. But my friends' interest encouraged me to continue with my storytelling. Sometimes when I came across difficult words, I constructed the possible meaning based on the progression of the narrative, depicted in the pictures and dialogue bubbles. The story that emerged through my interpretation and the pictures in the comic books was greatly appreciated by my friends.

The Khuman road also became one of the places where we gathered for our gossip sessions. The road was flanked on both sides by a thick growth of tall bushes, Caesar weeds, and Chinese chaste trees, small trees that came into bloom in the hot weather. During the dry season, Caesar weed seeds stuck to our clothes, and on rainy days leeches sucked on our skin.

Another remarkable sight on the Khuman road was the big mango tree. We were not the only ones that frequented that forsaken spot. The place was also a refuge for another visitor, a madman. The madman, from Lamlong, was Poison's age. Every evening, he came and sat under the mango tree, incessantly murmuring something unintelligible. Poison told us that the madman was his classmate at Lamlong Boys School. It was said that he become mad after an encounter with *helois*—exquisitely beautiful nymphs that are supposed to possess seductive charms and evil capabilities—while playing at the foot of the mango tree, and his routine visit to the mango tree was a rendezvous with the *helois*. A similar story was recounted to us by Pupu, my grandfather, about Tachou, Baba's younger brother. Tachou also encountered *helois* at the foot of the mango tree. According to another version of the same story recounted by Eney Meilambi, one day while he was going towards the mango tree to tend the cows, a white shroud fell on him. After this incident Tachou fell very ill. Pupu was a very famous maiba in Khurai at that time, but even after Pupu's intervention, Tachou's condition did not improve, but gradually deteriorated. Eney Meilambi had a storehouse of such supernatural stories which she was always ready to tell us.

We could not meet at any public place of our choosing, we were constantly censored in the eyes of the world. Whenever people saw us together, they called us 'inauspicious' or exclaimed, 'homos, just die'. Such cruel words caged us and restricted our movements. This was the reason why we met at strange places like the spooky Khuman neighbourhood.

As time went by, I started buying different kinds of magazines from Kesho's shop. I read these magazines diligently. Baba wanted me to read English newspapers. Notwithstanding his harsh treatment of me, he was willing to do everything for my education. He had little education himself, which must have made him very enthusiastic about mine. He was not a man who would pursue fashion and glitter. He believed in acting promptly, nothing was ever procrastinated. During my childhood, whenever I cried, he used to say, 'Have you seen heroes in the English films crying? Men do not cry.'

While I was growing up, I had no courage or desire to talk with Baba. If there was anything I needed to buy, my requests for money had to go through an intermediary, and Ema was the only person who acted in my favour. I have a distinct memory of where Baba kept money—inside his MSRTC (Manipur State Road Transport Corporation) identity card, a yellow-coloured card the size of the palm. Whenever Ema asked for money, he pulled out old paper notes of one and two rupees. Ema gave the old notes to me along with a few pieces of advice, 'Use this money carefully. The shop owner gave it to your Baba to buy tea for himself.' Ema's words inspired me to work hard. In my desire for success, I imagined myself in many roles—an officer, or a woman wearing a *phanek* and sunglasses coming back from the office. Baba would see me occupying these admirable positions. Why would he not be pleased?

Around that time, I started becoming notorious among the homos of Lamlong. The reason was my bold act of wearing make-up openly. My friends were no longer keen on socialising with me, and studiously avoided me in public places. It appeared that they did not want to be my friends anymore. I was aware of their efforts to avoid me. In fact, whenever people looked at us, my friends blamed me for attracting unnecessary attention. This was the same attitude the onlookers had about me, I was treated like an attention-seeking, ill-bred, shameless homo! I was marked out by people, they avoided me in the street and kept a distance from me. In truth, I was the only one not only to dress like a woman, but to walk openly in the street wearing women's clothing People had to say something, they called me '*kasubi* (slut)' and other names like *lamsha, besha*, all terms referring to promiscuous or immoral women.

Inspite of this, I continued to dress the way I wanted to. My desire to be a woman, a beautiful, fashionable woman, was so strong that I was not afraid of challenging anything that came in the way of my feminity. I felt that I could bear anything but I could not live like a man or like a woman who was not beautiful!

My unique way of dressing was inspired by Western films and popular artists that I read about in English-language magazines, such as *The Weekend* and *The Sun*. Boy George, Diana King and Julia Roberts were a few of my favourites. The dresses I wore were bought from Alu Galli for ten or twenty rupees. In my hands, those dresses transformed into different designs, which meant opening up the seams, redesigning and tailoring. The same friends who tried to avoid me on account of my bold fashion statement, ironically, came to me when they wanted to borrow the beautiful, feminine dresses in my fashion arsenal! Amongst these friends, only Bob praised my sense of dressing. He was very appreciative of the way I talked and carried myself in those stylish dresses. He often said that I looked like the heroines in English films.

One afternoon, a beautiful rainbow appeared on the horizon just after the rain, the streets looked clean and fresh. My friends and I were going somewhere, so it was an occasion for me to wear my signature dark eye make-up. Just as we reached Lainingthou, a man's voice could be heard from behind, 'Devebrata, that one looks hot and fun.' The comment was clearly directed at me, and it was Yaikhom Pritam who uttered those derisive words. Poison giggled and said, 'Enough. You yourself are so ugly, I could poop in your mouth.' The man must have heard Poison's equally derisive dismissal, which was rendered more humiliating by our laughter. He insulted us and we insulted him, and he was silenced. After walking on ahead for some distance, Poison turned towards me and said, 'Santa, he was making that comment because of your eye make-up.' He added, 'Why do you wear such loud make-up? Don't you feel embarrassed? People are making fun of you. Don't you hate that? You are doing it in broad daylight. You should be friends with Tom, he is from Kongba. He is just like you.' That was the first time I heard the name—Tom.

Since my friends told me that I had such an affinity with Tom, I was eager to know more about him. My friends told me that Tom was as uninhibited as I was, meaning he was not afraid of wearing make-up and feminine dresses in public, which also meant that he was a fearless person.

They had seen Tom at the Konung during a *jhulol* ceremony at night. The Konung was the king's palace where there were small temples or shrines for performing religious and cultural activities. Jhulol is a festival celebrated in August which commemorates the relationship bewtween Radha and Krishna. This festival is celebrated by the Meitei Hindus but people who follow the Sanamahi religion also join in to enjoy the food and dances like the Rash Leela.

Tom was standing alone by one of the pillars at the Konung, holding a torch in his hand which he constantly beamed on his face. He was not accompanied by any friends, he seemed to be enjoying his own company. My friends thought that it was very brave of Tom to be seen at Konung, standing alone so nonchalantly. The manner in which my friends described Tom established his courage and originality, and I was totally intrigued by him.

My friends' criticism and disapproval of me did not elicit any vindictive reaction from me—anybody could have an opinion, like me or dislike me. My only desire was to be able to wear whatever I wanted. Meanwhile, Baba had been witnessing the radical changes I was going through. On his part, he had decided to distance himself from me. Whenever his friends came to visit him, he shared his disgust and condemnation of me with them. He would say, 'A man should stay as a man. Behaving like women, like *ngamarak shamarak* will not bring any glory to a man's life. These men will forever be despised by people and society.' *Ngamarak shamarak* was a metaphor used for describing odious objects, it was clear to me that according to his philosophy of life, I was a living example of failure, someone to be vilified and ridiculed. His opprobrious words filled me with indignation. He nurtured such a hatred for his own child! Moreover, his words gave licence to the neighbours to openly ill-treat and reduce me to nothing. Any desire to show love and affection towards him died anew each time he denounced me with such contempt. I did not even want to greet him anymore.

It was not my fault that I wanted to dress as a woman or that I desired men. I was born as a man but a man that had the inner desire to be a woman. And for this reason I was disrespected by society! Nobody was aware of the woman that lay within me. The woman in me could neither be vanquished nor hidden somewhere in order to adjust myself to a world that was replete with selfish people and their selfish criticism. Sometimes repeated condemnation compelled me to think that I must be wrong or I must be suffering from mental delusions. To which rung of society did I belong, which I could claim as my own?

I could be oblivious to Baba's cruel words and abuses, but I felt betrayed by my own friends. I understood their love and concern for me, and I also reciprocated their affection. However, their constant cautioning me about the way I dressed and my bold attitude created an unnecessary and deep-seated stress in my relationship with them. In order to silence harsh comments from people, they tried to live like men as far as possible. Their two-faced attitude, embodying two different identities, one at night and one during the day, was not acceptable to me. Even though they were just like me, they always set me apart from themselves. Indeed, they did not hesitate to display their disapproval of me. My choice to stay on amicable terms with them was not born out of any weakness or delusions on my part. Regardless of my disappointment and their opprobrium, they were the ones I valued the most. It was only in their company that I felt alive, unlike the stinging gaze of the neighbours and strangers in the street.

One day Bob told me that *Pretty Woman* was showing at the Asha Cinema. Ever since I read a review of the film in *The Screen* magazine, I had dreamt of watching it. I immediately proposed to Bob that we must go and see it. Bob was also an ardent admirer of Western fashion and films. Two days later, Bob and I found ourselves outside Asha Cinema hall, waiting to buy tickets. There was a huge crowd of people outside the hall, all trying desperately to procure a ticket. Women were selling tickets in black at twice the actual price. Bob joined the male queue at the ticket counter, and I stood at a corner. He wore a blue hat that day, at a cursory glance nobody could tell that he was a homo. While he was waiting his turn in the queue, people coming to the cinema hall could not stop staring at me, and the stare was inevitably accompanied by gestures and whispered conversations. I was wearing a yellow crop top and tight jeans, with high-heeled brown boots. I had bleached my hair blonde and hadn't combed it for many days to get a messy look that was in fashion, and I had applied a thick layer of kajal in my eyes.

Their behaviour perturbed me and I wanted to get inside the hall as soon as possible to ecape from their gaze. Bob came back after a while, perspiring profusely. I was relieved, thinking that we would be going inside the hall. Instead, Bob informed me that he had dropped the ticket money somewhere and only realised it when he was about to pay the ticket seller. He was crestfallen and I was frustrated and annoyed—money lost, time wasted, and we did not get to see the film. I had had to lie to Ema to get the money for the ticket—I told her that I needed it to buy books. We returned without watching the film. Already, I was occupied thinking of pretexts for getting more money from Ema.

The next day, I ate my morning meal earlier than usual.

I went to Ema and told her that the money she had given me the previous day was not enough to buy the book I needed. Ema gave me more money. Bob and I went to Asha Cinema for the second time. Having learnt our lessons from the previous day's mishap, we were extra cautious with the money. The tickets had to be bought before they were sold out. It often happened that towards the end tickets were sold at a higher price to people who were willing to buy them at any cost. To avoid such a situation, we reached the hall very early. We managed to get two front row seats. I was utterly charmed by the movie. It felt like every man must be like Richard Gere, kind-hearted and handsome.

Immediately after coming out of the hall, I wanted to go to the bazar to buy clothes. Bob said with a knowing smile that I must be thinking of dressing like Julia Roberts. He assured me that Julia Roberts' style would suit me. 'Your figure and complexion are good. You can dress in any style, any dress will compliment you,' he said encouragingly. We went to Paona Bazar in a rickshaw. I bought a red-coloured fabric, three metres long, at an affordable price. From Paona Bazar, we went to Selection House at Alu Galli. There were piles of clothes on display in the shop. I turned these piles over, again and again. Finally, I spotted a loose white shirt, like the one Julia Roberts had worn in the film. I showed it to Bob, and asked, 'Will this look do?' In the veritable euphoria of *Pretty Woman*, no explanation was needed, Bob understood what I meant. He gave an affirmative nod, 'All right, nupi.' I found my version of Julia Roberts' iconic white shirt on the day I watched *Pretty Woman*. I bought the shirt for fifteen rupees. It was a very good day, a small segment of my dream seemed to have come true.

On our way back, we could not stop talking about *Pretty Woman*. We seemed to reach home in no time.

Bob's favourite character in the movie was Julia Roberts' friend. I was obsessed with the last scene in which Richard Gere walks in the rain, holding an umbrella, looking for Julia Roberts. The way Julia Roberts' character dressed, her attitude, her poise, all seemed very sexy to me, I was deeply and truly inspired. Also, the the scene in which Julia Roberts hitches a lift from Richard Gere left a lasting impression on my mind.

From that day onwards, I modelled my style on Julia Roberts' in *Pretty Woman*. The small sum with which I had bought the red material and white shirt in the rapturous aftermath of the film was the last bit of money in my possession. I did not buy any book. Anticipating Ema's questions, I borrowed a book from Bob, which I held in my hand for Ema to see. Before reaching home, I stopped at Ta Nando's house. His father was a tailor, and I wanted to get a pair of half-pants stitched, *a la* Julia Roberts. Nando's father did not have much idea about the design I wanted. He showed me an old catalogue that had Chinese models wearing different cuts and designs of pants. We flicked through the pages of the catalogue to find the style I wanted, but none of the designs resembled the half-pants of my dreams. We chose a style that we thought was somewhat similar, for lack of a better option. He said that it would take him four days to make the pants. I asked him to do it in one or two days, but he said he could not do it in less than three. A day less was not enough to quell my impatience but I had no choice but to wait.

My mind constantly went back to the piano scene and the last scene of the movie. The scenes haunted me even when I was eating my evening meal and when I went to bed that night. The following day, I visited Nando's father, and for the next couple of days I continued to visit him and sit with him for a while till the moment the half-pants were ready and delivered into my hands. I was there when the fabric was being cut into the required shape, and when he began stitching it. Noticing my childlike impatience, his daughter asked me, 'You come here every day! What kind of dress are you getting made?' I replied that it was a pair of half-pants. Then I began to worry that my ridiculous visits would be reported back to my family, which would definitely lead to questions being asked and create many problems for me. To circumvent such troubles, I presented Ta Nando's father with a few sticks of *bidis* that I had stealthily removed from Baba's *bidi* packets. He said that I could visit him without the *bidis* too. Despite his protests, I continued to offer him *bidis*, in the hope that he would stich the pants sooner, and also reduce his charges as much as possible.

As soon as the pair of half-pants was ready, I changed into them and went to Poison's house. Poison was highly impressed by the sheer boldness of my attire. I told him that my style was directly inspired by Julia Roberts in *Pretty Woman*. What did he think about the pants? He said that in the bright daylight, the red colour of the half-pants shone redder. That day, Poison had a request to make to me, 'I want to borrow your dress on Yaosang. Please don't lend your dress to anyone else before I wear it.' Yaosang was the Manipuri equivalent of Holi.

I cannot explain why, but the radical change in my style of dressing was accompanied by visible changes in my mannerisms. My voice became more feminine. Not surprisingly, my family and the neighbours interpreted me as some kind of joke. My likes and dislikes, what I thought and felt, was ignored, as I was not considered a respectable human being. This was a challenge to whatever I was and stood for. Their challenge was met with an aggressive passivity—I ignored all, everyone who did not care to understand or respect me.

I was not simply unique, I was extremely provocative too. The dresses I wore would not be worn by any Meitei woman. Once I shaved off my hair; this could be considered a culmination of my style statement that already included heavy make-up and multiple piercings. I had six piercings on each side of my ears, two piercings on each side of my nose. Each piercing was adorned with a piece of jewellery. I went everywhere dressed in this way; predictably, everyone stared at me. One day I roamed in the Lamlong Keithel area in tight, skimpy hot pants and a turquoise blue halter top. I became the cause of an accident that day—a middle-aged man kept staring at me with a look of hatred, and drove his scooter straight into a traffic pole on the road. It was justice delivered, I thought!

Meanwhile, in Khurai, I became famous, or rather notorious, as Santa Khurai, who dressed like a woman in broad daylight. Nobody talked about me with affection or goodwill. From the time I started wearing feminine clothing both at home and in public, hostile stares and harsh words followed me everywhere. Only the open roads on which I walked became my constant companion, and I continue to walk towards my destination. The criticism coming from common people infuriated me. But when the criticism came from my people, my homo friends, I could not be angry at them, rather I tolerated and understood their criticism. But no matter how forgiving I tried to be, my friend's unfavourable comments inflicted deep emotional wounds on me.

Once, Bob, Poison, Ronu, Maibi Macha, and I visited the Wangkhei constituency candidate Irabot's house to play a game of carrom. The preparation for general elections was underway at that time, so candidates used all forms of entertainment to bait the voters in their favour. Playing carrom appeared to be a tradition during the elections. We also met Manimohon, our friend from Kongpal, at the candidate's house. Everyone present looked at me as though I had fallen from the sky. After a while, my friends disappeared elsewhere, leaving me alone. I soon grew bored and went to join Poison and Ronu who were talking in a corner of the *sangoi*. They told me that Maibi Macha and Manimohon had gone to the Porompat PD complex that was under construction then. It was not difficult to locate Bob's whereabouts. I went to the place where a few persons were playing table tennis. Bob was very fond of table tennis, and I knew that he would be there.

For a while, I explored the place on my own and came across a group of men who were discussing the elections. They did not show any kind of negative reaction towards me. In fact they were well-dressed and looked dignified. Surprisingly, one of them already knew me. He called me to his side and introduced me to his friends. He said that I was a junior of one of his friends at Don Bosco school, Chingmeirong. They showed interest in meeting my friends, and invited us to a meal that was arranged for everyone there. Gladdened by their respectful treatment of me, I told Bob first about the invitaton. Bob told me that he would complete the table tennis match that was in progress first, meanwhile, I could tell Ronu, Poison, Manimohon and Maibi Macha. I found Poison and Ronu in the same place where they were before. Maibi Macha and Manimohon had not returned from Porompat. Poison and Ronu were not interested in talking with the men; rather they found it a bit embarrassing to be in their company. Besides, Poison was sure that some men from his locality must be loitering at the same gathering. 'Are you seriously interested? Those men must be the losers from Chingam Leirak,' he said. Bob persisted that we could at least go for a while and then leave the place if it turned out to be uncomfortable. In the end, it was Poison against all of us, and we prevailed over his reluctance. It happened that Poison did know a few of the men. They asked if we wanted to drink *yu,* locally brewed wine, which we declined. We did not eat with them, but sat separately. We left the place shortly after the meal.

On our way back from the candidate's house, we had to pass through Porompat. The Porompat road looked deserted at that time of the night, there was quietness all around. The sparse landscape made the night feel lonelier. More than human habitation, small ditches and marshes with thick clusters of reeds proliferated the area. During the daytime, horses grazing in the meadows made the place haunting and beautiful at the same time. We liked such deserted places where there was nobody to persecute us. Such places fetched us the freedom we longed for—we delivered film and drama dialogues and sang songs, every blissful movement was accompanied by a dance of freedom. Our laughter boomed out in the silence. We were the performers, we were the audience, too.

Halfway between Irabot's house and Lamlong, there was a *tomal* tree. As we were approaching the tree, three men appeared suddenly, as though they were apparitions. They commanded us to stand in a line. Each of the three men was carrying a bamboo stick. All the laughter and fun we had enjoyed a little while before vanished; it was as though that short-lived freedom had been a prelude to the terror that had suddenly seized us. I thought of overpowering the men, snatching the sticks from their hands and beating them to death, and then dumping their corpses in the surrounding marshland. But of course, no such thing was possible.

One man asked aggressively, 'Hey, where are you coming from?' Nobody replied, we hung our heads in silence. Again he asked, 'Are you dumb?'

Poison replied, 'We are coming from Irabot's house.'

Another man said, 'Why are you laughing so loud at this time of the night?'

They examined each one of us as we stood in front of them. Just as their gaze fell on me, one of them asked, 'Are you a homo?' He asked me that question as though 'homo' was my name, I knew he wanted to humiliate me. He asked me the question again and this time, I nodded in reply. Yes, I was a homo. My nod of consent was not enough to quell his thirst to insult me. In a loud, angry tone, he commanded me to answer him aloud. In the next few seconds he started hitting me with the bamboo stick. Angered by his conduct, I questioned their motive for treating us in this manner. My temerity in speaking up for myself offended his sense of superiority that gave him the right to humiliate and torture us. He pointed a gun at my head (I did not know that he was carrying a gun), and said, 'Are you begging me to shoot you, to finish you off right this second?' I was certain that my end had come, talking more could radically shorten my life. So I fell silent.

In the moments that followed, I was severely beaten, while my friends huddled at the side of the road. After satisfying their rage, the three men released us with the command to run to save our lives. We ran as fast as we could and as we ran, we could hear them laughing at us. As we fled the scene, Maibi Macha, who was running behind us, screamed, 'Nupis, stop.' We all stopped and waited for him to catch up with us. Even in those horrifying moments of fear and flight, Poison laughed, 'Tonight, Maibi's prediction is turning into reality.' This was a joke amongst us, because maibis traditionally make prophecies and tell people's fortunes, and his name was 'Maibi' Macha. So we used to tease him that he could make predictions.

Fear, exhaustion, and the precarious chance to live again erupted in a burst of uncontrollable laughter. I was in splits, my stomach ached. We started running again. Just as we were turning towards Yangoningthow, Mabi Macha, who was still struggling to keep up with, us said angrily, 'You *kasubis* (sluts), I was imploring you to wait for me.'

Without answering him, Poison said, 'Was not the spirit of *tomal* Makhong furious?' Maibi Macha could not register the meaning of Poison's statement immediately, but within a few seconds he replied, 'Enough, you *kasubi*.' It was believed that evil spirits played in the *tomal* tree, and Poison was trying to frighten us by reminding us of this folklore. Maibi Macha's panic-stricken cries as he ran behind us made us laugh all over again.

My meek acceptance of the thrashing inflicted upon me by the group of men was also a cause of laughter among my friends. It was remarkable that we were able to generate humour at our own expense. However, my laughter was a facade, a desire for revenge was being fuelled within me even as I laughed outwardly—I will take revenge when the time and opportunity arrive, I told myself.

Engrossed in telling us humourous anecdotes, Poison followed us beyond the gate of his house. When we reached the point where Lamlong main road split into four different streets, I asked them to accompany me till the gate of my house. Bob replied, 'You are not scared of wearing make-

up and showing attitude, but you get frightened easily!'
His derisive words filled me with a new sorrow, and out
of this pain and disappointment, a loud curse escaped me.
I knelt on the ground, hit my palm on the concrete road,
and said, 'If I am not wrong, you will die a miserable
death.' Poison must have realised he had hurt me; instead
of retaliating, he simply told us another funny story that
calmed me down a little.

It was an unspoken rule that we did not share stories of
dangerous encounters with anybody outside our group. In
truth, we considered these incidents shameful; we concluded
that we must be beaten because of our ugly looks, or some
fault in us. This was self-denigration bred out of fear and
insecurity. But though I encountered so much brutality from
people, I healed myself by recalling those moments when I
was able to tease men, buy snacks and suchlike for them
to mock them. Most trans people were too shy to approach
men publicly, but I had the courage to do so, even though
I was a very open trans, and this was my pride.

Men did not like me very much. My friends said I
had a horse face, I did not look feminine at all, and so I
would repel men. Often their words kept me away from
developing romantic feelings for men. Who would welcome
rejection! Some men did like me, but the problem was that
my idea of romance and relationships was influenced by
Hollywood movies, and these men could not communicate
with me in the way I wanted, and so the relationship did
not last for long.

Once my friends and I met outside Poison's house. It was
the Lai Haraoba season. Poison told us that Surjit from the

Laibung Committee of Lainingthou Lai Haroaba wanted to put up a dance drama performance. Poison and Ronu were no strangers to such performances, they had participated in dance dramas before. But I had never had an opportunity to be a part of such festivities. I shamelessly begged Poison to get me a role in the dance drama. Poison said, 'There is nobody to take the role of the *hingchabi* (witch). Do you want to do the role?' I said, 'I don't want to play the role of a *hingchabi*. I want to dance in the role of a beautiful woman.'

Poison said, 'Listen, nupi. In this drama, the *hingchabi* transforms into a heavenly dancer. You will be able to charm men with your dancing skill.'

I agreed to play the double role of *hingchabi* and heavenly dancer. For three days I rehearsed my part in Hero's courtyard. I danced to a popular song '*Mitchannaba Thoklaba Nangi Mityenga kana leiri ngairoidaba nangumba*' from the Manipuri film *Umangi Mi*. Even as I rehearsed, I imagined people in the Laibung Committee being charmed by my dance. I eagerly waited for the day of the performance.

Meanwhile, thoughts about the costume to be worn in the performance occupied my mind. I was sure that nobody could have imagined the kind of dress I had in mind. The only problem was the total absence of money to buy the dress. As usual, money would be given to me only when I had to buy books and stationery items. It had been a while since I had got any orders for drawing embroidery designs for bedsheets and pillow covers. This was one of my talents, and the only source of pocket money for me. But even if I had money, who would stitch the dress? It would have to be someone totally unknown to my family, any unfortunate revelation about my part in the dance drama would earn scorn and protest from them. My family would not be happy with me playing a woman's role, they would surely stop me from participating in the dance drama. Nobody in my family must know about my latest venture.

Another concern of mine was my short hair. I would need to borrow a wig. At that time only Shumang Leela actors possessed wigs and good make-up items.

A few days later, when I reached home from dance rehearsal, Ema told me that Eche Memcha, who ran an embroidery business, had come to meet me. I instantly knew that she must have come to give me an order for embroidery designs. This was a godsend, an opportunity to earn the money that I sorely needed for my costume. I immediately went to meet her at her house. Indeed, she needed designs for two different sets of bedsheets as soon as possible. We settled the price of the design at twenty rupees per set. She gave me sixty rupees more, as an advance for future orders. That night, under the dim beam of the light bulb, I drew the designs for the two sets of bedsheets. The following morning, I went to Eche Memcha's house to deliver the drawings. She was satisfied with the designs and said, 'These designs are very good. I will not take much time to fill in the stitches.' She generously praised the intricate flower patterns I had drawn.

As I walked out of her house, I continued to think about who would be the right person to stitch the dress, the right tailor to match my imagination and at the same time, be willing to keep my secret. Eche Santa's name came to my mind, she could do the job. Besides her family did not talk disapprovingly of me. Her brother whom we respectfully called Oja Ebomcha, was highly regarded by Baba. I believed that even if my father came to know about the whole affair, the worst scenario, Oja Ebomcha would speak in my favour. After a careful calculation of all the possible consequences, I concluded that Eche Santa was the right person to stitch the dress for me.

At Eche Santa's house, the first person I met was her younger sister, Ebecha, who was sitting in the *mangol,* softly singing to herself. She was unaware of my approach. When I greeted her, she turned towards me and said, 'Hello, dear Santoor! What are you doing here?'

I asked, 'Where is Eche Santa?'

Ebecha replied jokingly, 'Like you, she must be somewhere, looking for a man.'

I replied, 'Enough, crazy girl. Where is Eche Santa? I have some important work with her.'

'Cool down! She is in the toilet.'

Ebecha was a light-hearted girl, she could joke about any grave matter. But that particular day I was not inclined to respond to her banter. The dress, its details and my expectations of it, fully engaged my mind. Ebecha repeatedly enquired why I wanted to meet her sister, and each time I replied that I could only talk about it with Eche Santa. After a short while, Eche Santa appeared. She asked, 'What is the occasion for your visit, dear? Are you in the mood for some make-up?'

I said, 'No. I have come to discuss something with you.'

Eche Santa said, 'How grave an issue is it now! Do you want to borrow my bra?'

I said, 'Not that. This is about a dance drama performance I will be participating in very soon.'

Ebecha burst out laughing, 'Poor Modhu Singh! This time you will be at Santa's knee.' Modhu Singh was my father's name. Though he disapproved thoroughly of my feminity, he could not do anything to control my behaviour. By this remark, Ebecha meant that I had defeated my father, seeing me in the dance drama in the role of a woman, would bring him to his knees.

Then Eche Santa enquired, 'Where is this dance drama happening?'

Ebecha joined in, 'It must be at the Lainingthou Ahanba, I saw many homos playing kho-kho at the ground. Ta Surjit must be encouraging them to participate in the drama.' It was true many young homos played kho-kho at the Lainingthou Ahanba ground. Ebecha was also a skilled kho-kho player herself. She played on the same team as Bob, Ronu and Poison. She was a very close friend of Ta Surjit's daughter.

Eche Santa said, 'I will stitch the dress for you, whatever design you choose. As soon as I finish stitching the dress, I will show it to Sanahanbi.' She meant my mother; the two sisters often teased me by saying that they would expose my secret activities. But they never did so.

I said, 'Let's be serious. If you don't stitch the dress for me, I will go to Lamlong and find someone to stitch it for me.'

Eche Santa said, 'Sure, go ahead. Let's see who will make a dress for you.'

This flippant conversation between the two sisters infuriated me. In a gesture of defiance, I turned my face away and started walking away from them. I was aware that Eche Santa and Ebecha were laughing at me.

As I continued to walk away, Eche Santa called out, 'Wait, child. I was joking with you. You come here everyday to wear make-up. Did I ever tell your mother? If I had ever revealed it to her, she would not even allow you to step outside your house.'

Reassured by her words, I returned to them.

Eche Santa asked, 'Who else is participating?'

I replied, 'Four men and two homos.'

Ebecha asked inquisitively, 'Who is the other homo?'

'It is Poison.'

Eche Santa now asked, 'Who is Poison?'

Ebecha answered her. 'Poison is Ta Jadumani's younger brother, Ta Debebrata.'

Eche Santa asked again, 'Will he look good in dresses and make-up?'

I replied, 'We will have to wait and see. Poison is going to be the heroine.'

Ebecha asked impatiently, 'And what will be your character?'

I replied, 'I will be the *hingchabi*.'

Ebecha burst out laughing. 'That is very unfair. Poison is playing a cunning game with you. He will play the heroine's role, and you are made to play the *hingchabi*. You should not agree to it.' Eche Santa laughed at Ebecha's words.

The sisters were not aware of the script of the dance drama, so I reassured them,'Do not worry. I am not playing an ugly *hingchabi* only. This *hingchabi* is going to transform into an alluring woman and then she will charm the king, with a dance. Got it?'

As usual, Ebecha had no dearth of witty rejoinders in her arsenal. 'Really. How much more beautiful can you be? Your eyebrows are already shaped like leeches.' I told her that my performance would give a fitting reply to her taunts.

Eche Santa finally asked me, 'What kind of dress do you want for the role?'

I replied, 'Maybe a blouse. I will borrow a *phanek* from you.'

Ebecha did not spare this reply as well. Turning towards Eche Santa, she said, 'Eche, lend him Ema's old *mayanglang phanek*.'

At that time, I did not know what a *mayanglang phanek* looked like and on what occasion it was meant to be worn.

Rather I thought it must be an exquisite garment and was excited at the thought of wearing it. 'That would be so nice. What colour is it? Let me see.'

Eche Santa said in an amused tone, 'You are so eager to look like a woman, but you do not even know what a *mayanglang phanek* is! If you dance in a *mayanglang phanek* at Lai Haraoba, people will greet you with a hailstorm of stones.'

I asked her what she meant—why would they throw stones at me?

Eche Santa said, 'A *mayanglang phanek* is the one women wear when they are mourning the death of a person. If you ever dance wearing a *mayanglang phanek* during a *laibow*, everyone will call you crazy and beat the hell out of you.' All the while Eche Santa was explaining to me what a *mayanglang phanek* was, Ebecha was mercilessly laughing at my expense. She was truly one of the naughtiest girls around.

Eche Santa asked me kindly me if I had money to buy the fabric for the blouse. I told her about the money Eche Memcha had given me for the embroidery designs. Eche Santa told me to go and buy the fabric. I told her that our programme was just a day away, and there wasn't enough time to go to the bazar to look for the fabric. I had hoped that she would have some fabric in her house.

Ebecha said, 'Then you should buy a white long cloth, stitch a blouse with that, and then dye it.' She meant the thin cloth made of cotton thread that people used as a bath towel or in ritual activities.

I asked, 'Will I get long cloth in Lamlong?' Eche Santa said that I would.

Ebecha had an ingenious suggestion. 'Eche Santa, you can take a bigger measurement, so that the seams can be double-folded. This will prevent the seams from coming apart. It is such a thin cloth that it can easily tear.'

Eche Santa agreed with Ebecha's idea but she had a doubt. 'But if the seams do come apart even then, do not blame me. You are not giving me much time to make the dress,' she said. Since there was not enough time to go shopping for the right fabric for the blouse, I thought it more practical to agree with Ebecha's suggestion.

I said, 'Where will I get the fabric? And how are we going to dye it?'

Eche Santa told me, 'You will find the fabric at Rupini's shop, or maybe Sama's shop. The dye is sold at Ram Singh's shop, buy a colour of your choice, and buy for two rupees only.'

As I got up to go, I entreated them, 'Eche Santa and Ebecha, please do not let my family know about this.'

At Lamlong Bazar I bought a long piece of long cloth from Rupini's shop. And I bought a red-coloured dye for two rupees. After buying these two items, I visited Poison at his house. I was eager to know how his preparations were going. Poison was sitting on the bench by the pond. It surprised me a little to see how nonchalant Poison was—he did not seem to be at all anxious about the performance the next day.

Ronu, who was with Poison at that time, said sarcastically on seeing me, 'Our artist for tomorrow has also arrived.' I asked Poison about his preparations. He told me that he would be wearing a *phanek mapal naibi*. I asked, 'What about the hair?'

Poison replied, 'I will secure my hair tightly and wear a long *shambandong* (hair extension, made of real hair and worn as a pony-tail). What will you you wear?'

I replied, 'Almost the same as yours.'

I did not stay longer at Poison's place. I hurried towards
Eche Santa's house to gave her the material for the blouse.
It was agreed that the blouse would be ready by morning
the next day. It was only after making all the arrangements
for my costume that I returned home.

That night my mind was occupied with thoughts about
my performance that would be witnessed by many people.
I went to bed immediately after the meal. Everyone was
asleep. But I was awake, humming in my mind, while my
body and hands responded to the rhythm of the song. In
the morning, I pretended to be studying for a while, but
thoughts about the blouse and dance drama had blocked any
concern for books. Just then, it happened that Oja Ebomcha
walked past our *shumang* on his way to Thoidingjam
Bem Bem's house, where he was giving private tuitions to
children.

I asked, 'Oja Ebomcha, what was Eche Santa doing
when you were leaving?'

'She was sweeping the *shumang*,' he replied.

I pressed him further, 'You did not see her stitching?'

Oja Ebomcha said, 'It is too early.'

His reply set warning bells ringing in my mind. Eche
Santa must not have stitched my blouse. I needed to know
what she was doing at that time. As usual I had to devise
a plan. Human will is strong, it always finds a way. I told
Ema that I wanted to eat *tal,* a local delicacy, from Ebok
Ashangbi's hotel. Ema gave me two rupees to buy *tal.* With
two rupees in my pocket and the blouse on my mind, I went
straight to Eche Santa's house. She was not to be seen in the
shumang. I went inside the house. She was in the kitchen,
cooking. Ebecha was sitting on the bed that was kept in
the kitchen, studying. I said despairingly, 'Eche Santa, you
did not stitch my blouse?'

Ebecha giggled, 'Your eyes are teary, you are almost crying. So fragile, like a flower.'

Eche Santa said, 'Look at you. You are going to cry. Who said that I did not stitch your blouse? I have already stitched it.'

I rushed towards the sewing machine. I was overcome with happiness when I saw my blouse. I gave Eche Santa ten rupees for the blouse but she refused to accept it. 'Leave it. Do not give me money for this. But you must draw a design for a piece of embroidery for me.'

I replied, 'I will definitely draw designs for your embroidery and will also buy *kwa* for you. But what about the colour of the blouse?'

Eche Santa replied, 'I will dye your blouse immediately after the morning meal. Just pray that it does not rain today, we have to dry the cloth in the sun.'

Ebecha promptly said, 'I am waiting for a heavy downpour today. It would be fun.'

I walked towards Ebecha who was still sitting on the bed, nonchalantly playing with the strands of her hair. Sensing that I was going to attack her, she jumped off the bed and evaded my grasp. My toes jammed against the foot of the bed while I was chasing her around it, making me yelp in pain. Ebecha said that I was being punished for doing things without the knowledge of my family.

Eche Santa asked me to try on the blouse. 'Let's see if the blouse fits.'

I removed my shirt to try on the blouse. Seeing my bony frame, Ebecha said, 'You really look like a *hingchabi*. You look like a mad *hingchabi*.'

I replied, 'Listen, I might be thin, but my body structure is considered fashionable by international standards.' Ebecha retorted, 'Truly international. You look like you have been fasting on an international level!'

The blouse turned out to be a little loose. Eche Santa marked out the extra material with a chalk, which meant she would alter it to fit my size. I could have my blouse fully ready by noon. Ebecha said, 'I am coming on time to watch you dancing. You must not fail.' I said confidently, 'Leave it to me.'

Towards the evening, I visited Eche Santa's house again. My blouse was finally ready. I borrowed a *phanek* from her to pair with the blouse. Both sisters had decided to come and watch me perform.

The blouse and *phanek* were not the only things I needed—I needed make-up and cosmetics as well. So I helped the sisters to collect firewood, with the motive that I could then ask them to lend me some make-up. Ebecha gave me a face powder called Spring Song and a red lipstick. Both the items were old and used up. When I told Ebecha this, she gave me another lipstick and counselled me that if I wanted good make-up, I should take help from the male maibis. 'They have all the make-up items,' she said. I put all the materials Eche Santa provided in a polythene bag and headed towards Poison's house, but he was not at home. One of Poison's sisters-in-law told me that he had gone to the house of a friend to prepare for the dance drama, but she didn't know where the person's house was and neither did I. I went to Ronu's house to ask his younger brother about Ronu and Poison's whereabouts. I knew that all my friends would have gathered around Poison. Poison's brother told me where Ronu had gone. When I reached there, Poison was already halfway through his make-up. I saw that Poison had good make-up and dresses. My long cloth blouse and the borrowed *phanek* and cometics seemed shabby and cheap beside his, like the difference between an ocean and a pond.

As there was nothing I could do about this, I started applying my make-up. The first item I used was the face powder. Maibi Macha exclaimed as though I had committed a crime, 'Santa is directly applying the powder to her face.'

Ronu explained, 'Nupi, you have to apply the paste first, otherwise the powder will smudge all over your face. Where is your paste?'

I asked, 'What is paste? I do not have a paste.'

'Really? How will you apply make-up then?' Ronu asked in surprise.

Ronu took a small amount of paste from a packet with KOSMIC printed on it, from Poison, and applied it on my face. Meanwhile, I could not stop looking at Poison. Poison had got a real hair extension from a Shumang Leela Nupi Sabi called Bijoy. Nupi Sabis were homos who played the role of women in the Shumang Leela. The homos who took part in the Leelas were very beautiful and feminine. (To explain—the term 'Nupi Sabi' was used for homos who did not take part in the Leelas also, but the difference was that the non-Leela homos did not like to be called by this term and saw it as an insult, whereas those who took part in the Leelas accepted the term.)

The make-up, dress and hair extension made Poison look very beautiful, like a vision. All our friends who had gathered there appreciated his appearance. On the other hand, everything went wrong with my make-up. Bob, Ronu and Maibi Macha tried to correct my horrible make-up— one would come and say I was doing it the wrong way, while another applied another layer over the previous one. This process continued for a while. The repeated application of the Kosmic paste made my cheeks fiery red. Each person's fingers seemed to have left marks on my face. The make-up did not make me look beautiful, my face looked distorted.

I did not feel beautiful, I felt like an alien creature. But the determination to dance and enjoy the dance drama was stronger than my despair over my ugly face.

Finally, the moment arrived. Our dance drama was introduced and announced on the loudspeaker. Along with other artistes my name was also repeatedly announced— 'Playing the role of the *hingchabi* is Santa'. As the announcement continued, more and more people gathered to watch our performance. By the time the performance started, the Lai Haraoba grounds were overflowing with people.

The long-awaited dance drama finally started—the king and his minister were visiting a forest. On seeing the king, the *hingchabi*, my character, was lured by the desire for him. She worked magic on the minister who immediately lost consciousness. Probably I looked like a real *hingchabi* because when I appeared on the stage, everyone in the audience laughed. As soon as I started dancing, my blouse tore, which made them laugh even more. The entire *laibung* was filled with the raucous laughter of the audience. The dance drama was not supposed to be funny, it was meant to be solemn; the laughter assured me that something was greatly amiss. Ashamed of everything that was happening to me, I ran inside the small room reserved for the maibas and maibis. Poison continued playing his part on the stage.

Backstage, everyone was praising Poison's beautiful appearance. As far as I was concerned, my fellow players did not even come near me or speak to me. After my utter humiliation at the hands of the audience that could not stop laughing at me, I silently left the play before it got over. At first I was scared of going home alone, but I could not stay at the venue any longer. I walked back alone with fear and the heavy feeling of self-pity and defeat in my heart. At that time of night, there was no one to be seen, and a light rain made things worse. I dipped the torn, red blouse in the puddles on the roadside and used it to wipe the make-up off my face. I threw the torn, wet blouse in a corner of the Lamlong market, then I continued walking towards home. It was very dark. The sound of the *penna*—a traditional musical instrument—from the distant *laibung* made the lonely environment even more eerie. Disappointment, shame and fear of what my family would say preoccupied my mind, my legs were shaking. Despite all this my only concern was to reach home. Songs playing on megaphones could also be heard from the direction of Khutlembi Lai Haraoba ground. When I reached Lukhoi's dukan, I saw a light approaching from Khutlembi ground. I thought that it must be the headlight of a truck, and felt greatly relieved. The light was fast approaching me, and each moment it drew nearer, it got bigger and brighter. I don't recall what happened after that, the only thing I could remember was that when the light reached me, I felt as though it had wrapped itself around my body.

I must have reached home in a trance-like state. When I fully regained consciousness, I was at the edge of the *mangol*, I could feel Ema's hand tenderly touching my forehead. I couldn't make out if Ema was talking to me or asking questions. Whatever she uttered was only faintly comprehensible to me. I asked what had happened, and Ema seemed to be asking if I was conscious. It seemed as though I was inhabiting a totally different world. I could barely remember my name. My mother was saying that she had gone to the Lai Haraoba venue to watch me perform. 'I went carrying a rod, with the intention of beating you. It was Keina who stopped me from doing so.' She said that my antics were outrageous, if Baba came to know about this, he would not spare me. She also said that I must thank my luck, as Baba was away from home on night duty.

The next day, I went to Eche Santa's house and scolded her for her shoddy stitching. My outrage did not have any effect on the two sisters; on the contrary, they laughed hysterically. Unlike the laughter of the audience the previous night, the sisters' laughter did not make me angry. Instead, my anger slowly subsided and I also started laughing with them. Eche Santa informed me that Ema and Ema Keina had also come to watch our dance drama. Somebody also told her that I fainted in the aftermath of my *hingchabi* role.

I said, 'I know. Ema told me everything.'

Ebecha said, 'It was not only your mother and Ema Keina, many people from your neighbourhood also came.'

I asked, 'What did Ema say after seeing me?'

Eche Santa replied, 'Your mother laughed and said that you were very ugly. She also had a wooden rod in her hand.'

I said, 'Since she is ugly, I am also ugly.'

Ebecha chipped in, 'Indeed, you do not look like a woman, you are very ugly.'

I replied, 'That is enough. I look much better than you.'

After spending some time with the sisters, I visited Bob's house, with the intention of collecting more information about the dance drama. I took a shortcut through Laishram lane to reach Bob's house. Bob was asleep, but I woke him up.

I asked, 'Nupi, how did I do last night?'

Bob laughed, 'You looked like a torn sack of rice.'

Inspite of all my pain and humiliation, I could not help laughing heartily at Bob's description of me as a torn rice sack. We went to Poison's house and found him folding the dresses he had worn at the dance drama. Seeing us, he said excitedly, 'I got an offer to join the leela.'

Bob said disinterestedly, 'Good for you.'

Poison could not stop talking about the applause he had got from people after the performance.

In the period following the dance drama fiasco, I fell sick periodically. The symptoms of my sickness could not be diagnosed, they were so weird and unique. My ailing condition made Ema cry a lot and Baba's face looked noticeably worried. Ema told me about a few of the incidents that had happened during this time. In one incident, I did not come home for two days. While everyone was searching for me, a few people found me wandering at a desolate place in the Kangla fort area. These people finally brought me home. Ema also said that I did not eat a single meal for a week. Another time, I came home completely naked. Ema said that I had walked in that naked state all through Lamlong. Baba and Ema consulted doctors many times, but my sickness persisted. Then Ema described my symptoms to a maiba from Uripok. He said that my sickness was the initial stage of becoming a maibi.

It was at this time that a small *laishang* dedicated to our *sageigi lai* or ancestral deity, Ebudhou Pakhangba, was built in our homestead. From early morning till noon, many people visited me every day. They also offered money, flowers and fruits to Ebudhou Pakhangba. When they wanted to know the misfortunes that would befall their families, I closed my eyes and prayed to Ebudhou to reveal their fate to me. As soon as I closed my eyes and said some initial invocations, a strange, unnameable process happened—a serpent-like creature seemed to raise itself perpendicularly from the lower end of my backbone. As this energy touched the zenith of my head, I became unaware of my surroundings, and I was led into a different world of dreams and unusual visions. This new world was alive with abundant flowers and fruits, and my sole companion in this world was an old man who talked to me. When I regained consciousness, I retold the conversations with the old man to the person who sought my advice. The words spoken in that dreamlike state were considered sacred and full of wisdom by the people. My visitors believed that I was telling them insightful truths on the matters for which they were seeking answers, and that was the reason why more and more people came to seek knowledge about their life from me.

After recovering from my illness, I visited Poison again. By then, my friends had started talking about me as a maibi. Another tag was added to my name; in their words, 'Homo Santa has become a maibi.' Each new epithet was accompanied by laughter. Now, everyone looked upon me as a maibi. People offered me money to read their future, the kind of thing for which maibis were usually sought after. People perceived me as a medium to whom money, sacred flowers, and sacred fire had to be offered to divine their future. Their perception alienated me from the ordinary world of men and women, I felt lonely and isolated.

Since the time I came to know about maibis, I had decided that I never wanted to be one. Maibis were looked upon as capable of causing evil things to happen to people, they were particularly regarded as individuals possessing the power to connect with *lais* or spirits. People were scared of the form they took when possessed by a *lai*.

Despite my aversion, I became a maibi, and nothing could be done to disown my new form. The sacredness of a maibi came with many restrictions, principal amongst them being diet. I was only permitted certain foods, others were forbidden. I was made to learn *laihourol,* a sacred chant of the maibis, from a few revered maibis and maibas. If I failed to follow these precepts, I would suffer from aches and pains, and even the guardian *lai* could overpower and make me go insane, or so I was told. I learnt *laihourol* from a maibi in Uripok. The *laihourol* helped me control and understand the new world of fear, the unintelligible language and actions that were flowing from the state of *lai tongba,* a state in which the maibi is possessed by a deity.

However, the manner in which people perceived me and the changing attitude of my friends distressed me greatly. One day I told Ema, 'Ema, tell these people not to come to me anymore.' Ema said, 'I have told them so. But it would be rude to turn them out. Your Baba's situation also distresses me a lot. It seems that his friends also talk negatively about your condition.' I was already a homo and I had become a maibi, too. Truth be told, it must have been a great ordeal for him.

I said, 'Let's consult the maiba who treated me before. We can ask him to bring me back to a normal condition.'

Ema said, 'He said that it is only after the *lai* is suppressed that you will be fine again. But before the process is finally completed, the spirit will manifest itself in you now and then. The spirit will not leave you easily.'

It must have been for three or four months that I was the custodian of this gift of the medium, which proved to be an immense encumbrance for me. The fear of being judged harshly by society made me spend most of my time within the four walls of the house. I ate all the food proscribed so as to negate the sacred knowledge that was supposedly destined to flow through my soul and body. The result was not what I expected, the wilful disobedience did not release me from the unwanted power and divine privileges that were afflicting me. Whenever I ate the forbidden food, I fainted and fell sick. My deteriorating condition greatly worried Ema. She started consulting many other maibas and maibis.

One day, Ema took me to Uripok in a rickshaw. She said that we were going to meet the same maiba who had previously treated me. She believed that only he could control the *lai*. We did not know the exact address of the maiba. We got off the rickshaw at Uripok Lai Khutlembi. We went inside a small *laishang* and asked a middle-aged man who was sitting there for directions. He told us that the maiba lived in the house adjacent to the *laishang*. When we arrived at the house, we could not see anyone around, so we opened the gate and entered. The maiba was reclining between the pillars of the *mangol*. Ema addressed the maiba as 'mamma'. He asked us who we were, it was clear that he did not remember us. He looked very old and it seemed that his eyesight had become weaker. Ema reminded him that I was the boy from Khurai that he had treated before and she was my mother. Ema and I stepped into the *mangol*. Ema touched the feet of the maiba before sitting down on one of the stools his son offered us.

The maiba asked us the reason for our visit. Ema replied, 'Mamma, my son is very young. We cannot always look after him. He eats food that he should not eat. His health is becoming worse day by day. Sometimes he faints. I am here with the hope that you would be able to control the *lai* in him.' Ema and the maiba spoke together for a while.

A *phak* or reed mat was spread in the middle of the *mangol*. I was made to lie down on my back on the *phak*. Then the maiba intoned the *laisol*, a sacred chant, over my body and pressed down on my stomach with his open palm. After checking my pulse, he called Ema aside and spoke to her. I was not allowed to hear their brief conversation. After this interaction, we did not stay at the place for long.

On the way, before we reached home, I asked Ema what the maiba had told her. Ema said that my condition was a bit grave, but we had to continue the treatment to suppress the deity that had possessed me.

A week after our visit to his house, Baba brought the maiba home. Our family treated him with great respect and care. Eche and Ema cooked his meal, and Baba caught a big fish for him from our pond. Our small *laishang* was thoroughly cleaned before the maiba's arrival. Ema put all the offerings of flowers and other items that were needed in the *laishang*. Once the maiba had seated himself at the shrine, I was made to sit beside him. After a prolonged chanting of the sacred words, he repeatedly stroked my body with a small twig of mahogany. My body gradually felt a release, as though something heavy had been lifted out of me. It was some form of miracle. The maiba turned towards me and asked, 'How does your body feel?'

I replied, 'I feel very light.'

He turned towards Ema and said, 'Everything will be fine now, do not worry. Be sure that he does not eat the proscribed food.'

The maiba ate the meal Ema and Eche had cooked for him. After he had eaten, Baba took him back to his house at Uripok. I was surprised that he was taking all this trouble for me, he had never till then expressed any affection for me. So, when he showed worry and concern about me, it baffled me. Why would he even think about my well-being! Was his concern on account of the shame that I had become a maibi? Or was it Ema's motherly love for me that had compelled him to do all this?

From that day onwards, the sickness that accompanied the characteristics of a maibi gradually disappeared. I started going out of the house again. Whenever people asked me to read their palms or divine their future, I replied that my *lai* had been suppressed and I did not have those powers anymore. My consistent response to their requests made their nagging and negative attitude towards me eventually stop; I was no maibi that could see their future. My homo friends also gradually stopped thinking of me as a maibi. Our friendship returned to its former footing, nobody was a maibi amongst us.

One day, a few months after the maiba from Uripok treated me, my friends and I were at Poison's house, it was one of our usual gatherings. Poison suddenly said to me, 'Nupi, you must be careful.'

'Why?' I asked

Poison replied, 'Some men were enquiring about you. They also asked your address.'

I was surprised and asked Poison why they had asked about me, but he did not know the reason.

I asked, 'Do you know anything about them?' Poison replied that he did not know any of them, but that they had looked vexed.

Bob joined the conversation, addressing my anxieties, '*Naharols* are searching for homos who openly dress and behave like women. Tom, from Kongba, was beaten up by them.' Bob's reply did alarm me a bit. I had heard stories about beatings and warnings by people who called themselves *naharols*, such as shooting a gun at the thighs of women who wore pants, or *kwa* eaters' lips being slashed by a blade, or video cassette shopkeepers being shot on the suspicion that they were filming pornographic videos. I do not know if they were authentic *naharols*. Fear and anxiety made those stories appear real. I said, 'Why did they ask for me? What could be the reason?'

Poison said, 'You must be more careful from now on. You should dress more soberly, your style of dressing must be provoking them.' Bob seemed to concur with Poison. 'Indeed, you are too much, the way you dress,' he said.

The rest of the afternoon, I thought about what they had said about my clothes. I ruminated over two possibilities— were they telling me the truth? Or were they telling a convenient lie to stop me from wearing my dresses? My suspicion against my friends was fuelled by their outright disapproval of my way of dressing and my make-up. My resentment towards them stemmed from their silence every time people disparaged them. I wondered why they did not acknowledge their desire to wear women's clothing in public. If we could stand together against those who demeaned us, they would at least not insult us in public. We were made weaker hourly and daily by open mockery from others. Nevertheless, Bob's and Poison's joint warnings made me more cautious than before.

Fear and anxiety again caged me inside the walls of the house. The immediate effect of this self-censorship, or rather censorship from everybody else, was the lack of companions who would empathise with my loneliness and listen to my words of despair. In this situation, writing poems and short stories became a source of expressing my my innermost feelings.

Another manifestation of this loneliness was a newfound attention to my studies, which impressed my parents very much, but they were strangers to the inner turmoil I was struggling with. They saw this new development as a desire in me to reform myself. Ema was on top of the world at this turn of events. I came to know about Ema's happiness from a brief conversation with my Ebok. 'You are a precious child. At the time of your birth, your Pupu said that you would not be an ordinary child. Even if you have wasted some time, it does not matter. Concentrate on your studies from now on.' It was not the first time that I was hearing comments about the uniqueness of my life. When I initially started manifesting my feminine identity, Ebok repeatedly told Ema that the circumstances of my birth were not ordinary and that I could turn out to be contrary to what people expected of me.

One evening I was reading a story called 'The Last Day of Pompeii', which was a chapter in my sister's English textbook. I remembered being fully engrossed in the story. Suddenly Ema, who was in the *shumang*, told me that my friends had come to meet me. I was sure that they must be Poison, Ronu and Bob, but it was an unusual time for them to visit me at my house. We avoided visiting each other in the evenings. Wondering what could have happened, I went out to meet them. To my surprise, the fellow standing in the *shumang*, waiting for me, was not any of my friends. In fact, he was not anyone I had seen before. Puzzled and curious, I asked, 'What is this about?'

He spoke to me as though we had been best buddies for ages. 'Pal, how are you? Look, there is a little something I have to tell you. Should we walk towards the gate?' The stranger's behaviour immediately created doubts in my mind. But I did not want Ema to think that there was anything amiss. I complied with the unknown youth who was posing as my friend for whatever reason. As we reached the middle of the *shumang*, the man put a gun, hidden from Ema's sight, to my back and whispered threateningly, 'Tell your mother that you will be back in a while, tell her you are not going too far away.'

I followed his instructions. 'Ema, it is my friend from MBC. I will be back in a while.'

Ema replied, 'Come back as soon as possible. Do not go beyond Ebok Ebetombi's house.'

The stranger did not remove his gun. We continued walking towards the gate. Dusk was falling and the thick growth of cedars and acacia trees made our locality ominously dark. There was no public lighting system in our locality in those days, the entire neighbourhood was completely dark after dusk. As the stranger and I walked towards the far end of the lane, I saw three more men were waiting for us.

One of them asked, 'Is this the one?'

The man who had led me out of my house mockingly replied, 'Yes, this is the one.'

Another man said, 'You miserable homo. His legs must be crippled.'

They pushed me further towards the Laishram neighbourhood. At the far end of Laishram was a vast paddy field, which was quite deserted at that hour. Just before the stretch of the paddy field began, there was a thick grove of bamboo. One man plucked a bamboo branch with which he started lashing at my legs.

He asked, 'Tell us what are you? Man or woman?' In that very instance, another man kicked me from behind. I fell to the ground. One of the others slapped my face, I was mercilessly assaulted from every direction. My misery and abjectness seemed to be complete. It was strange, but at that very moment a kind of rage rose up inside me, and it clamoured to be heard. 'Who are you? Why are you beating me?' I managed to say.

My questioning them betrayed a courage and defiance they were not expecting. One of them punched my mouth. 'You dare question us! We are the ones made to punish and educate people like you.' He took my ability to speak up for myself even as they were assaulting me, as an insult.

One of them commanded, 'Lie on your stomach.' There was no way that I could not comply. I could only hope for somebody to show up on the street. More than hope, it was a silent scream of utter despair—not a single soul heard me or saw me in that humiliating state of desperation. They continued beating me with the bamboo branch until I was raw and bruised all over. One of them forced me to hold out my hands. Seeing my painted nails, all of them laughed and spat in my face. Then, calling me 'Shameless homo', the first man pushed my hands to the ground and smashed my nails with a brick.

I was forced to say, 'I am a man, and I can fuck women.' They made me repeat this line several times. The torture continued for a while, without interruption. They appeared to have gone mad with rage.

They warned me against telling anybody about the incident. 'If we ever find you walking in the streets in women's clothing, that will be the end of you,' one of them said. With this threat, the ordeal came to an abrupt end. The entire encounter was executed as a punishment. Punishment for even existing as a human being!

Somehow, I managed to reach home in that injured state. Ema was clueless about what had happened, she asked, 'Who were those people?' I did not want to talk about my ordeal. 'I do not know,' I replied curtly, no emotion in my voice.

Examining my swollen face, she anxiously asked, 'What happened? Who did this to you?'

I replied, 'Those people who just came did this to me.'

Ema pressed me, 'Why did they do this to you?'

I said matter-of-factly, 'Because they say that I wear women's clothing.'

At this, Ema broke into a wail. 'We have been trying to tell you your behaviour is not acceptable. Ours is a difficult time. Many pose as *naharols*, guns are also easily available. You should be careful. Be afraid.'

I said, 'I am not scared. This is happening to me because you brought me into this world.'

Ema wiped my bruised and bleeding face. 'You have to be very careful. We are living in very bad times. A few days before two fake *naharols* tried to collect money from Konsam Leikai. Good thing they were arrested by Meira Paibis.' (Meira Paibis are the 'torch-bearing women' of Manipur—they carry bamboo torches at night and guard and protect people against attacks from the armed forces and the state. The Meira Paibis play an important role in the social movement in Manipur.)

I replied coldly, 'I don't care. I will retaliate.'

'Well then. You are courting your death,' Ema said with a sigh. 'Do not let the neighbours know what happened to you. Try to understand.' I sensed the hopelessness of a mother in her reply.

I replied, 'I do not care about death now.'

That night I could not sleep. A desire for revenge, to kill those men who had done this to me, kept me awake. Their only advantage was that I was outnumbered, otherwise, it would not have been so easy for them to inflict hurt and humiliation on me. They were actually cowards.

Some days after this incident, my friends and I met at Poison's house. They did not know what had happened to me, I did not tell them anything about the beating and warnings I had received at the hands of the strangers at Laishram Leirak. I held myself responsible for the incident. It was my decision to live my life so openly as a woman and dress the way I did; I internalized the blame. I knew that not a single person in my family or amongst my friends would support me or encourage me to live like this.

Bob began to talk about a matter of interest for all of us. 'Nupis, shouldn't we all start visiting the bazar area from now on?' It sounded as though he was proposing something special, but what could that be? We had all been to the bazar for one reason or the other many times.

Bob continued, 'It was great fun. Many came yesterday.'

Poison asked, 'What do you mean?'

Bob replied, 'There were homos from many different places. We all gathered at the gallery.'

'Was there also somebody called Kalu from Singjamie? I heard that he is very beautiful,' Ronu said, joining in the conversation.

Bob replied, 'He is very beautiful. His complexion is unparalleled. The delicate beauty of his skin is as though one could see water slipping down his throat.'

Poison asked, 'What about Tom from Kongba?'

Bob replied, 'I did not see him. I heard that he mostly hangs out with girls.'

This conversation excited me a great deal. Bob had an extraordinary talent for narration, he knew how to hold an audience. I came to know that homos wore women's make-up and beautiful clothing when they had exclusive gatherings like the one Bob was talking about. Each story Bob told revealed something new and exciting. I told him that I would love to join the bazar gatherings. We decided to go the next day. All of us would meet outside Napoleon's shop from where we would go to the bazar.

It was the winter season. The days were getting shorter and dusk fell much earlier. I left home hurriedly around 4.30 p.m. I wore the same dress inspired by Julia Roberts in *Pretty Woman*. Just as I was leaving, Ema appeared on the *mangol* and asked where I was going. My only reply was that I would be back soon. I was the first one to reach Napoleon's shop, Ronu, Bob and Poison had not yet arrived. I thought perhaps they had stood me up, but I decided it was better to wait for a while. There was a paan dukan run by two Mayang, that is, non-Manipuri, men near Napoleon's shop. I decided to go to the dukan to buy a quid.

I approached the narrow wooden counter of the dukan. Only the shopkeeper's head was visible, he must have been looking for something below the counter. I called out, 'Bheiya?' 'Bheiya' was the term we used for non-Manipuri mainland men. On hearing my voice, he lifted his head and replied, 'What?'

I said, 'Give me a *talab*.'

The man covered his head with a scarf in the manner women did. His voice and mannerisms were very feminine. I had come to the bazar many times before but it was the first time I was seeing him. Even so, his manner towards me was very warm.

I paid him two rupees for the *talab*, which he declined, saying, 'Leave it, my dear friend.' I was taken aback by this expression of endearment coming from a person who was a complete stranger to me. So far only my friends had spoken to me with such affection. I said, 'No, bheiya, you have to take the money.'

He said, 'Do not call me bheiya. I am Sri Devi.'

Puzzled by his statement, I laughed. He also laughed. His Mayang accent was clearer than many other Mayangs. After talking for a while, I came to know that he had come from Bihar with another man who also happened to be his partner. They had left Bihar together almost ten years ago. He also knew Bob, Ronu and Poison very well, in fact he said that he had gone to watch the Shumang Leela in their company.

Sri Devi asked, 'My lovely friend, what is your name?'

I replied, 'My name is Santa.'

'Where are you from?'

I replied, 'I am from Thoidingjam Leikai.'

Sri Devi said, 'Then you live nearby.'

I said, 'Yes, it is not very far from here.'

Then Sri Devi asked, 'Where is your man?' His question made us both laugh.

I replied, 'I don't have a man.'

'You are beautiful. You should have a good man,' Sri Devi responded.

I replied, 'Nobody loves me. I am very unfortunate.'

Sri Devi said, 'Poison's lover is very good. He visits here often, to eat *kwa*.'

It surprised me that Sri Devi knew about Poison's intimate life, while I did not. It also hurt me a little that Poison told Sri Devi things he did not share with me. Though we talked about many things, he had never told me about his lover.

I said, 'The man must be Poison's friend.'

Sri Devi said, 'No, not a friend. They are lovers, and sometimes they fight.'

Sri Devi's company made the wait for my friends less frustrating. After a while, Poison and Ronu arrived, followed by Bob and Mohonsingh. I was surprised to see that none of them wore any make-up, they all looked as they did on any ordinary day. Their unglamorous appearance was at odds with what Bob had said the evening would hold. Bob and Mohonsingh stood under the gulmohar tree near the paan dukan, while Poison walked upto Sri Devi and me. 'Sri Devi, is my friend beautiful?' Poison asked.

Sri Devi said, 'Yes, beautiful. He said he has no lover.'
Poison replied, 'His man died.'
Sri Devi asked in alarm, 'How?'
Poison replied, 'He fell into a ditch and died.'

Poison's flippant reply conveyed to Sri Devi that the story about my dead lover was just a joke. He thought for a second and replied, 'Then find another man for him. Poison, where is your man?'

Poison replied, 'He went to Ukhrul for work.'

Poison and Ronu looked at each other and laughed. But I still believed in what Poison had told Sri Devi. I demanded that Poison tell me about his relationship. Poison explained to me that the man was his cousin, and the boyfriend story was only a joke. This cousin would ask Poison for money, and sometimes this was the cause of their quarrels. Often, these quarrels took place in front of Sri Devi's shop. When Sri Devi asked Poison about the cousin, Poison said that the man was his boyfriend, and Sri Devi believed him.

After a short while, a bus arrived. All of us boarded the bus one by one. Mohonsingh waved at Sri Devi from the window and called out, 'Mein Dilli gayi haun (I am going to Delhi)', which seemed to impress Sri Devi.

Inside the bus, none of us spoke. We got off at the Minuthong bridge. It was still too early for us to come out in our full glory. Bob, who was the expert in the new venture, said that we must wait until dusk. We crossed the Minuthong bridge to sit on the deserted bank of the Imphal river. Mohonsingh's humourous chatter kept us entertained for the while. When darkness began to spread over the afternoon's saffron sky, we were ready to leave the river bank; by then the street lamps had been lit. Under Bob's lead we crossed the Minuthong river again. At the intersection of Tellipati and Hatta, there was a barber shop run by a Mayang. Going by the ease with which he led us inside the shop, it appeared that the barber was a good acquaintance of Bob's. No explanations were asked for or made. When the barber closed his shop for the day, we started applying make-up.

Bob took out a tube of Fair & Lovely cream from his bag. With skilled hands, he squeezed some cream out of the tube, rubbed it on his palms and applied it on his face. On top of this foundation he applied a thick layer of Pond's talcum powder. He was also carrying a kajal pencil that looked like the ones available in Moreh. He ran several strokes of kajal on his eyelids, constantly wetting the tip of the pencil with his tongue. Next, he fixed a pair of false eyelashes to his eyelids with the help of a glue. Finally, he removed the cap he was wearing and pull down his curly long hair on one side of his shoulder. When he was done, Bob did not look like the everyday Bob; that night he looked different and gorgeous, like a beautiful, coy young girl. I was envious of his beauty. I also started putting on make-up, but it was not possible to attain Bob's beauty and allure, regardless of the amount of kajal or lipstick I wore. Moreover, I did not have long, false eyelashes, my hair was short, and my features were not as fine as his But I had to be content with the results.

Unlike Bob, Poison and Ronu did not wear heavy make-up. Poison wore a light eye make-up and a thin layer of powder on his face, while Ronu was satisfied with just a light touch of face powder. Ronu was very beautiful, like a young girl who blooms in pristine beauty without a touch of make-up. In another corner of the room, Mohonsingh too was occupied in dressing up. He held a small mirror in his hand throughout the time he was putting on the make-up. Mohonsingh had a dark complexion, the cut of his face was like that of Grace John, the famous female Black model who looked like a man; his hair was short but slightly long in the front. Mohonsingh worked at an automobile workshop, which made it impossible for him to keep his hair long, his job demanded that he look masculine, a proper man. None of these external circumstances could lessen Mohonsingh's charismatic nature. Whatever he did attracted attention, his style was magnetic. He did not spend a lot of money on cosmetics, he managed to achieve the look he wanted at an affordable cost, something that I admired.

He took out two lumps of sandalwood paste, of different colours, from his trouser pockets. On my enquiring, he said that the yellow sandalwood paste was to be used under the tubelight and the whitish sandalwood was to be used in ordinary lighting. He chose the yellow sandalwood for the night. He took the blade used for shaving men's beards from the barber's counter, with which he scratched off an abundant amount of sandalwood flakes. In the next step, he rubbed the powder on his face with both hands.

After putting on his make-up, Mohonsingh busied himself fixing his hair. He took a few drops of water in his palm and wetted the front part of his hair, probably to smooth out the curls, but it still looked very curly. Then he removed the thin shirt he was wearing over another shirt. With this thin shirt he fashioned a stylish headpiece and covered his short hair with it, leaving a fringe of long hair in front. It gave him an ultra stylish look. Mohonsingh was truly resourceful.

He suddenly grabbed the small knife which was lying within his reach, put one leg on the foot of the chair and aimed it under my chin. In this provocative pose, he pronounced, 'License to kill.' Then he added, 'Now you see Zeenat's prowess!' We were heartily entertained by this impromptu performance. We all agreed that Mohonsingh looked like one of those heroines in American movies.

Together we walked in the direction of the bazar. The road was deserted at that time of the evening, which meant that we could walk freely and confidently, without fear of any humiliation or harassment that could suddenly strike us from nowhere. Our first stop was the Indira Park. At the park we saw a sizeable number of homos. They sat in small groups—some were singing songs, others dancing. I could recognise a few homos from Khurai in one of the groups. Many more homos arrived at the park in a matter of minutes. Some of them came on bicycles. The park that was located at the heart of Imphal city was soon swarming with a joyous crowd of homos as the nocturnal hours passed by.

At that gathering, nobody was a stranger. Not a single trace of mockery or hatred raised its ugly head. Nobody lived in the shadow of fear and guilt, there was freedom and more celebration as the night gathered pace. We walked through each and every galli of the city. We were never silent, we talked, laughed, and marched on through the night. But whenever we heard the sound of the vehicles carrying Army personnel and the Manipuri commandos, we immediately fell silent—our laughter momentarily disappeared even as the *langmeithanbi* disappeared in the air (according to the local belief, *langmeithanbi* is the mysterious light emanating from the marshes in the paddy field, and it is believed that it holds evil spirits). We resumed our laughing and talking within seconds of the vehicles driving away. That night, I experienced pure freedom for the first time in my life. I had never imagined that there could be so many homos in Manipur. Seeing so many people like myself, wearing clothes of their choice, laughing at their own jokes and stories, and walking in freedom gave me courage to live life on my own terms, I was convinced that I was not alone in this world.

This feeling of pure freedom and the accompanying bliss made me want to stall time, I did not want the night to end. It was getting later and later, but nobody bothered about time. Nobody thought of going back to their homes. But Poison reminded me that we had a long way to go. Hence we all left Indira Park and began the journey home. When we reached the four-way crossroad at Lamlong market, I asked my friends to walk with me till my house. Ronu and Poison said that it would be better for them to take a shortcut from Lamlong market, and hence they would not be able to accompany me. But Mohonsingh and Bob agreed. All the way till we reached my house, Mohonsingh narrated a series of stories from horror films—from *Evil Death* to *Ali Baba Chalees Chor*. Mohansingh was not content with mere oral retellings. He narrated every story with actions—sometimes he stuck out his tongue to look like the devil, sometimes his hands eerily grabbed my hands and shoulders from behind. Such antics, far from being scary, made him look comical. They left me outside my house and then took a shortcut through Laishram Leirak to reach their respective houses.

It must have been around midnight when I reached home. I stood on the edge of the *mangol* for a while. I hesitated to approach the door and knock on it, I knew no one would welcome me at that hour. I could feel their annoyance already. But I still had hope in my mother. Without knocking on the door, I softly called out her name. She opened the door as quietly as she could, without saying a word to me. I headed towards my bed, without asking for food. Ema said angrily albeit in a hushed tone, 'Eat your meal.' She put out a plate of food for me and stood beside me, watching me while I ate. We did not exchange a single word. There was a palpable sadness overshadowing her face. I went to bed immediately after I had eaten. I must have slept as soon as my head touched the pillow. When I opened my eyes, it was morning.

———

From that time onwards, my routine changed—daytime visits to friends were replaced by a nocturnal freedom at night in the Imphal bazar. My thoughts were mostly preoccupied with what dresses and make-up I would wear at night. By late afternoon, I would be filled with both anxiety and excitement in anticipation of the euphoric moments that were going to follow. My happiness must have been visible to Ema, the one who opened the door for me at night when I returned home from my tryst with freedom. Her anxiety was different from mine, hers was accompanied by worries and fears—she repeatedly asked me where I would disappear every night. But she was asking a forbidden question, and I could not give her any answers.

Every afternoon my friends and I met in front of Sri Devi's shop, then we boarded a bus to the bazar. We were like government employees going to office every morning, except that our office timing happened to be evening. During the summer we went to the bazar around 5 p.m, on winter days we went a bit earlier, around 4.30 p.m. After repeated practice of the same routine over many days, sometimes I went alone without waiting for my friends but we always came back together.

In due course, our nocturnal rendezvous at Indira Park came to an end. The Manipuri commandos who were posted at various night stations of Imphal city began to arrest homos from the park. The arrests would be followed by harsh beatings. We had to look for other places to continue our meetings. Some homos went to quiet, lonely places like the river banks or deserted grounds. A few others roamed through the Paona Bazar lanes or took a lift with men driving by in cars or scooters. Many of us sought out *yu* vendors. After drinking a copious amount of *yu*, we would become bolder in our flirting with men. The *yu* vendors were a new discovery for us, we realised we could meet many men at the liquor vends. Brave new world! The Imphal Polo Ground also became an alternative destination. The wooden gallery of the ground became our new nest. The polo ground gave us some logistical advantage—we could wait at the polo ground until the men started arriving at the liquor vends, without having to sit at the vends for hours. Easy passage between the gallery and the vends made our life less complicated. Before heading to the polo ground gallery, Bs had a good dose of *yu* from the vends in the vicinity of Usha Cinema. 'B' was the code word we used for each other, derived from the term 'Nupi Maanbi', meaning those whose given gender at birth was male but whose expression and identity was feminine—we shortened this to 'B'.

Around the time we started meeting at the polo ground, the Assam Rifle regiment was stationed inside the Kangla complex. This regiment was an addition to the Indian Army personnel that were guarding the Governor's residence. The Army presence at both places made Imphal City heavily militarized, especially during the night, and became a hurdle to our nocturnal meetings in and around the city. Many times the Army personnel beat up the Bs. Despite this, homos continued to gather at the polo ground at night—

they were like *helois* that haunted Imphal City at night. They wore attractive make-up and tried to lure men, they sang and danced. Many of them came to be acquainted with the Army personnel stationed in and around the city. But the men who gave the homos company never took them seriously; after satisfying their desires, they would drop off the homos at exactly the same place from where they had picked them up. Knowing well that society never wanted to see them with men, homos had surrendered to the impossibility of marriage and conjugal life with men. Sometimes, this topic occupied an entire evening's conversation.

Homos, in their varied clothing and make-up, gave a distinct flavour to the night life in Imphal City. Some performed a catwalk in the old wooden gallery of the polo ground, while some gave company to men, others strolled home through the gallis of the city. Every B had a different story. These different stories were told in the mode and tone best suited to the teller's persona. Each story was a manifestation of an inner desire and talent.

Some said that television was coming to Manipur for the first time, that is to say, the government was going to set up a DDK Imphal station that would be used for local telecasts. Until then, we would get telecasts only from Delhi. This caused great excitement amongst the Bs, who thought it would give them a chance to showcase their talents on a public platform. Mohonsingh said that he would be presenting an advertisement for *chenghi,* the traditional hair wash prepared with rice water and local herbs. Mohonsingh acted out the script which he created extempore. First, he acted as though he had long hair, which he dipped in water, then he splashed the long hair with *chenghi,* and rubbed the strands of hair between his palms; pretending to fix his gaze on the audience, he rolled out the catchphrase of the advertisement: 'Chenghi infused with sangbrie (white-flowered pogostemon) leaves...Manipur.' His performance was met with much laughter and applause from the Bs. DDK Imphal came in 1998, but alas, Mohonsingh never got a chance to present his act!

The men who met Bs at the polo ground were mostly the Army personnel stationed in the vicinity of the ground, but there were a few Meitei men, too. Sometimes, if Bs wanted to meet Meitei men, they had to go to the Usha Cinema or the yu vendors of Kakhulong. However, the polo ground was the only place where Bs could spend a longer time with the Meitei men.

Sometimes, around 11 p.m, after drinking yu, Bs proceeded from the gallery to the bank of the Nambul river that ran behind the Paona Bazar. During winter, we collected empty cartons that the shops in the Paona Bazar had disposed of, to make a bonfire near the Usha Cinema. The fire kept us warm through the night. Near the Usha Cinema was a small stall run by Komon's wife. Komon was a Shumang Leela Nupi Sabi, he used to play female roles in the Leela. Waikhu bora, a deep-fried delicacy made with crab and gram flour, paknam, a cake-like delicacy, and singjum, a local cuisine prepared with vegetables and herbs mixed with Ngari—feremented fish—could be bought from her stall. She kept her stall open till late at night, to earn more money. Yu drinkers came to her stall to buy the snacks as an accompaniment to drinks. Additionally, her stall was a good nest for Bs. There was also an old woman's potpham or open stall, outside the polo ground. Whenever we drank yu very late at night, we bought waikhu bora from her stall. Waikhu bora was very cheap and lasted longer when accompanied by yu, a perfect combination.

It seemed that in the world of homos, day and night were reversed—nights spent in the vicinity of Usha Cinema became our day. The place was like the promised land for us. As we claimed the night, we claimed the universe, too. Whenever we saw any non-B on the street at that time of the night, we laughed at them, we despised them, we intimidated them. It was our fairy tale world!

In this time of freedom and love, Ronu's relationship with a man from Keisampat was becoming deeper. The man's name was Taton, he was a shopkeeper in Imphal city. Ronu often went off without us, to meet Taton. It was only later that he would say where he went with Taton—sometimes they stayed at a hotel, sometimes on the bank of the Nambol till dawn, and sometimes at Taton's shop at Keisampat. They could not live without one another; rain or shine, heat or cold, they met without fail. And whenever they met, they fought, intense quarrels, as though they would never meet after the fight. But in reality, they met the following day. Sometimes, after a nasty quarrel, they stayed together at one of the Leela offices or a hotel. Ronu's passionate relationship with Taton seemed to have distanced him from us.

Bob had a different story, he was very clear and definite in setting his own agenda. He was very beautiful, his beauty shone at night when he was seen in his best make-up and dresses. His looks lured many men into desiring him. However, he did not take relationships and men seriously. Bob was more interested in enjoying life as much as possible. One of his talents was singing. Bob demonstrated this talent in singing competitions with the men who sought the company of homos. Very often this friendly competition happened on the bank of the Nambol river. The men loved Bob's voice, they were willing to wager every penny they had to hear him singing. Bob's favourite song was a beloved Manipuri classic sung by Ashem Bimola, *Chakliba lanmei*. Bob could sing this song to perfection—the rhythm, the lyrics, the tune, everything veritably rivalled the original version.

One evening, Bob, Poison, and I went to the Imphal polo ground. As soon as we reached the bazar, it started raining heavily. We took refuge from the downpour in the nearest *yu* vend, that was owned by Ingo. Oddly enough, there was not a single homo at the liquor vend that day. We did not have enough money to buy a large amount of *yu*, we had to manage with a quarter of a litre. As the rain cleared up a bit, we headed towards the polo ground to check the scene. We did not see any other Bs at the ground too, the place was remarkably empty. Moreover, the rain had turned the grassy ground into a field of mud and slush, it was quite a messy affair to even step on the ground.

There was no point in hanging out in that lifeless place, so we went towards Indira Park in the hope of bonding with other Bs. There was a small shop run by two brothers outside Indira Park. Usually, the shop had many customers and remained open till late. If Bs wanted to buy cigarettes and *kwa* late at night, this shop was the only place we could go. Poison wanted to buy *kwa* before entering the park. The interior of the shop was well-lit, everything stacked inside was clearly visible to the customers. Poison asked for a *kwa* from the shop owner. In reply the shopkeeper said, 'Dear woman, you are flirtatiously smiling from ear to ear, but little did you anticipate that your smile would snort mucous.'

We looked at Poison, and it was only then that we saw that his dark eye make-up had smudged and run all the way down to his chin. Poison looked hideous and comical. The darkness of the rainy night might have concealed it from us or any other onlooker, but in the bright lighting of the shop, it was clearly visible. We exclaimed, 'Your make-up!' Poison walked up to a small mirror that was fixed on the wooden frame of the shop to check his face. Far from being embarrassed, he merely shrugged and said, 'It is not my fault, it is the rain.' With these words, he skilfully wiped off the spoiled make-up on the hem of his shirt. Then he took the *kwa* from the owner but not before he delivered a flirtatious remark: 'My face might be smeared black, but I still have my charm.' Laughing at the manner in which Poison had turned the situation in his favour, we all entered the park. But the Manipur commandos were patrolling around the park, they would surely arrest and beat us. We returned home.

One day when we were sitting at the polo ground gallery, Bob suddenly disappeared, without telling us where he was going. One of the rituals of our friendship was that we would always go home together, so we waited for him. As more time went by and he did not return, we began searching for him in the lanes of the bazar, but he was nowhere to be found. Eventually, we decided to return home. On the way back, we kept looking over our shoulders in the hope that he was following behind. Even in those anxious moments, Mohonsingh put on a comic act. He pretended that he was lamenting for Bob, 'Dear lovely friend, where are you? Silence and slumber have descended on the polo ground and the gallis of the bazar. In the garb of the thick night, even the commandos have deserted Indira Park. Would you call our name from behind the sheet of the clouds! And if you happen to know good, kind men, bring me one too.' Every line he spoke was delivered to perfection, a laugh riot.

Just as we reached the Public Works Department office, we found Bob running out of one of the lanes behind the building towards the main road; he was panting and seemed to be shaken. We stopped him and asked what the matter was. In a trembling voice, he said, 'I almost died today. Hurry, let's go.' His agitated behaviour alarmed us. Without asking for further explanations, we also hurriedly walked by his side. He did not say anything until we reached the Minuthong river.

Slowly, Bob started narrating his story. 'While I was buying *waikhu bora* from the old lady's *potpham*, I met an Army man. I did not understand his language, but he was hinting at me to follow him. I did not want to go with him, but his gun scared me and so I followed him. He took me to the Army bunker inside the PWD premises. Then he woke up other Army fellows. They grabbed whatever tool was at hand and surrounded me from all sides. They told me that I would have to do whatever they wanted me to do, or else they would beat me. The only way I could think of to get out of the situation was to tell them that I had to pee. I pretended to be peeing in the toilet at the back of the building, and finally managed to escape by wading through the dirty water of the drain behind the building.'

Mohonsingh was the first to speak after hearing Bob's story. 'They are very dangerous. Once at the radio station, one Army fellow tried to hit me with the butt of his gun without any reason whatsoever. But I somehow managed to dodge him. If his barrel had hit me, it would be The End for me. Be very careful whenever they are around. They are very unpredictable and dangerous.'

Truly, Bob had suffered an ordeal. The fetid smell coming from his feet was testimony to the difficulty he had undergone to escape. Bob needed to wash his stinking feet before he reached home. He went down to the river basin, while we waited for him on the bank. His spirits revived as he washed his feet in the river water and he exulted in his lucky escape. As he climbed up to the river bank, he was singing a song from the Hindi film *Satyam Shivam Sundaram*, '*Bol barey panna ghattapey*'. The song did not go waste on Mohonsingh. He immediately removed his shirt and twisted it and tied it around his chest in the style of a bra. Then he walked towards a mound in the Chingambam burial ground, stood on the mound and danced. We taunted him, 'Your ugly face is going to resurrect the dead.'

Mohonsingh turned towards me and said, 'Hey, you stupid. You look like a *nanapi*,' meaning, ear tops worn by women. He said half the sentence in English and half in Manipuri.

I said, 'Why are you sitting on the burial mound at this time of the night? Don't you think it could be a bad omen?'

Mohonsingh replied in a dramatic manner, 'I am the thick root of the tree growing on the mount of the Nongmaiching Hill.' This delivery was done in the manner of a James Bond girl—sultry, sexy and confident, at complete odds with the time of night and the place. His antics made me laugh till I reached home. The road from the bazar to Khurai was very long but that day we hardly noticed how we reached Khurai. Bob's dangerous encounter with the Army and Mohonsingh's hilarious antics had lifted the tedium of the journey.

That night, the front door was left unlatched from inside. Ema must have got used to me coming home late on most nights. I could enter the house without waking her up, and this relieved me. I closed the door softly behind me and immediately went to the kitchen. My food was kept in the *samuk*, a traditional container made with wicker to store food and objects. I removed the plate, it was fish curry. But what a strange sight! A thin layer of ash was sprinkled over the fish, making it impossible to eat. Ema must have done this to teach me a lesson—or perhaps one of my other family members. I sat with the plate in front of me, tears rolling down my cheeks. I was hungry, but the maddening sight of the inedible food incensed me. I thought of burning down the house and killing my family and myself. In the moments that followed, I thought—why should I die? I am innocent. Sitting with the food lying before me, I ruminated—it was better to die; I should search for a rope to hang myself. But at the time of cremating me, people would see my body and then they would mock me. I dressed like a woman but in reality, I was a man! The fear of people seeing my body was repulsive enough to assuage any suicidal feelings that night. If I had to die, I must die in the body of a woman. In those few moments of extreme hunger and humiliation, my only consolation being a distant dream that I would one day acquire the body I desired, I comforted myself by eating a humble meal—rice mixed with water. I went to sleep in a state of high emotion.

The next morning, the outrageous act of the previous night lacerated me afresh. I did not have any desire or hunger to eat. I went to Bob's house, determined to tell him about my family's callous conduct. From his house, we went to Mohonsingh's house together. Things were better at his house, no prying eyes of family members and neighbours trying to fill our minds with guilt. We found Mohonsingh carrying logs of firewood into the kitchen. We sat in the room on the eastern side of the house. It was a very small, cramped room, like a caterpillar's cocoon, and it was untidy and messy. The pictures on the walls of the room were clippings of English films cut out from *The Weekend* magazine. As soon as Mohonsingh entered the room, he posed against the wall, and said in a provocative manner, 'Give me my stuff.' His delivery was nasty and sexy and comic at the same time. As usual, his antics made us laugh. I asked, 'Mohonsingh, if *naharols* come to warn you against behaving like a woman, what would you say?'

Mohonsingh said, 'If they shoot me, I would collect my blood oozing out of the bullet wound and then write on the wall, "I did not act in porn films."' Mohonsingh had no schooling; he spoke in a thick accent; he lived on daily wages. These circumstances, which people ordinarily considered poverty, did not lessen his spirit, he seemed to be grateful for his circumstances, he never showed a glimmer of sadness and helplessness, never uttered a word of discontent. His attitude to life was truly enviable.

I asked again, 'Mohonsingh, who is your favourite actress?'

He replied, 'Zeenat Aman and Julia Roberts.' Even his serious answers sounded comic.

Then Bob said, changing the topic, 'Let's arrange the New Year's party at Top Moirankampu.'

Mohonsingh asked, 'Will there be many people? If the party is happening at Top Moirangkampu, Denao will surely join us.'

Bob replied, 'The party will happen in the paddy field at the back of his house.' After talking for a while, all of us went into the kitchen. When the pot of rice started simmering, Mohonsingh looked for a ladle to stir the rice. He didn't waste time in trying to find one, he dipped his fingers into the pot of boiling water to stir the rice. His action surprised Bob, who exclaimed, 'You will surely die.'

Mohonsingh removed his hand from the pot and said, 'No. This is a university, right?' We did not know what he meant by university, nevertheless we laughed. I asked what he meant.

Mohonsingh said, 'I am saying that this is a lesson I learnt from university and hence I will not be injured.' He was making a joke at his own expense, we all knew he had never been to university.

I had not eaten the morning meal, and it seemed that laughing on an empty stomach could make one famished. I accepted Mohonsingh's invitation to eat with him. Bob had already eaten, so he did not join us. After the meal, Bob and I went to Bob's relatives' house, to play Ashok Chakra, a game in which a coin is flipped to decide head or tail. It was a game that needed money. I listlessly watched them playing, I was excluded from the game by my utter poverty. Bob continued to play enthusiastically. How long could I watch my friends playing while I just sat around? I left, but not before Bob and I planned to visit Sri Devi's shop in the evening.

In fact, visiting the bazar in the evenings and my friends' houses in the morning had become my daily routine. Drawing embroidery designs for bedsheets and pillow covers remained the sole source of my income, but such opportunities came my way only once in a while. I tried to avoid staying at home as much as possible. Avoiding home meant avoiding conversing with my family members. I interacted only with Ema. Sometimes I took solace in a dream that I was living in a commune with my friends at the foot of a mountain, far away from home. This was the only way to live peacefully. It was not only I who would be happy then, my family memers would be happy too. After all, I was the fly in the pot of their happiness.

———————

On New Year's morning, we arranged a party in the paddy field behind Denao's house. The Iril river ran at a little distance from the paddy field. Towards the south and north of the paddy fields was a village. Winter was the harvesting season. The only greenery was a grove of banana plants in the middle of the paddy field, the rest of the field was covered by paddy stumps. At that time of the year, the place was deserted and serene. On the morning of the party, Ronu, Mohonsingh, Bob and I rode to Top Moirangkampu on bicycles. Denao was already waiting for us in the *shumang*. Two cooking pots and a few banana leaves had been kept ready. The major attraction of the party was the rooster, reared at Denao's house, that had saffron-coloured feathers. All of us went to the paddy field to cook the rooster and have a feast. Each one of us contributed a little bit of effort—we dressed the bird together, some of us collected dried leaves to light a fire, some went to fetch water from the river. Nobody complained about anything, a spirit of happiness prevailed over the paddy field.

Denao and I happened to be the best cooks of all. The heat from the temporary hearth raised the temperature in our modest kitchen in the wilderness. I removed the black, high-neck shirt I was wearing and put it aside. A photo session after the feasting was the crowning glory of the party. As soon as the photo session started I needed to put on my shirt. But it had miraculously disappeared, even though I had put it in a safe place! Despite a thorough search everywhere, nobody found the shirt. Denao had to lend me his *haophi*, a woollen shawl, which I threw over my shoulder as a poor substitute for the lost shirt. Then, after the photo session finally got over, Mohonsingh handed me something. It was my shirt! The black cloth wrapped around his head throughout the photo session was indeed my shirt, and I had thought that it was his scarf. Outraged, I turned towards him and said, 'You are disgusting.'

Mohonsingh replied, 'No. I had to wear your black shirt as a wig, otherwise, Julia Roberts' bad hair would be your shame.' My shirt had saved Mohonsingh from a bad hair day!

We went to the river to clean the cooking pots and other utensils. Together we worked and together we returned to the field. As we rested after the cleaning session, Mohonsingh entertained us with another of his performances—in the middle of the field, he sang, danced, and delivered dialogues. When the party ended, I returned home on my bicycle. That evening, we did not go to the bazar.

The next day, Ronu, Poison, Mohonsingh and I visited the bazar. Surprisingly none of our fellow homos could be seen in the polo ground. At the Paona Bazar *yu* vend, we met two Bs from Thangmeiband. We also ordered our *yu*. The B friends told us about an incident that had happened at the polo ground gallery on the night of 31st December. It seemed that a few Bs were beaten and taken away by the Manipur commandos, while a few managed to run away. Meanwhile, another B from Moirangkhom arrived, he said that we had had a lucky escape on the wretched night of 31st December. 'Dears, you are so blessed not to have come to the polo ground on the night of the 31st.'

Bob asked, 'What happened on the 31st night?'

The B replied, 'The polo ground turned into a black sheet, like it was covered by a flock of crows.'

Bob asked, 'Were you also there yesterday?'

The B replied, 'Yes. We lit a bonfire in the middle of the ground to celebrate New Year's Eve. We were just sitting around the bonfire and talking, nothing more. Suddenly, out of nowhere a convoy of commandos arrived, and started beating us.'

I asked, 'Didn't you hear the sounds of their vehicle approaching?'

The B replied, 'No. We did not hear anything. They did not allow us to say anything, too.'

Bob replied, 'Didn't you have time to flee the scene?'

The B replied, 'Yes, some of us had time to run. I ran swiftly, but unfortunately, many Army personnel had surrounded us even in the direction in which I was running. I climbed up the nearest wall to escape them. But they pulled me down from the wall, beat me and kicked me. My body is still aching from their punches.' Saying these words, the B turned towards Ingo and ordered his *yu*. After Ingo had handed him a glass, he continued, 'Then Manipuri commandos arrested us and put us in the jail.'

I asked, 'Did they give any reasons for the mass arrest?'

The B replied, 'No, they did not give us any reasons whatsoever. Inside the jail, the commandos called us "homo, big anus", and repeatedly beat us. One commando even burned a B's hair with a matchstick. This B is from Singjamei.'

I said, 'You should have been able to ask why they arrested innocent people in that manner.'

The B replied, 'Santa, how on earth do you think anyone could have asked in that situation? If you were there, would you have done so?'

I said, 'The commandos were wrong. If I were there, I would have asked the reason.'

Ronu turned towards me, 'Enough. Don't try to act fearless. When we were thrashed at Porompat, you did not say a single word.'

I replied, 'No, I did not stay dumb. I asked why we were beaten, remember?'

The B continued, 'Leave your arguments. Listen to what happened next. All of us were released around dawn. Maybe they did not have enough food to feed us.' He laughed. 'As we were coming out of the stinky jail, I saw a telephone in an unattended room. I was determined to retaliate, so I walked into that room, removed the telephone cord from the socket, and took the telephone with me.'

I said, 'Hurrah! That is the spirit.'

We all laughed appreciatively at the B's act of defiance. In the meanwhile, Dipu, the son of my Edomcha or maternal aunt, from Uripok, also arrived at the liquor vend. Dipu exchanged a knowing glance with the B and laughed, 'Remember what happened last night.' Pointing at the B, he said, 'This fungus-looking B lifted a telephone from the police station last night. If they investigate now, we are most likely to die. One day they will come to the polo ground, looking for the telephone.'

The B said, 'I don't care. Since they treated us in the worst manner, for being homos, I am also doing what is within my capacity!'

Dipu said, 'You are a superhit! I feel scared going out with you. You once luckily dodged death itself. Didn't you almost blast a bomb on yourself?'

The mention of the bomb made the rest of us very curious. We wanted to know the story. The knowing glances and giggles exchanged between Dipu and the B fuelled our curiosity even more. Dipu called the B a dangerous *hingchabi*. The B, who was quite a good storyteller, finally agreed to tell us about the incident. 'Yes, it is true, the bomb incident happened near the BOC.' He was referring to the Bharat Oil Corporation oil pump. He and Dipu burst out laughing again.

Ronu, who seemed to have had enough of the mystery, said, 'Why don't you just continue with the story!'

The B said, 'One day Dipu got angry after his mother shaved off his hair. He came to the polo ground to release his temper, his face was...' He left the sentence incomplete, and laughed. After a bit, he continued, 'I told him that he could stay the night at my house. We were heading towards my house when, as we went past the Secretariat, we came across a few men who flirted with us. Dipu was ashamed of his bald head, so he rushed into a corner. I went into another corner to give a blow job to one of these men. While pleasuring him, I saw an alloy ring falling out of his pant pocket. I thought that the ring must have fallen out from the man's wallet. I put the ring on my finger, and nonchalantly pulled the thread connected to the ring. Suddenly the man slapped off my hands and shouted, 'It is a bomb. We are going to die.' I said that I had only picked up the ring because I thought it was some junk that had fallen out of his pocket. This is the story about the bomb.'

The small audience gathered at the vend heard the B's story with rapt attention. The incident could really have caused the death of the man and the B, but we all laughed. What if the bomb had exploded! That day we did not go elsewhere, we sat at the vend. Made doubly cautious by the incident of the 31st night, we decided not to visit the polo ground for a few days. We thought it prudent to inform other Bs to stay away from there too.

The beating and arrest of Bs by the Army and the Manipur commandos became a regular affair after the incident on New Year's Eve, with the polo ground becoming the main target. Bs from Khurai had slowly stopped visiting the gallery. Even if we went to the bazar, we did not proceed beyond Ta Ingo's *yu* vend that was located conveniently outside the walls of the polo ground.

One day after a quarrel with my family, I went to the polo ground alone. Anger and disappointment could make the mind numb to the need for company. I feared neither the commandos nor the Army. If I had to face them single-handedly, I would. Entering the polo ground all alone that night was driven by the frustration that had become a part of my life. Indian Army and CRPF personnel were at their usual posts at the polo ground, and so no Bs could be seen. After a while Bunty, a B from Lamphel came; he was wearing tight jeans, his head was covered. When we saw each other, he asked, 'Khurai lai, who else have you seen?'

I replied, 'Nobody else.'

Bunty said, 'The situation here is not good. Let's go. We can sit at Ta Ingo's vend.'

I said, 'Why should we be afraid?'

Bunty said again, 'We must go, it is better to be at Ta Ingo's.' On his insistence, I followed him to Ta Ingo's. We found many more Bs at the vend, but instead of the usual sounds of laughter and gaiety, the atmosphere was subdued and tense. Everybody looked sad and depressed, and appeared to be engaged in a serious conversation. We asked them what was the reason for their sombre mood.

Thoiba replied, 'Did you know Leishabi? He is dead.'

I replied, 'That is very sad. How did he die?'

Thoibi said, 'He was found dead below the gallery

today. People saw his dead body during their morning walk.' After a heavy pause, he continued, 'It is said that his head was badly injured, his skull was cracked too. It might be that he was murdered.'

Tomba, another B from Khagempalli, said that Leishabi and he had sat at Indira Park till late at night after which he left for home alone. Leishabi had stayed behind in the park. 'Then how was he found dead at the polo ground? Is this not very suspicious?'

The news made everyone very sad. Who could have murdered him? Many of us suspected that it must have been the Army. The only people who could be seen around the polo ground throughout the night till dawn were the Army personnel. The terrifying thing was that news about such deaths was becoming more frequent. The stories of beatings and arrests made us slowly avoid the polo ground gallery. The freedom we had enjoyed at the polo ground was short-lived. Like the Laimeidong or hornbills that flocked together, we used to have happy gatherings at the gallery. But the untoward incidents that started happening there made us drift apart from one another. In the absence of a place of our own, we were lonely and isolated creatures. The freedom we had enjoyed in the past three years disappeared.

━━━━━━

In the absence of these nocturnal gatherings, I stayed at home. Staying at home also implied a considerable reduction in the ugly quarrels with family members, as they no longer had cause to get upset by my coming home late at night. In those years, parents sent their wayward sons outside Manipur in the hope that they would learn discipline and add value to their lives. Another route to inculcate decency in sons was marriage. Still another valid reason for sending their sons outside Manipur was to prevent them from becoming *naharols*. Moreover, getting a degree from colleges and universities in other states was considered a matter of dignity and respect, it was a very desirable social status. But I had seen that those who had spent years studying elsewhere mostly returned with drug addiction, besides a degree. But the lure of an Outside Degree overcame the parents' misgivings about drug addiction!

Our neighbour, Daddy, was also one such parent who sent his son to a college outside Manipur. Daddy's example encouraged Baba to send me to Hyderabad to pursue a college education. This was in 1994, and I was around twenty-one. In fact, Hyderabad was my idea, Baba would have been content with any place outside Manipur. Ema discussed the matter on his behalf since Baba and I were not on talking terms. It was finally decided between Ema, Baba and me that I would go to Hyderabad to enrol for a B.A. degree at Osmania University. Ta August, my eldest sister's husband, was to travel with me to Hyderabad to arrange for my college admission.

The Blue Hill bus service was newly introduced in Manipur around that time. We left Imphal early in the morning and reached Guwahati the next morning. At Guwahati, Ta August struggled to book train tickets to Hyderabad. First, he tried to book the tickets through 'tatkal', I had no idea what that meant. But he was not able to do so. Ta August was a very kind man, his concern was to make my journey easy and comfortable. While he ran from one source to another to procure train tickets to Hyderabad, I stood alone at a corner of the railway station. Every sight appeared new and intimidating to me, except for a Meitei-looking boy a little older than me, who was approaching me. He had a companion, a girl. He asked me, 'Are you a Meitei?'

I replied, 'Yes.'

He asked, 'Where are you going?'

I told him I was going to Hyderabad. 'Have you got tickets?' he asked.

I said, 'We haven't got tickets. I came with a relative, he has gone to arrange for the ticket.'

The boy said, 'We got tickets on RAC. But I have to make sure that the reservations are confirmed. Please stay with my sister in the meantime.' That was when I got to know that the girl was his sister.

The girl and I started talking. She asked where I was from and when I told her Khurai, she said, 'I am from Top, near Moirangkampu bridge. So, we are practically from the same place.'

Suddenly I was reminded of Denao who was from Top. 'Do you know Denao? He is from Top,' I said.

She replied, 'I do not know many people in Manipur. I have lived mostly in Hyderabad.'

I did not believe her. She might not have lived in Manipur for a very long time, but how could she not know her neighbours! I concluded that she was only trying to show off the fact that she had lived in Hyderabad for a longer time.

Ta August finally returned. He was very surprised to see me seemingly friendly with another person. He asked the girl, 'Are you leishabi's friend?'

The girl was visibly surprised to hear the word 'leishabi', the common term for an unmarried woman, being used for me. She replied, smiling, 'No, we just met.' Ta August asked her a few more questions, then he said some good things about me, 'This is also a smart leishabi from Khurai. It is good that you two met.' Ta August had no problem with my feminine nature. He always called me leishabi, instead of derogatory words like 'homo'. He only advised me to take my education seriously, he did not seem to be driven by any negative attitude towards my kind. Sometimes my sister said that his calling me 'leishabi' was a mockery, but it did not appear like that to me. After a while, the girl's brother also came back with the tickets. We formed a small group and stayed together throughout the journey.

The train started at 11 p.m. As soon as we had safely boarded the train, Ta August asked me to be always mindful of my luggage and also not to talk to strangers. We could manage to get only two tickets on reservation, which were given to me and the girl. Ta August and the boy did not get seats to sleep at night, they had to manage as best as they could. During the daytime, they managed to sit in any vacant seats available. The boy and Ta August bought food for us. Even when the girl and I visited the washroom, either Ta August or the boy stood on guard outside the bathroom. We reached Hyderabad amid great inconvenience. The siblings left for their place in an auto-rickshaw, Ta August and I went towards the city in search of a hotel.

Ta August booked a single room in a small hotel. That night, before going to sleep, he said, 'Leishabi, tomorrow we have to wake up early, we will go to the college to enquire about the admission.'

After a pause, he continued, 'People in south India are generally agreeable and hospitable. But do not make your feminine nature very obvious. People in the college might be unpleasant to you. Choose your friends wisely. Also, we must use money carefully.

'Be sincere with your studies. If you are good at studies,

nobody will look down upon you, even if your manner is feminine.'

I obediently listened to his kind and sincere advice. Exhaustion from the motion sickness during the train journey kept me awake. Even though I closed my eyes, I could not sleep. But Ta August slept peacefully. In my sleep-deprived state, I remembered my homo friends from Khurai. I wished we had come together. If I had come here with my B friends rather than Ta August, I would have been much happier. I did not think much about my family. Throughout the sleepless night, each one of my homo friends' faces seemed to flash in front of me.

The next day, Ta August and I went to Osmania University in an auto-rickshaw. We returned to the hotel immediately after buying the admission form. According to the admission criteria, I stood a good chance of getting admission. But it bothered me that completion of the B.A. degree would take a lot of time, at least three years. This raised a few questions in my mind—would I be able to visit home regularly? What about the hardship of bus and train journeys? Where would my parents get the money to pay for the course? The answers to these questions were not easy. The university building also did not look attractive. Ultimately, there was no strong factor that could compel me to take admission at the university.

That evening, when Ta August and I were trying to fill in the application form, I said with a sudden resolve, 'Ta August, I don't want to do the B.A. course.' My statement came as a shock to Ta August. 'What happened now?' he asked.

I replied, 'The B.A. course is going to take many years to complete, and the financial situation at home is not good. It would be better to look for a course that can be done in a year.'

Ta August said, 'No. A Bachelor degree surely takes time to complete. Do not count this as an inconvenience. Moreover, what will you do in Manipur? Your father will arrange for the money somehow. You only need to be sincere in your studies.'

I insisted, 'What will more studies do? It would be better to join a course that would directly help me get a job as soon as possible.'

He did not listen to me. I also withdrew my hand and dropped the pen. I did not even eat the food Ta August ordered in the hotel room. Seeing my rebelliousness, he must have thought it better to talk to Baba, and went outside to make a call. I do not know what he said to my father, but when he came back, he said, 'Leishabi, you can choose between lab technician or D.Pharma.'

I asked, 'How many years will it take?'

Ta August said, 'Lab technician is for a year and D.Pharma can also be done within a year.'

I did not know what a lab technician could do, but I knew well about D.Pharma. Ta August had a D.Pharma degree, and he was employed at the 7th MR. When he visited our house, he would sometimes tell us about the medical-related work he did in his professional capacity. Once in a while, he gave us clean cottonwool and antiseptic ointments. My worry was not about a beneficial course that would get me a job. My impatience to return home governed any choice I made at that time.

The next day, we took the train to Guntur. Compared to Guntur, Hyderabad was quite a posh place. I immediately hated Guntur—the place was dirty, it did not even have a proper market. I did not tell Ta August about my instant hatred of Guntur, doing so might enrage him. The next day we went to the college where I would be doing the lab technician course. The college building and its location almost made me cry in disgust. No, it did not even have an autonomous building, all it had was a semblance of a premises rented inside a big building. The name of the college, Siddhartha, was painted on a board outside the premises. Automatically, my mind went back to the college at Osmania University, to which I wanted to return immediately. At that moment, a B.A. degree that was going to take three years appeared more attractive than a one-year lab technician course in this godforsaken place. The hostel at Guntur did not even have a name board. The well at the back of the hostel was the only source of water supply to the hostellers. The dirty toilet reeked of a nauseating smell. No amount of renovation could improve the place's deplorable condition. Where had I brought myself! Everything was shabby and dirty.

On reflection, though, I thought that it may be better to see how things went once the session started. I got admission at Siddhartha, without a protest but with a reluctance that only I knew about.

After securing my admission at Siddhartha, Ta August left for Manipur. After a few weeks, some Meitei men and women came to study at the same institution. We stayed in the hostels run by the institute. The women's hostel was located across the wall of the hostel I stayed in. We Meiteis care for each other in everything. They knew that I was a homo but they did not do anything to hurt or insult me.

Among the girls was one called Rebecca whose house was not far from mine in Manipur. She already knew me, and through her, other Meiteis in the institute also came to know about me. Every day we went out sightseeing. Sometimes we cooked and ate together. My uneasiness about the place grew less day by day. With these new friends, Guntur became quite a tolerable place, and I no longer regretted my decision not to take admission at Osmania.

I stopped wearing heavy make-up, but I continued wearing feminine clothing. Fortunately nobody criticised my choice of dress, probably because the institute was low-key. Sometimes I borrowed *phaneks* from Rebecca when we went sightseeing. My hair had also grown longer.

I would often meet a person wearing a sari outside my hostel in the afternoon. The person was a hijra, a transvestite, but at that time I did not know this term, I thought he/she was a homo. The homo had only one hand. He always sat outside a grocery store, he never looked at me once, but I could not stop myself from staring at him. I closely observed his sense of dressing, way of speaking, the way he clapped. Mostly he wore a sheer yellow-coloured sari, he looked clean and well-groomed. I envied his attitude, the courage to wear women's clothing without caring for society. I had not seen anybody like this person around Guntur. I wondered if he had any friends. He reminded me of my homo friends at the polo ground.

Guntur was not as advanced as the other cities, but for me it was like America. I experienced a lot of freedom in that rather insignificant place. College gave me happiness, I made new friends who were very supportive. Siddhartha taught me a new feeling—the sadness I felt if I missed any class—which meant that I would miss the company of my friends.

One day our happiness was interrupted by Rebecca's sudden illness. She complained of severe stomach pain, and we had to rush her to Guntur Hospital. The doctors said that her appendix had to be removed to save her life. Rebecca's parents' or one of her family member's signature was needed for the operation. The doctors refused to let us sign on the behalf of her family. Our insistence that she was very close to us and we could sign for the permission fell on deaf ears. Meanwhile, Rebecca's condition was becoming more critical every minute. She was taken inside the ICU. It was unthinkable that Rebecca's parents would arrive the next day to take care of her. It would be a long train journey before the family finally reached Guntur. Finally, Bimol, a friend of ours from Khagnabok, went to the institute to talk with the principal. We waited at the hospital for him to return with a solution to the crisis. Throughout this time, we kept taking updates from the doctor; the permission for the operation had not yet been given. Bimol arrived in great haste with a look of anger and disappointment on his face. When we asked him what had happened he said, 'Mayangs are bullshit. I am very angry. Students in his institution are suffering but he is not willing to show sympathy.'

Tayai, one of our senior friends from Utlao, asked him what the principal had said.

Bimol replied, 'He said that we did not inform him about Rebecca in the first instance, and he did not give permission for admitting her in the hospital. So he cannot take a risk now.'

Tayai held his head with both hands. 'This is the end. He is not willing to show even a bit of sympathy. What should we do now?' he said in despair.

We huddled together in a corner of the hospital. Our condition was hopeless and in hopelessness, we asked questions that could never be answered. We kept on insisting that the doctors start the operation, but the only reply we got was that they could not do so without permission from the guardians. They told us that the patient would have to keep suffering in agony, or we must get the signature of consent from the family.

Jeeten suddenly said, 'Isn't there anybody from Manipur working in this hospital?'

Tayai replied, 'Yes, we can ask. This is a good government hospital, so one or two Meiteis must be working or studying here.'

Bimol asked the doctor who was treating Rebecca about Meiteis in the hospital. The doctor said there was a doctor from Manipur who had been working in the hospital for almost five years. We were relieved to hear this. We took the number of the Meitei doctor's room and immediately went to meet him.

In the room, we saw a tall man, he indeed looked like a Meitei. There were some patients in his room at the time. Tayai asked him if we could enter. He looked up from writing a prescription and said, 'Yes, what is the matter?' His pleasant manner gave us a slight hope. His attendants brought a few chairs for us to sit on.

Bimol first told the doctor about Rebecca's case, then he told him we were from Manipur and had come to Guntur to study. The doctor told us his name and address in Manipur—his name was Pratap and he was from Uripok. He had been working in the hospital for the past five years. He agreed to come and examine Rebecca. He talked with the doctor who was treating her. The doctor finally agreed to start the operation on the condition that one of us signed on behalf of Rebecca's guardian. Tayai signed the consent paper. The doctors were finally ready for the operation. Rebecca was shifted from the ICU to the operation theatre. We followed her as she was wheeled on a stretcher towards the OT. Rebecca did not open her eyes, she did not speak a single word, her face was considerably shrunken in pain. Our only hope was that she would recover after the operation. When Rebecca was finally taken into the operation theatre, Dr Pratap went inside along with the other doctors.

After a short while Dr Pratap came out of the theatre, he looked down and did not look at us, he looked very sad. We thought that the operation had got over very soon. But I doubted the look on his face. Finally, he said, 'She could not be saved.'

His words struck us dumb. In despair and anger, Tayai and Bimol hit the walls with their fists. The rest of us tried to calm them down. Our tears and rage were completely impotent in the face of death that put an end to our little hope that had flickered in Rebecca's last moments. She could not be brought back to life.

We did not have friends and support in Guntur. Differences in food, apathy from the Mayangs, and the distance from our own homes combined together to isolate us. We were a minority with a different culture and habits, fighting for our survival in an alien environment. There was no one to listen to our woes, we could not even cry to our heart's content. Every human has some complaints against the forces that separate friendship by death and misfortune. Sometimes we articulate such complaints and sometimes we do not. We could not ask anyone why we felt miserable that day. Only tears relieved us of the burden of voiceless complaints.

Rebecca's body was kept in the morgue. We were faced with the difficult task of conveying the news of her tragic death to her family. Her sudden death and the circumstances in which it had taken place, had drained our spirits and wits. We stayed in the hospital in that state of hopelessness till the evening. Tayai finally suggested that we should try to find the phone number to contact her family in his diary. Doctor Pratap, visibly saddened by Rebecca's death, also stayed in the hospital for some time. Before he left, he gave us his phone number to contact him in case he could help us.

At the hostel, Ebecha and Surbala were planning to cook food for all of us. The reality of death had not cast a shadow over them yet. They were washing the vegetables while a song called '*Aja kalapao jamin paar*' from the movie *Ghar* was playing on a small stereo taperecorder. They greeted us cheerfully. Surbala asked, 'Is she better now? Is she in the auto?' Nobody answered her. We tried to hide the signs of our tears. Tayai replied, 'She has to stay in the hospital for a while.'

Tayai's reply was heartbreaking. We could no longer hold back our grief. I started crying, calling out Rebecca's name. The others also began to cry. Alarmed, Surbala and Ebecha screamed at us, 'What happened?' Nobody could actually put in words that Rebecca had passed away in the operation theatre.

I finally replied, 'Sur, Rebecca is no more.'

'What are you saying?' said Surbala disbelievingly. Then she and Ebecha began to cry, like the rest of us.

Our sadness was like a tunnel with no end in sight. Rebecca had succumbed to a health issue, but the suddenness of her death was difficult to accept. She was amongst us just a few hours ago, now she was dead! Who could believe it! When we were finally able to talk, a few thoughts tormented us afresh: 'If the operation had started a little earlier, she could have been saved', 'She died because the doctor refused to perform the surgery on time', 'We should kill the doctor and that will give us peace'.

We searched Tayai's diary but could not find a number

to contact Rebecca's family. Perhaps she had noted down the number somewhere in her diary or a notebook. But where? Then Surbala suggested that someone from one of our families could go to Rebecca's house to inform her family about her death. Her suggestion struck me with an idea—Rebecca had earlier told me that we came from the same neighbourhood in Lamlong. I told everyone that my family could directly inform Rebecca's family.

We went together to the telephone booth nearby, to make a call to my family. It was around 10:30 p.m. Back home, everyone must have been asleep by then, winter nights are cold in Manipur. There was no telephone connection at my house. I had to make a call to Oja Randhir, who lived across the road from our house first, and request him to call Ema or Baba. It would take Oja Randhir a while to go to my house, and then to bring Ema or Baba to talk to me on the phone. The entire process would take at least half an hour. But I wondered if Oja Randhir's family would pick up the phone at that time of the night in the first place. Who would like to wake up in the middle of a cold winter night and go out to fetch Ema or Baba from my house? However, death is the end of everything, besides we lived so far away from home. I believed that someone from Oja Randhir's side would do us the favour, regardless of the weather and the lateness of the hour.

We reached the telephone booth. I dialled Oja Randhir's number. Luck must have been in my favour, Oja Randhir's wife picked up the call—her sick child had kept her awake. I requested her to connect me with one of my family members. It was a very lucky coincidence that just that day, she had been thinking of fetching my grandfather, who was a well-known and respected maiba, to tend to her sick child. I had to wait for another half an hour for my parents to reach Oja Randhir's house. It was an ordeal to wait through that half hour. Surbala, Ebecha and I could not stop weeping, though everyone around us was staring at us. Around 11.30 p.m, I called Oja Randhir's telephone number, again. It was Ema who answered the call. Hearing her voice made me cry aloud, which alarmed Ema. She asked me anxiously, 'Ibungo, what happened? Has something bad happened?'

Jeeten took the telephone receiver from me and said, 'Is it Santa's Ema? Ema, one of our classmates, Rebecca, passed away today. She is also from Khurai. We are calling to request you if it would be possible to inform Rebecca's family about this.' Jeeten gave the receiver to me on Ema's request. By then, I had controlled my tears and was able to speak.

My mother said, 'How did this happen? It is very sad. Whose daughter is the girl?'

I replied, 'She was the daughter of one of Tachow's friends. The friend is from Lairou.' By Tachow I meant my uncle, my father's younger brother.

Ema said, 'Your Tachow has many friends. How would we know which friend? Do you know the friend's name?' I told her I did not.

Then Ema asked, 'Do you know the address?' I gave her the address of Tachow's friend.

Ema said, 'I will go with your father now and try to find the place. Try to call us more often. Take care of yourself. You never send us letters, and I sometimes get worried. How will the girl's family contact you?'

Without replying to any of her complaints, I said, 'Try to convey the message as soon as possible. The body is in the morgue now. We will feel very uneasy until she is given a burial.'

She replied, 'Yes, I will try. Your Baba is also here. He wants to talk with you.'

I told her I didn't want to speak to Baba, but she said, 'Your Baba is worried about you, at least talk.'

With great reluctance, I agreed. I waited for him to speak first. 'Ibungo, be careful. Concentrate on your studies. Do not be distracted by other things,' Baba said.

I replied, 'Yes.'

I did not want to hear that voice, his voice failed to arouse any trace of affection in my heart, on the contrary, it annoyed me. I cut short his advice and his effort to show concern by asking him to give the phone to Ema.

When she came on the line, I said, 'Ema, you must go now to find Rebecca's family and convey the message.'

Ema said, 'Yes, I will go directly from here. It is getting very late, but can you wait for us to return and contact you again?' I told her we would wait at the booth and call again after some time.

The tense telephonic interaction concluded for the time being. We sat together at one corner of the telephone booth, waiting till it was time to call my parents again. That night none of us ate, we felt no hunger. It was getting late and the booth would be open only till 1 a.m. We decided that we would wait until it was time for the booth to close, and then we would make the final call. Even as we agreed, I called again and again as I just could not summon the patience to wait. Sometimes, a worried Oja Randhir received the call. Every time I called I was asked to wait. As we waited, we talked about the problems besetting us—the difficulty of staying in contact with our families once we left Manipur, the problems of connectivity between Manipur and other parts of India. Jeeten gave his answer to these problems, 'If all the educational facilities were available in Manipur, Rebecca would not have died today.'

Tayai added, 'It seems like it would be better to be a part of Burma. It is easier to commute to Burma through the Moreh road by bus.'

At midnight, I dialled Oja Randhir's number again and this time, Ema answered the phone.

Ema said, 'Ebungo, I am with a family member of the girl. Talk with him.'

A man spoke in a broken voice, 'Ebungo, how did everything happen?'

I could hear the voice of a woman lamenting in the background, 'My daughter said that she would come back and look after her younger siblings. Now, what has happened to you? I want to go to my child, take me to my child.' Her lament made me start weeping again. Tayai took the telephone receiver from me and told the man everything about the circumstances in which Rebecca died.

On the way back to the hostel, Tayai told us that the relatives would come to take the body. They did not tell him the exact day. I said, 'I hope they come fast because knowing that her body is lying in the morgue makes me feel that Rebecca is still beside me, alive.' Moreover, how could we carry on with our lives while a friend's body was lying at a morgue?

It was only a few hours before dawn when we reached the hostel. Surbala and Ebecha did not return to their rooms. All of us stayed in Tayai's room that night. We talked about peforming the final rites for Rebecca. Tayai said that we should wait for at least a week for her family to arrive in Guntur. Meanwhile, we must go to the hospital daily to inform the morgue keeper that the relatives would be arriving soon. We also called the number given to us by Rebecca's father. When we called the new number, Rebecca's uncle received the call. He was extremely saddened by the news of Rebecca's death. It was this uncle who had sent Rebecca to study in Guntur, her parents were poor and did not have enough money to arrange for her studies. I thought the uncle would come to Guntur.

Surbala told us that Rebecca talked with this uncle regularly and sent him letters too. She believed that Rebecca was adopted by her uncle. 'Rebecca did not talk much about her own family,' she told us.

The tragedy of Rebecca's story affected me, physically and mentally. I did not wish to participate in their discussions anymore. I wanted to be alone. 'I am tired now. I will see you tomorrow,' I told them.

Tayai said, 'Yes, take a rest for a while.'

I lay on my bed, thinking about the events that had happened. No matter how tired my body and mind were, I could not sleep. The images of Rebecca the previous morning, alive and healthy, repeatedly flashed in front of my eyes. I closed my eyes, but thoughts streamed into my mind one after another, each thought was a torturous one. *If the surgery was performed half an hour earlier, she could have been saved; doctors did not think about patients, they cared for their money only. What would have happened had I died in place of Rebecca? If I died my friends would feel the same sadness and grief that was being felt now, my family would also be devastated.* Thinking about their sadness made me think that it would be better to die. Suddenly I longed for the anguish, love and separation they would experience in the event of my death. I longed for their heart-wrenching cries, the despair of not seeing me again, the desire to win me back from death. In the next moment, I thought death would be the end of everything, nothing could happen after death. Being alive was a greater advantage. I must die after serving society so that I could leave behind a legacy.

What caused me the most anguish was the reluctance of the doctors to perform the surgery on time. Nobody lent us the support we needed at that time. I could not forgive the doctor—he did not allow us to sign the consent form; notwithstanding his awareness that we were students coming from far off places, far from our families, he insisted on a family member's signature! These considerations compelled me to think that his action was deliberate cruelty. I felt challenged and despised and this was accompanied by a rage to kill him. I wished I had an iron rod with which I could destroy his office. I wanted to expose his irresponsibility as a doctor and to insult him to my heart's content. Moreover, the college principal's refusal to help us in that dire situation filled me with a seething indignation. The intense emotions burnt my body, in that sleep-deprived state my mind and body were afire and I wanted to scream. Could anybody control themselves in such a situation? I could not. I got up from my bed and marched off in the direction of Tayai's room. Standing outside Tayai's door, I called out his name loudly and pounded on his door.

Ebecha opened the door. Seeing my state, she looked alarmed. Inside the room, my friends were either sleeping or were trying to sleep, I did not pay attention to them.

I said, 'Wake up, you all. Tayai, we must go to the hospital now.'

Surbala said, 'What has happened, Santa?'

I replied, 'Nothing. But we must meet the doctor now.'

Tayai said, 'The doctor will not be there at this hour. What will we do at the hospital just now?'

I replied, 'Let's just go there. I will not cause any trouble. I just want to talk with the doctor.'

Tayai tried to pacify me, 'Yes, we will talk with the doctor. But we must go in the morning. We will decide

what to say to him together in the morning.' In desperation,
I began to sob. My friends assured me once again that we
would go in the morning.

The first thing I wanted to do the next morning was to
go to the hospital. Tayai advised me that we must inform
the principal first. The principal arrived at the college only
after 11 a.m. My feelings vacillated from one emotion to
another. One moment I thought it better to wait for my
friends, all of us united in one cause, to vindicate Rebecca.
The next moment, I wanted to confront the principal right
away, whether the others came with me or not. Meanwhile,
Surbala and Ebecha asked me to accompany them to the
market to buy bread for breakfast. I was reluctant to go
anywhere, except the hospital to talk with the doctor. I
could not rest until I had asked him to explain the actual
cause of Rebecca's death.

It was my customary habit to shave my face every
morning, before setting out. That morning I did not care
to attend to this routine. Surbala said, 'You are too angry.
Your beard is showing.' I told her that I did not care.

While everyone else was eating the bread Surbala and
Ebecha bought, I sat sulking in a corner. They repeatedly asked
me to eat, which made me angrier. Anger, disappointment,
despair drove me into a raging hopelessness, I did not
know what I was thinking or doing. My friends left for
their respective rooms, and I tried to pass the long hours
by pacing up and down, in and out of my room. When
the clock struck 10.30 a.m, I hired a rickshaw and went
to the Guntur Hospital without telling any of my friends.
The rickshaw dropped me just outside the hospital. I went
directly to the office where the doctor who treated Rebecca
sat. When I entered his office, he was with a few other
fellow doctors. His very appearance overwhelmed me with

anger, I shouted, 'You killed my friend, he killed my friend.' A few people who were present at the scene dragged me out of the room. Everything blacked out at that moment, I could not recollect what happened after that.

When I regained consciousness, I was in a hospital bed. Surbala was sitting beside me. My body ached from head to toe, it was as though someone had physically assaulted me. On closer inspection, I realised I was on a drip. I wanted to speak, but Surbala stopped me. 'Take rest,' she said in a gentle voice. Her manner was caring and affectionate. I asked about Rebecca. Surbala replied that Rebecca was stable and resting on a bed in another room. I believed her. From that day onwards, I had frequent spells of fainting. A psychiatrist called Phani Bhushan treated me. He gave me multi-coloured red and black tablets called Spectran 25. My Meitei friends came to meet me regularly.

Inside the Guntur hospital complex, there was a huge park that was fenced off from all directions. A few trees grew inside the fence. Patients from the psychiatry department could be seen playing and walking in the park. The family members of these patients visited them frequently, bringing snacks. My friends would take me to that park when they came to visit me.

Whenever I had a fainting spell, I could not remember anything after I regained consciousness. It appeared that my condition was gradually worsening. One day Tayai visited me and told me that I should go home to Manipur for a while. Tayai said, 'We have many days before the exams start. We can go to Manipur and come back to Guntur in time for the exams. I have talked with your family, too.' I had no desire to go home. But on everyone's insistence, I left for Manipur with Tayai. I do not quite remember how we reached home. As far as I can recall, we could not get train tickets from Kolkata to Guwahati. We travelled on a bus from Kolkata to get there. From Guwahati too we would have had to travel by bus as there is no train serive from Guwhati to Imphal.

It was very difficult to remember the course of events during that time, it was as though I was running after a faint, fleeting shadow that eluded my control. Sometimes it felt like I had been saved from a nightmare. After staying at home for many days, I began to recover my senses. My sister-in-law told me that Rebecca had been cremated at Guntur, the family did not have money to buy train tickets to bring her body to Manipur. Her father and her uncle went to Guntur to perform her last rites. The *sorat* ceremony, a ritual observed after the death of a person, was observed at her home in Manipur.

Once I began to get better, Ema started encouraging me to study so that I could complete my training and find a job, and make a comfortable life for myself. But I was not allowed to go outside the house.

At the end of two months, I went back to Guntur to write the final exams. Everything looked unfamiliar and alien. The place I had known seemed like a distant memory, the sights and sounds did not feel intimate like before, it felt quiet and lonely. The hostel looked old and dilapidated. The big tree outside the college had also spread its branches considerably. It appeared to me that a tangible crevice had appeared between my friends and me. A sense of guardedness had replaced the earlier candid conversations we used to have, they seemed to talk with me sparingly. The new differences were overwhelming. Such a drastic change in such a short time! As though an intimate relationship was suddenly snapped and then wiped away. However, no change can achieve a totally clean slate. Despite all the perceived changes, certain things did remain unchanged—we ate together, we discussed issues, we visited places together.

After two months, I finally wrote the exams and returned home immediately afterwards. A few of my friends stayed back to wait for the results. Some others planned to apply for jobs once the results were declared.

The second time I returned home, a new mood had set in. As I waited for the examination results and certificates, there was the anticipation of finding employment—the possibility of getting a job was thrilling. This was an altogether new direction for me.

In Manipur, my friends had also entered a new phase. They had newer stories to tell me. The number of Bs had increased, a new generation of Bs had arrived. However, the increase in the number of Bs did not deter people from humiliating us in broad daylight, on the roadside. In that repect, nothing had changed, only the population had increased.

In truth, the stories of insult and torture meted out to Bs were a form of entertainment for the Manipuris. Each story vilified the Bs involved. Without even the slightest effort to get to know our side of the story, we were conveniently blamed for every wrong society could conceive of. There were many stories of Bs being deserted by their male lovers, which resulted in more incidents of suicide among the Bs. Nobody expressed sorrow for those unfortunate deaths. Rather, people justified these deaths as just retribution for our fatuous imitation of women. We were victims, but we were blamed for bringing death unto ourselves. We tried to distance ourselves from love, the very emotion of love felt like a premonition of death and accusations. Even in death, we were blamed for choosing death.

In these changing times, people looked upon me with disgust and repulsion, as before. However, now I had a silver lining—my education often rescued me from damnation. Many parents approached me to tutor their children, this was an iota of respect left in my life. Undoubtedly, my schooling and the brief stint outside Manipur were the basis of this newfound respect and trust. I had heard it said that human beings respect and fear those who occupy a higher position but this was the first time I had encountered the truth of this precept. According to such beliefs, my education was truly a boon—I was popular and respected among the people, I had earned a certain recognition. The quality of my educational expertise was of course a different matter, known only to me. Taking advantage of my new relationship with my neighbours, I reached out to the younger Bs to advise them. I encouraged them to get a good education and earn respect from society, like me.

Parents who hired me as a home tutor were aware of my feminine nature. However, they wisely chose my education and ability to teach their children as being more important. People make choices that benefit them. So, they overlooked my make-up and skirts, and other women's clothing that I wore.

I had grown friendly with a few women in my neighbourhood. Amureima, an elderly woman who lived across the street from our house, was one such kind woman. She rented out *potloi* and lent me dresses for Lai Haraoba. Her two sons, Biren and Amuba, also hired me to tutor their children. In fact some people did not want to hire any person other than me as a trustworthy tutor for their children. Private tuition became a good source of income for me. When a few wayward children performed well in the school exams under my tutelage, my stock rose.

As my reputation as a tutor grew, my relationship with the people who employed me also changed, they had no reservations in talking with me. I also became friendly with a few men in my neighbourhood. In Ta Amuba's neighbourhood, I was known as Khoinou, a traditional term used by women for their women friends. The sobriquet had a reason—whenever I saw any women from that locality, I addressed them as 'Khoinou eta'. My new name came from my manner of addressing them.

The boys in my neighbourhood requested me to write love letters and messages in greeting cards for their girlfriends. I throughly enjoyed this task. One day, Enaobi, a relative of Ta Amuba, requested me to write a love letter for his girlfriend. After a few days, I was informed by Enaobi that the girl told him that it was a beautiful letter, and she wanted to know who had written it. Motilal, an acquaintance of mine, also approached me for the same task. He had been in love with a girl he met at the coaching centre, but he could not express his feelings for her. One day he told me everything about his feelings for the girl, and then asked me to write a letter to her. I wrote a letter expressing his feelings and the helplessness of his inarticulate love for her. I do not know if it was a result of this letter, but the girl agreed to his love proposal. Motilal was very happy after this. My reputation as a writer of love letters spread like wildfire. Many young men, mostly my age, in the neighbourhood from Lamlong to Lairou came to know about the beauty of the love letters I wrote.

My neighbours now appeared to be more accepting of my homo friends who sometimes visited me. This change in their attitude might have been an extension of the little respect I commanded among people at that time. They referred to any homo seen in the neighbourhood as Khoinou or Santa. A relative absence of homo-bashing made my neighbourhood a class apart from other neighbourhoods. Sometimes, I introduced my homo friends to the young men in the neighbourhood, and they became lovers later on.

Many women in Lamlong regarded me as a very learned person. One of them, Koijam Thoibi, and I became very good friends. She was a dancer at the Sangeet Kala Sangam and was also a theatre artist. I visited her very often at her house. Her father though was disapproving of my feminine nature. Was it a coincidence that he knew Baba well! The contrast between Baba and me was a raw disappointment for him. He was very concerned about my future. He frequently chastised me in these words, 'You are a very smart boy, why do you waste your talent?' Sometimes his disapproval compelled him to chase me out of his house. On these occasions, I hid in the back verandah of the house. Whenever I visited Eche Thoibi, I made sure that her father was away at the workshop, his presence in the house created tension for me. I avoided visiting Eche Thoibi if I knew he was at home but on some unfortunate days, if he happened to be there, Thoibi secretly signalled me that he was around. Sometimes when I could not escape his fury, I hid inside the mosquito net of Eche Thoibi's bed. I would come out of hiding only after he had left.

Thoibi had a sister called Eche Pey. She had a boyish haircut and always wore men's clothing. Everyone called her 'Pey' which in contemporary language, was the term for a trans man or boy. Wild in her ways, she did whatever she wanted to do. She fearlessly spoke her mind, never deterred by where she was or who she was with. I was not particularly close to her, because she teased me a lot and argued with me. Besides she was much older than me. One day, I saw her sitting in their *shumang*, looking preoccupied. The moment she saw me, she said, 'Nupi, the day I get a penis, I will climb up to the top of the Noimaiching hill and pee down the slope. Wouldn't you like to see?'

I did not know how she invented such outlandish ideas. 'I don't wish to partake in your laughable ideas. What you just said is not much different from proposing that the sun rises in the west!' I said.

My reply enraged her, 'This homo is impudent, I'm going to kill you.' Then she chased me to the pond in front of the house. I managed to escape and ran towards Poison's house.

One evening Eche Pey asked me to go with her, to meet her girlfriend. I did not understand what she meant by 'girlfriend'—she was a girl, even though she wore boys' clothing. It all sounded mysterious to me, and I refused her offer. She grabbed my wrist and threatened me, 'Get on the backseat of the Luna right now.' Then she said in a friendlier tone, 'I'm offering you a chance to meet a future sister-in-law.'

This reference to a sister-in-law made me understand that she was referring to a romantic relationship. I obeyed and sat on the backseat of her Luna. After riding along the river bank, she finally turned into the small lane that lay between Kongpal bridge and the Lai Hiden. Just as we reached the lane, a thatched house came into sight. The house was surrounded on all sides by mango and citrus trees. The periphery of the house looked neat and clean, the verandah, backyard and courtyard of the house were well-maintained and it was obvious that they were swept every day. As we walked towards the *mangol*, Eche Pey called out loudly, 'Sapna, Sapna'.

A young girl came out and invited us inside the house. There, we saw many girls sitting on a bed. I did not know who among those girls was Sapna. The moment these girls saw Pey, they wanted her to buy them delicacies of their choice. Pey asked them to say what they wanted one by one, as though she was taking orders from customers. The girls laughed at every word Pey uttered, for what reason, I did not know! One girl asked if Pey had hit a jackpot, that she had so generously offered to buy whatever they wanted. Pey replied that it was not a jackpot, she had taken money from her father. The girls wanted Pey to buy *singju* and *kangao*, and Sapna would make tea for everyone. Pey gave the little girl who had greeted us at the *shumang* money to go and buy the snacks.

One amongst the group of noisy girls was a married woman. In a voice of authority, she said, 'Sapna, go and start making tea.' Her statement afforded me the opportunity to see which of the girls was Sapna. A girl sitting on the edge of the bed coyly stood up. She was Sapna, beautiful and well-built. She had not spoken much throughout the time we were there. She looked like the heroine of the film *Samphabee*. Obeying the married woman's instructions, she went inside the kitchen to make tea, while the other girls and Pey continued talking. One girl wanted to know if I was one of Pey's relatives. Pey replied teasingly, 'Not a relative, but a *sanou*'. 'Sanou' was the term used by a man to refer to his female lover. They were full of playful curiousity, the next thing they wanted to know was, 'Is he a homo?' They laughed at their own question. They were asking a question, but it appeared that they already knew the answer. Why did they laugh? I directed my anger at Pey, which impelled her to modify her previous answer: 'I'm only joking. He is like a younger sibling to me. I roped him in for my visit here. He is very good at studies.' Her reply cooled my temper a little bit.

Having clarified our relationship, Pey went inside the kitchen. The rest of us in the room could hear Pey and Sapna talking in the kitchen. The girls' gang, who seemed to know everything about Pey and Sapna, started giggling, 'See, they have started, again.' The married woman, who talked more than the rest, said aloud in the manner of addressing the two people in the kitchen, 'Haven't you done with your chit-chat?' Pey replied from inside the kitchen, 'Yes.' Then Sapna came out of the kitchen, with tea for everyone, closely followed by Pey who looked visibly angry.

The married woman asked, 'Pey, what happened? You look annoyed.'

Pey replied, 'Somebody is being very independent these days.'

The married woman replied, 'No. It is that man's fault, chasing Sapna all the time. She does not do anything to encourage it.'

Pey replied, 'She hides a lot from me.'

In a soothing tone, the married woman said, 'Don't worry. We will monitor her whereabouts.'

All of us ate *bora* and *kangao* together. Finally, it was time for Pey and me to leave for home. The girls accompanied us to the gate of the house. Just as we reached the gate, Pey told the married woman, 'Eche Pishak, this time I am putting my trust in you. You must be responsible. Don't let her go to the *Thabal Chongba*. Otherwise, you will be the one to be blamed.' One of the girls replied to Pey, 'Then you have to make a big monetary contribution to the *Thabal Chongba*.' Pey replied, 'Yes, I will make a handsome contribution on the condition that she will not be allowed to go there.' Regardless of the tension and arguments, the overall mood was a happy one. On our way back home, Pey asked if her girlfriend was beautiful. I replied in the affirmative, and I was not lying. Sapna was indeed very beautiful.

Around that time, I made many more new friends. I started spending less time with my homo friends and this created a distance between us. Baba was the most relieved at this relative absence of homos in my life, which he perceived as a positive change. A new ray of hope began to glimmer in him; his behaviour and manner of speaking became more relaxed. He thought I had changed—which was not true—and hence he changed his attitude towards me. He even started talking about things he had not spoken about before—finding a job, building a new house, distributing his land and property amongst the three brothers. Indeed, his happiness was my happiness, but I could never be warm towards him again.

Almost two years had passed since I had returned from Guntur. I had finally procured the certificate of lab technician, but I was still unemployed. Who was there to help me? Procuring a job in Manipur cost a lot of money, and even that did not always guarantee a job. There were many stories of people who had paid money to unreliable sources only to find they had been cheated. The only way my family could dream of paying for a job was to sell a piece of land my father owned, and even that may not suffice. Besides, the most crucial point was not the money. I knew that my chances of being selected for a job were almost zero, given that I was a homo. This factor did not motivate me enough to find employment. Baba was not aware of the various conflicts competing with each other in my mind. He believed that everything depended on merit.

My lack of interest in finding a government job started annoying Baba. He frequently mentioned that I was not honouring the money, time and resources spent on my training and education. In his language, I had wasted my time and his money. Added to the already existing tension and anxiety, his words made me question myself—why did I go to Guntur to study? Whenever he expressed his discontent against me, he would give an account of how much he had spent on my education all those years. Sometimes, I replied, and we would get into a heated argument. I took it as a challenge—one day I must become truly successful to be able to give a fitting reply to him. I had the desire to be successful, but the road towards success was not clear in my mind, it was clouded with uncertainty. But I was convinced that the road Baba chose for me was already a blocked one. I pondered on the various courses of action that could adequately equip me to earn a respectable income. So far, my source of income was private tuition and embroidery art. Despite my impoverished state, I did not take money from my parents.

I thought of visiting hospitals and well-connected people to ask for jobs. Perhaps my certificate might make them consider my candidature. My constant reveries about what I could do still did not provide any clear solution. This daily tension brought back the fainting spells I had suffered in the past. This time, my family did not pay much attention to me. I was given the medicines prescribed by the doctor at the Guntur hospital and left to my own devices. This indifference created a loss of will to live. I asked myself— why should I, a human being, bear so much pain and suffering in life? What was the value of my life? To whom could I narrate my sad story? How could I attain a life of peace?

This was the time when many private firms were setting up micro-finance businesses. I gave job interviews for these firms. The twelfth standard certificate and my lab technician certificate were the only qualifications I had. At many places, I was rejected even before the actual interview—simply on the basis of my appearance. At other places, people asked me irrelevant questions, smiled at me condescendingly, and turned me out. One day I went to give an interview at a micro finance office that was located close to Rajkumar Chandrajit Sana Singh Open Gallery, near Keishamthong. A security guard stopped me and asked the reason for my visit. I told him I had come for an interview. He wanted to check my certificates, and so I handed him my file that contained all the documents. He looked at the file and said that no interview was scheduled that day, but I could see many people, each holding a file, sitting on a bench outside the office. I spoke no further and returned home, my heart heavy. I did not relate this story to my family. Had I told them, they would have asked me to find a job befitting my training.

That day I was not even given a chance to show my credentials. The rejection was not based on competency or incompetency. It was based on my appearance. If I had been allowed to show my certificates and give the interview, I could have been one among those eligible, qualified women. What are the qualifications of a lower division clerk? Or of a security guard or a constable? All of them had a respectable place in society. And I? I was insulted and turned away wherever I went. I was looked upon as an individual without a purpose. The utter disregard for my life went hand in hand with the daily insults at my own home.

Human beings stray from the path of truth. In their effort to show and wield their power, they exploit and exile the weak. Is this the way of the world?

I could not get any respectable employment. My family did not count tuition and embroidery art as jobs. I was a jobless person in the eyes of the world, and at home, I was a black sheep. There was an incessant stream of criticism against me. This hostile atmosphere nullified whatever little enterprise was left in me. I quit trying. I was lost, my life was in a very dark place.

During the daytime, I spent my time at Thoidingjam or Ta Amuba's house. The company of the married women brought some smiles and laughter amid my inner hopelessness. Their friendliness and acceptance of me eased the tension at least for a short while. Another haven at that time was Ebok Amureima's house, where I helped her and her daughters-in-law in decorating *potloi*.

I resumed visiting my homo friends, to ease my feelings of dejection and despair. I had lost all traces of anxiety regarding my family's opinion about my choice of friends. They continued to criticise me, I continued treading my path. Could I worry less about their opinions? How could I adjust my likes and dislikes for their comfort? A result of their infinite scorn for me was the courage to revel in everything I wanted to do and everywhere I wanted to go.

On most evenings I went to meet Poison. At other times, I was in the jovial company of Taton Ramananda. Ramananda was around fifty years of age. He usually wore a *khudei,* the traditional casual wear for Meitei men, instead of a shirt he used a *phadi*, a bath towel, as a scarf. Behind his house was some vacant land. On dry days, we played ludo on this ground, for a stake of five rupees. Ramananda had a very good source for financing the ludo games. He plucked vegetables from the homestead and gave them to his mother to sell in the market. Among the many things Ramananda did, one activity was permanent—fishing. Rain or shine, he cast his fishing *ein,* a kind of traditional fishing net, in the waters of the Kongba river. But I never saw him catch any fish.

One day I visited him while he was at his favourite task. He was holding the long rope attached to the *ein* and waiting for fish to be lured into the net underwater. On the other side of the river basin, a married woman called out to Ramananda and asked him how many he had caught that day. Raman replied, 'My *tungol* is overflowing with fish.' *Tungol* was the moveable container carried by fishermen and fisherwomen.The woman and I laughed, but Ramananda did not laugh. His attention was focused on the *ein* underwater. His young niece was also standing beside him. Ramananda and the girl looked like mother and daughter.

On another memorable occasion, he was picking the *chenkruk* or amaranth that grew on the land along the border with Sengjam. His niece and I had also followed him there. At the edge of the ground was a thick grove of bamboo plants. After picking *chenkruk*, he went towards the grove to uproot *ushoi*, the tender bamboo roots. He told the girl and me not to follow him to the grove. Since the ground of the grove was muddy, I listened to his advice, but the little girl followed him. As they came out of the grove, Ramananda suddenly asked the girl not to move. When the girl looked down, she saw a leech sucking on her feet, her skin had started bleeding. She started crying in fright and jumping up and down. Ramananda calmed the girl down and carefully removed the leech. As he did so, the girl started hitting Ramananda. Ramananda laughed and asked why he was being beaten. This playful and affectionate interaction remained in my mind for years to come. Ramananda had had a brief stint in Shumang Leela. I remembered that during the tenth standard farewell function at Don Bosco High School in Chingmeirong, I had borrowed a wig and dresses from Ramananda for a dance performance. I had come to Ramananda on the recommendation of my homo friends.

One day I reached Ramananda's house early. I ate the morning meal at his house and rested for a while on his bed. In those days I sported a pixie haircut (inspired by Diana King) and my face had become very fair from repeated usage of a cream called Promina supplied from Burma (Myanmar). But the skin around my neck was dark. This was why I wore a scarf to hide my neck.

My eyebrows needed to be shaped in a manner that would compliment my chic look. While Ramananda was plucking my eyebrows with a pair tweezers I fell asleep. I was roused by the sound of his younger sister, Ebecha, shouting loudly, 'Taton, there is something in your bed.' Ramananda was also laughing. Ebecha continued, 'Taton, bring seven flowers of different hues, seven different fruits, and let's put them together on a banana leaf and offer it to the spirit.' Saying this, she burst into laughter. There was a background to Ebecha's little drama. People thought that I was from the Thoidingjam clan which had a presiding female deity, and Ebecha was referring to this goddess when she talked about offering fruit and flowers to the spirit. Meanwhile, Ramananda had plucked my eyebrows into two thin lines, making me look like Spook from *Star Trek*. I did not look chic at all!

Unexpectedly, Bob and Dijen also arrived at Ramananda's place. They exclaimed at my eyebrows, 'Ho, Ema!'—Oh!

Mother!—Dijen said jocularly, 'Nupi, we should not be seen together in public for two years.'

All of us sat together in Ramananda's room and thought about where we could go for the evening. There did not seem to be any option more attractive than the Chingjoibi Lai Haraoba. I had bought a short, sleeveless top from Selection House and told my friends I would wear it that day. 'Hey, nupi,' Ramananda teased, 'be careful or you might fall flat in the *thirei* bush.' He meant a kind of wild flower which people planted around the house as a fencing. Everyone laughed. I said that I was joking and I would certainly not wear the top. However, the moment we decided to go to Chingjoibi Lai Haraoba, was the moment I decided to wear the sexy top. At home after taking a bath, I wore the top under a big T-shirt. I left the house dressed like this. Before I headed to Ramananda's house, I went to Khumukcham Ebecha's house to borrow an eyebrow pencil and darkened my eyebrows. Then I walked to Ramananda's house, carrying myself with pride. Many people stared at me as I walked down the road. Each stare emboldened me, I held my head high.

Ramananda was getting ready when I arrived. I watched as he carefully extracted a modest amount of powder from a lump of sandalwood. He then applied the powder on his face. He was wearing a pair of old, worn-out pants and a red polo neck T-shirt. Dijen and Bob had not arrived. The moment Ramananda saw me, he expressed approval of my modest dressing. 'You should dress like this. Otherwise, your skimpy pants look like a deflated balloon. Your shirt befits a scarecrow,' he said. In response to his sarcastic comments about my clothing, I told him that he did not appreciate my style statement. He replied, 'Is it in fashion to wear skimpy clothes, then? If so, you might as well go naked.' I told him that such a time would also come soon. While we were engaging in this light banter, Bob and Dijen also arrived. They were dressed in the latest fashion of young men those days, and looked neat and clean.

The moment we reached the Chingjoibi Lai Haraoba ground, I removed the big T-shirt to reveal the top that was awaiting its moment of fame—or should it be notoriety. I stood under a lamppost and struck a pose so that my style and attitude would be noticed by all who came there. Ramananda, who had been witnessing my actions from behind, thumped his chest with his fist and exclaimed, 'I did not expect this. You are a *hingchabi*.' Saying this, he moved to another part of the crowd, distancing himself from me. Bob did not say anything, but he laughed at Ramananda's observation. Probably he had a similar opinion about my dress! He followed Ramananda and both sat together in a corner.

I did not shift my position. A few boys came and stood near me. They poked at me with a stick and asked me what I had inside the top in an attempt to humiliate me. They were not content with entertaining themselves alone, they invited a few other friends of theirs to come and bully me. One of them said, 'Hey, you homo, you big-anus bullock. You should just kill yourself.' For the next few moments, they continued hurling insult after insult upon me. They surrounded me from all sides as though I were a thief caught in the act. I was not cowed down by their comments, however harsh. I traded each insult with one of my own, to just stand there quietly and listen to them would have been the act of a coward. The tension between us reached the point where both sides were on the verge of a physical fight. It was wiser for me to avoid a physical brawl as I was vastly outnumbered. So, I headed to the corner where

Ramananda, Bob and Dijen were sitting, and told them that it was time for us to go back. They were all upset with me. Dijen said, 'I warned you before, not to provoke people.' Ramananda added, 'Because of your goddess-like attitude, we cannot even watch Lai Haraoba peacefully.' Despite their annoyance, they agreed to leave immediately.

When we were half way through Pheroijam, those troublesome boys turned up again. They indicated that they wanted to talk to me, so I stood apart from my friends. I asked, 'What bullshit do you want now, you lazy good-for-nothings? I can spit into your faces right this moment.' My lack of fear and ability to speak so boldly must have come as a rude shock to them. Two among the losers gang unzipped their pants and urinated on my feet. They couldn't do anything more than this, they called me 'homo bastard' and ran away. They were not brave at all! It was quite an anti-climax. I found the courage to chase them to retaliate, but failed to catch up with them. When I came back to where my friends were waiting, Dijen said, 'This is fascinating. Nupi, you are a good racer. You are no less than P.T. Usha.'

Ramananda said, 'Very bad boys. But your dress and attitude provoked them!' I clenched my teeth and convinced myself that one day I would teach them a lesson and avenge myself.

I could not sleep that night. Various arguments and viewpoints played themselves out in my mind—if I were a girl, such an incident would not have happened to me; if I were a girl, people present at the ground would have punished those boys; since I was not a girl, I did not get help from anyone; even if I had shouted and asked for help, I would be the one to be blamed, they would have said, 'Why do you wear such indecent clothing? Why do you act like a woman?' I wanted to establish a court to judge and punish offenders like those boys. Amidst these arguments and counter-arguments, I fell asleep.

Such incidents happened to me often, leaving pain and discontent in the pit of my gut. Only the company of my homo friends could push these unpleasant feelings into near-oblivion. All depressing thoughts and anxieties disappeared whenever we were together. We wanted a space exclusively meant for us, a *Thabal Chongba* event would have been ideal. We also started planning beauty pageants for homos. In this field Bob was always ahead of me, he along with Ronu and Poison had actually gone thrice to watch a *Thabal Chongba* where homos were allowed to particiapte in the Senapati district. On all these occasions they wore women's clothing. Since Senapati was a hilly region, with very few Meitei people, there was no criticism from anybody. The few Meitei villagers living there thought they were dressing like that just for fun. Ramananda also talked about a beauty contest for homos that happened at Khagempalli, sometimes he would talk as though he himself had participated in such contests.

My friends had started talking about a medicine for enlarging breasts. The existence of such a medicine raised my hopes to a whole new level. My friends told me that some Bs had started using the medicine. I wanted to see the medicine with my own eyes. Bob was the one who possessed all the information, he told me that the name of the medicine was Depo Provera, it was an an injection available in vials. Bob said said he would go to Moreh (on the Burma border) to buy the medicine, and in a few days he left on this mission.

For the next three or four days, I went to Bob's house daily, to enquire after him. I also went to Poison's house to ask him if he had heard from Bob. The desire and excitement in the days between his departure and return to Imphal filled my heart with warmth. Time and again, I checked my sultry-looking tops. I imagined how I would look in those tops, perfectly fitting my luscious breasts. The tension of waiting was soothed by the prospect of the desire that would be fulfilled, it would be a fitting reward for the long wait. After a week I went to Bob's house, sure that he must have returned by then and indeed he had. I was very happy to see him. Excitedly, I asked, 'Nupi, did you buy any?'

Bob sounded discouraged. 'Nupi, I did not get any. I just wasted my money.'

'But why?' I asked.

Bob replied, 'Actually, I placed the order with Harku, a Nupi Sabi from Burma. But Harku did not come to see me. I have requested Ta Sanaremba to bring the medicines to Imphal once Harku delivers them.' Ta Sanaremba was an elderly person who would bring various goods from Burma and sell them in Manipur.

I asked Bob when Ta Sanaremba was coming to Imphal, and he replied, 'The day after tomorrow, by evening.'

I continued, 'Nupi, you look very tired. I will come later on. But do not forget to keep two vials for me.' Bob assured me that he would do so.

I went to meet Bob again the day Ta Sanaremba was supposed to return from Moreh. I went to his room without speaking to anybody else in the house. On the small side table next to his bed, there were five similar-looking vials with red caps. As I was waiting for Bob, I picked up one vial and checked the labelling. The label said 'Depo

Provera'. Imagine my excitement at the sight of those vials that promised magic! I ran down the stairs and looked for Bob everywhere in the house. Bob replied from the toilet, 'Stop yelling, bitch. I am here.' I stood outside the toilet and said, 'Are the medicines on your table the ones for breast enlargement?'

Bob replied, 'Yes.'

I asked, 'How much does it cost?'

Bob replied, 'Rs 120 a vial.'

A bit dismayed, I said, 'It is very expensive.' Bob replied that he was lucky to have got it. We went to his room together. I said, 'Give me my share, two.'

Bob replied, 'Look, I have just five vials. If you take two, there will not be enough left for me. Let's place your order with Ta Sanaremba.'

Bob's reply shattered my hopes. I had thought that if Bob bought the medicine for me, it would be possible to pay the money later on. If I had to place an order, I would have to pay the full amount immediately, something I could not do at that time. I concluded that he was not willing to share the vials with me. But I knew that arguing with him or even complaining that he had hurt my feelings would not be prudent at that moment. Without speaking further on the matter, I stayed for a while and talked about other things. Throughout that time, I held the vials in my hand. It was difficult to leave his house empty-handed, I did not want to return home. Unable to handle my disappointment, I went to meet Poison at his house. I told Poison about the medicine. Poison had not heard about Bob's return.

Poison asked, 'How many did you see?'

I replied, 'Five.'

Poison said, 'I gave him money for three. If there are only five, what are we going to do?' Poison's question increased my anxiety. Bob had said that all five vials were his, but now it appeared that Poison also had a claim to three of them. Poison was in hurry to meet Bob, but I excused myself, saying, 'I'll go now. I haven't eaten.' Poison and I parted along the way. That day, I thought that I would no longer be friends with anybody, and I would not trust in Bob anymore.

After Bob's successful visit to Moreh, Poison, Ronu and Manimohon also started going there. I was aware that they were going to Moreh to buy the medicine. But there was no way I could ask any of them to procure the medicine for me. If truth be told, I neither had the money to go to Moreh nor to buy the medicine.

Even in the midst of these impossible circumstances, I found a glimmer of hope. I had to get the medicine for breast enlargement! I knew that in order to do so, I would have to enlist the support of Ema. She was always on the lookout for smallscale retail businesses. I knew that she would be enthusiastic about starting a business in Moreh, if I could come up with a plan. Confident of success. I sat down to talk to Ema about doing business in Moreh.

I began, 'Cosmetics like Promina are very cheap in the markets of Moreh. I think in the Imphal markets people sell it at double the price.' Though I talked about Promina, which was for skin lightening, my motive of course was to procure Depo Provera for myself.

Ema asked, 'What is the profit?'

I replied, 'The price of one box of Promina in Moreh is fifty rupees, here it is sold at 150 rupees, at some places it costs 200 rupees.' I also shared a list of items from Burma that could possibly be bought in Moreh and sold in Imphal, like red chilli, tamarind and dried fish etc which would earn us good profits.

However my intention, which I kept secret from Ema, was neither the profit or loss but simply to buy Depo Provera. My other secret plan was to somehow take money from Ema to buy the injections in bulk and sell some of them at a profit, so that I would have enough for my own use at no cost to myself.

Ema said, 'The profit is good. It is worth trying.'

Sensing Ema's willingness, I exaggerated a bit. To lure Ema into my business idea, I projected unrealistic figures for the profit that could be garnered from the venture. I spoke with such confidence that Ema started believing in my bogus arithmetic. After listening to my impressive information, Ema finally said that we must go to Moreh first to get a better perspective on a possible business. Elated, I agreed instantly. In a few days, she fixed a day for going to Moreh.

We went to Moreh. But Ema kept all our money in a purse in her sole custody. I did not have a single penny in my pocket. Even at the hotel in Moreh, she kept the purse with her. I began to worry that I was not going to have any money to buy the medicine, which was my sole purpose for coming to Moreh. Ema looked for chillies, dried fish and tamarind that were available at low prices in the Namphalong market. However, she was not willing to visit the Tamu market, the first Burma market just after crossing the Manipur border. This was the place where I could buy my medicine. When we returned to the hotel that night after buying everything Ema wanted and had had our meal, I told her, 'Ema there is a medicine for skin lightening available in the Tamu market. People like it a lot. I think we can profit from this medicine. It costs only twenty rupees a pack here, and we can sell it at Rs 120 in Imphal.'

Ema replied, 'We will buy it in the morning. Let us sleep now.'

She fell asleep after a while. Her reply had given me hope and I said a prayer to Kondong Lairembi (an Umanglai female deity) for her blessings before I finally went to sleep.

The following morning, we went to Tamu market on a horse-drawn cart. I walked to the shops that sold the particular medicine and enquired about Depo Provera. The shopkeepers did not know what I was talking about, it was very difficult to communicate with them. When I asked a middle-aged woman, she repeated, 'Depo Provera,' (she pronounced it as 'Deplo Plovela'), while her hand gestured to her breasts. I was concerned that her gesture might arouse Ema's suspicions. Meanwhile, Ema asked me, 'What is she trying to say? She is touching her chest and trying to say something.'

I replied, 'Maybe she is trying to say that the first time the medicine is used, chest pain might be a side effect.' The woman showed me the vial, and it looked exactly like the ones I had seen on Bob's table. I bought three boxes of Depo Provero. To keep up the pretence of doing a business in skin lightening creams, I bought a few Promina packs as well.

Ema had planned to return to Imphal that day. As soon as we reached the hotel we hired a coolie to carry all the items we had bought to the bus station. The moment we reached home, I unpacked the bag that contained the boxes of Depo Provera and put them in my bag. My family members should not see the medicines, it would be a disaster if they began asking questions.

Now that I had the medicine, I lost my intention to sell some for profit and decided to keep the whole lot for myself. I did give some to my friends for free. Whenever Ema asked me about the money, I told her that the buyers would be paying me soon. For a long time, she continued asking about the money, but eventually she stopped. She probably had given up the prospect of benefitting from my little business venture.

I needed to buy some syringes to start taking the injections. In those days, syringes were freely available in the pharmacies, and no one questioned why I needed them. The injections made my skin fair, but my breasts remained the same size. But it worked on Poison and Manimohon. I complained to them that my breasts were not becoming bigger. Poison agreed that the size of my breasts remained the same as before. He had a different concern. He thought I would look too provocative in my skimpy tops if my breasts became bigger. I had worn a sleeveless top with a deep neck that day. Poison observed, 'Even now you are eager to show off your breasts that are the size of a dot on the wall. Imagine what would happen if they were bigger. You would create such a drama in public that it would be awkward to be seen together with you!'

My friends never encouraged me in anything I did. At times I thought that their views were not very different from the people who hated us. We had the same complaints and problems to talk about, nevertheless, there was a wide gap between them and me. Our likes and dislikes conflicted at times. I could not ascertain what caused the difference, I could only be upset about the lack of unity between us. I gradually realised that it was becoming impossible to get along with other homos. The way they viewed me was wrong. Or perhaps we had different roads to freedom and contentment.

I spent most of my time absorbing other people's

criticism of me. At home, quarrels and arguments with Baba continued to disrupt our domestic life. Peace remained a permanent absentee in my life. My family's disapproval of me had reached a new level by this time. Every member resented me, from every angle! They felt bitter about my supposed lack of interest in finding a job, in addition to my choice of friends and disengagement with education. I was an outcast both at home and in the world. I remained a black sheep for a long time.

My desire to continue studies was dimmed by my unwillingness to face the drama that would ensue if I did get admission in any college in Manipur. Things had been different in Guntur where there was a small handful of people from Manipur who had to stick together to support and protect one another in that place so far from our homes. Hence, my feminine nature and gender expression was accepted by them. But here in Manipur, it was a time when homos were very badly treated. Moreover, seeing someone like me wearing dresses and women's clothing in college, would be a phenomenon, and people would definitely target me for no other reason except that I was different.

Nevertheless, I had begun to realise that a college education was needed in order to get a job. Additionally, it was important to demonstrate that a homo could study in a good college. Based on this conviction, I started looking for a suitable college.

Ema did not want me to stay in Khurai. She finally decided to send me to stay with her younger sister, Eney Rani, at Uripok, ostensibly to give private tuition to her children. Ema had been talking with Eney Rani on this matter for a while, which showed that Ema was constantly looking for opportunities to send me away from home.

One evening, Eney's husband came to our house to take me to his home. I did not have a choice, Ema had already willed it so.

Edomcha Rani was the eldest daughter-in-law of Ningthoukhongjam Khelchandra, a renowned scholar and a Padma Shri awardee. People called Khelchandra 'Paji', and so I also called him Paji. My duty in his household was to help the children with their studies morning and night. There was nothing else to do. I did not have any friends in Uripok, it was a struggle to stay in that house in those circumstances—no friends, no activities. Sometimes, I watched programmes on their black and white television set, at other times, I read Paji's books in his library. In due course, his library and his books became a motivation for me to stay in his house.

Every day, from morning till evening, people stood in a queue to meet Paji. Some came to interview him, some talked with him, and others read in his library. Around that time, some people had started discussing the Meitei Mayek issue with Paji. This was a disagreement between Padma Shri Khelchandra and other groups regarding the number of alphabets in the Meitei Mayek language. Each side claimed they were correct. The only thing I knew was that all those discussions were serious and intellectual matters. I read about the discussion on Meitei Mayek alphabets in a local newspaper. Akaba from the Soibam neighbourhood was one of the persons who held a different view from Paji and claimed that the number of alphabets he said there were, was correct.

After four months, Edomcha Rani's husband brought me back home on his Luna. Once his children's final examinations were over, my duty to teach them came to an end. The first thing I did after coming back from Uripok was to go to Poison's house. Poison and some other friends were playing ludo, and Khoidong was leading the game. There was also a friend of Khoidong called Meitrabak. In due time, Meitrabak became a regular player.

Every day, after the morning meal, we played ludo in Khoidong's courtyard or the verandah, sometimes we split into two groups. We played for a stake of ten rupees. Meitrabak and I got acquainted with one another. He was tall and well-built, with black, silky straight hair, his face had a certain grace and attraction. I liked him a lot, but there was a huge age difference between us, which made it almost impossible for me to express my feelings to him. He must have been only around fifteen years old, and I was eight or nine years older.

Meitrabak was the son of the owner of the Vivek hotel at Lamlong. Vivek hotel had become more popular than Babu hotel by then. One speciality of Vivek hotel was its potato and chicken mixture snack that was popular far and wide.

One day I asked Khoidong, 'Khoidong, how many siblings does Meitrabak have?'

Khoidong, who stammered a bit, started counting the number of siblings in Meitrabak's family—'Sandhyarani, Vivek, Nilbir, Prithivi...four, and their cousin Surbala.'

I asked, 'In which class is he studying?'

Khoidong replied, 'Same as mine, he is studying in Class VIII.'

I asked again, 'How are his parents?'

Khoidong replied, 'I don't know. His father is always very good to homos. He used to tease me and say I would be his daughter-in-law one day.'

I asked, 'Do you regularly visit his house?'

Khoidong replied, 'Yes, I always go to his house to watch TV.'

I said, 'Khoidong, doesn't he have any other pair of pants? He wears the same pants every day.'

Khoidong replied, 'Yes, he wears that pair only, they are his school uniform. His father is very stingy. They use a toothbrush till the brush is flat and soft.'

At that time, I had eight hundred rupees, the amount given to me by Edomcha Rani's husband as remuneration for teaching their children. I could buy something for Meitrabak with the money.

I asked Khoidong if Meitrabak was good at studies. Khoidong replied, 'I don't think so. He is just a Tarzan knowing nothing about books.'

I asked, 'Can he read Manipuri?' Khoidong told me he could.

I said, 'I want to write something for him. Will you give it to him?'

Khoidong agreed. He paused for a moment and said, 'Ta Santa, it seems that you like him.'

I replied, 'Not like that. I just want to say something to him.'

Khoidong shrugged and said, 'Okay, you write it. I will give it to him.'

That night I wrote a long letter in Manipuri, addressed to Meitrabak. My message was not particularly about love and romance. I expressed my thoughts about his beauty and advised him to concentrate on his studies. I put the letter inside an envelope and placed it under my pillow.

The next day, I went to Khoidong's around 11 a.m. He was dancing in the verandah and a song was playing on a stereo player. The music was so loud that he could not hear me calling his name. I turned off the stereo player. Khoidong was startled and looked at me sharply. 'Bitch,' he said. Then, remembering our conversation of the day before, he asked, 'Ta Santa, do you have the letter now?' I handed him the envelope that contained the letter. I also gave him *kwa*. He put the *kwa* in his mouth and immediately left for Meitrabak's house. I told him that I would be waiting for him and so he must come back soon. While I waited for him to return, I sat with Eche Sheela, Khoidong's eldest sister, and chatted with her.

Khoidong came back very soon, walking rapidly. He was almost out of breath when he reached the verandah. I was relieved when he said that he had delivered the letter. He filled a steel cup with water from the pitcher and gulped it down. I was eager to know about Meitrabak's reaction when Khoidong gave him the letter. But it was embarrassing to ask in Eche Sheela's presence. Eche Sheela was the first one to break the tense silence. 'What did you give Naocha?' she asked. Naocha was another name for Khoidong. Before I could prevent Khoidong from answering, he said, 'I was delivering Ta Santa's letter to Meitrabak.'

Khoidong's revelation flustered me, and I said angrily, 'Shut up, child.' Eche Sheela burst out laughing and said to me, 'Oh, you, old woman.' We three looked at each other and laughed, the whole house rang with our laughter. I ran towards the backyard of the house and tried to calm myself down. I returned only after I had controlled myself.

Eche Sheela was very fond of talking about adult stuff. But though she talked freely about sex, she had not really had any romantic affairs or liaisons with men, her past was free of such things. She was a kind, sweet-tempered person. Now she said to me conversationally, 'Santa, you all want to be women. Don't you have an erection? When our Naocha was very young, every morning he woke up with an erection. Now he is a homo, so I do not have any idea.' Her honest curiosity angered Naocha, 'Stop asking

such things, vamp. I had made an offering of my organ to
the gods on the Cheiraoba (Meitei New Year) day.'

Eche Sheela appeared to take the whole thing about my
letter to Meitrabak very seriously. She said, 'I heard that
Devo (Poison) is in a relationship with Joykumar. You also
like Meitrabak. How do you have sex?'

Taken aback, I said, 'This is too much. I cannot believe
that you are asking me such a thing.'

Sheela replied, 'Indeed, I have been thinking about this
for a long time. I don't want to ask Devo about it. But I
do not mind asking you.'

Khoidong tried to intervene by talking about other
things. But Eche Sheela would not be diverted. She said,
'Shut up, Naocha. Tell me, what is the real thing, Santa?'

I said, 'You should listen to Khoidong.'

Sheela persisted, 'Do you do it from the back? It is scary
to think about it. Tell me, is it painful?'

I said, 'You, women, will not know about this. It is so
pleasurable. It is as though I am lying on a big boulder
in a calm place on a scorching summer day, while a cool
fountain of water lazily showers over my body.'

They laughed at my description. Poison arrived just
then and we told him what we had been discussing. Poison
turned red and said, 'I do not know anything about men
and relationship stuff. I do not want to be in Santa's league.'
He stared at me piercingly as he said this. His look told
me that he was raging at me. But what could his anger
do? What happened between two people in their intimate
moments could not be known. Besides, Eche Sheela knew
a little too much to believe in his claim to innocence.
Even though people did not talk openly, they did not stop
wondering 'how' and 'what'. One day people would surely
come to know. We carried on talking for a while when

Bob called us from outside. Poison, Khoidong and I went out to meet Bob. Poison suddenly turned towards me and said, 'Santa, you are extremely shameless.'

His remark surprised me. 'Why do you say that?' I asked. Poison replied, 'You sit and gossip with women. You have no sense of decency. We live with a certain sense of responsibility and modesty, and so we do not do anything that will belittle us in front of others.'

I replied, 'Poison, Eche Sheela was the one talking about it, my participation was accidental. I do not think it is particularly damaging.'

Poison replied, 'It might not be harmful to people like you, but it is harmful to me. You are looking out for men in the guise of giving tuition to children in your neighbourhood. Do not do it in our neighbourhood. Nobody will respect us.'

I was both surprised and enraged by his accusations. I said, 'Poison, you should not be saying such bitter things to me. No matter how angry you are, you cannot accuse me of things I have never done. You are trying to hide your relationship with Joykumar but everyone knows about it, even though they might not talk about it to your face. People laugh behind your back. The children that come to me to get tuition lessons are sent by their parents. You are the one luring men.'

My words outraged him, and he said, 'Don't come to my house ever again.'

I said, 'Well, you are very childish. You can lose your temper as much as you want. I don't care.' With these words, I stood up to leave.

Bob who had been silent for a while, said, 'Enough, Santa, you are too much. Do not come to my locality also. People talk about you a lot. Sometimes I try to hide when you come to my house.'

I replied, 'Well, Bob, losing your friendship will not cause any loss to me. You are not greater than me. So, your words do not bother me.' Saying this, I left the place.

Their words wounded me. I told myself that I would no longer seek the company of my homo friends. In the moments that followed, I started feeling the loss, a wave of loneliness and sadness engulfed me. They deceived themselves by walking the trodden roads, to me this was foolish and cowardly. Their disavowal of me and my perspective on life could never deter me—I would continue to wear the clothes I wanted, nothing would change.

From that day on, a visible distance developed between the homos of Lamlong and me. But I continued visiting Khoidong. He told me many things about Meitrabak—how he was doing, where he went, and who his friends were. Meitrabak did not reply to my letter, and Khoidong was the only person who could tell me the reason. He told me, 'He says he is shy about this.' I had to accept the fact that my hope for a reply from Meitrabak was unlikely to be fulfilled.

Meitrabak might not have replied to my letter, but I continued to think about him. I had an urge to buy gifts for him. I went to Khuman Lampak with Khoidong with the intention of buying clothes for him. I bought a pair of jeans for Meitrbak and a T-shirt for Khoidong. On our way back, we stopped at Lamlong. I wanted Khoidong to deliver my present to Meitrabak as soon as possible. I was eager to know his reaction. Would he accept my present? If he accepted it, what would he say? Would he happily take my present? I couldn't wait for an answer to my questions, I told Khoidong, 'First go and give this present to Meitrabak. I am waiting here for you.'

Khoidong always agreed to whatever I proposed. He took the pants and left for Meitrabak's house. I stood and waited for him at the Lamlong crossroad, near the electricity transformer. My heart was beating fast and my palms were moist. I silently prayed that Meitrabak would accept my present. My mind was telling me that my action was futile and I should not have given anything to him. In the next moment, the feeling of hopelessness was countered by the assurance that a gift was the only way to ascertain his feelings for me. I kept looking out for Khoidong. When he returned, Meitrabak was with him. I had never imagined such a possibility, my legs began to tremble. As they drew closer, Khoidong winked at me and said, 'Ta Santa, Meitrabak and I are going to Tompok's house to get a few books.' Tompok was one of their classmates.

Meitrabak did not look at me, he just smiled and stroked Khoidong's head. Khoidong said, 'Why are you shy? I am telling the truth.' I did not know what the two had secretly planned, but Khoidong suddenly suggested that we go to Khuman Lampak instead. 'Let's go to Khuman Lampak today. We can meet Tompok tomorrow.' Evidently, Khoidong must have hatched a plan that would work in my favour. Perhaps Meitrabak was a willing party to it. This raised my hopes.

We walked towards Khuman Lampak. Khoidong walked a bit ahead of Meitrabak and me, giving us a chance to talk to one another. I appreciated his mature behaviour in this. But Meitrabak and I did not talk much, we only talked about the jeans. We kept walking. When we reached Telepati bridge, we crossed to the other side and continued walking.

That day I was very happy. It was a new beginning in my life. I was overwhelmed with my love for Meitrabak. I thought about him constantly, I wanted to stay by his side all my life. I asked questions that I had not asked myself before—did he have a lover? What would I do if he got married? I did not even like the helpful and concerned Khoidong to be near him.

I tried as much as possible not to reveal my emotions and feelings to Khoidong and Meitrabak, I did not think it right. Most of the time, I pretended to be uninterested in Meitrabak. I also visited his family's hotel many times for no reason. Even though he was very young, he liked drinking *yu* a lot. In my effort to spend time with him, I accompanied him on his *yu* drinking trips to vendors. Every evening, Meitrabak and I headed towards the Ragailong neighbourhood at Khuman to drink *yu*. I loved it very much when he treated me as his woman, and this happened only after he drank *yu*. Another of our routines was to sit at the Puthiba ground. We never talked about love, just being in his company made me happy. Once, after getting drunk, he said, in English, 'Ta Santa you have no concern for other people's efeel.' I corrected him, 'Feeling, not efeel.' He accepted my correction and apologized for his mistake.

If we could not go to Khuman, we would go to Sangeet Kala Hall to buy the *yu* from the vendor in the vicinity. Everyone in Lamlong came to know our story. Khoidong told me one day about a conversation he had with Meitrbak's mother. She wanted to know if Meitrabak and I were in a relationship. Khoidong denied any such relationship between the two of us, and said I was only helping Meitrabak with studies. Khoidong also added that I might be a homo but I was very good at studies.

In fact, we did not share a physical relationship. But I felt him very intimately, I could recognise his footsteps and even the sound of his breathing. I wanted him to be a person worthy of success. But each time I realised that he could not be mine, I quarrelled with him for no reason. We never sealed our relationship with words of affirmation like 'I love you' but I could not be happy without seeing him. I could not hope for a stable and exclusive future with him, but for the moment he was my choice, my present. We drank *yu* together. I bought books for him, I closely monitored his school attendance. I bought boiled eggs for him. Like the branches of the plum tree heavy with abundant fruit, love filled my heart with the blissful burden of longing and desire. I was driven into desiring him by his simplicity. His word 'efeel' sowed a new emotion inside me. He was the rain that heralded the spring in the drought of my life.

His family came to know about our *yu* drinking ventures. One night when we were coming back together from a vend, his mother met us at Lamlong. It was closing time at the market, she must have been waiting to confront us. On seeing us, she said, addressing Meitrabak, 'Ebungo Macha, wait.' Both of us came to a standstill. In the next moment I was about to continue walking, but she stopped me, saying, 'Hey homo, you also wait. You are spoiling my son. Don't come near him.' Angered by her words, I replied, 'What? You cannot discipline your son. He is the one who taught me to drink *yu*.' While I was quarrelling with her, Meitrabak fled the scene. After some time I also returned home.

Upset by the confrontation with Meitrabak's mother, I sat for a while outside my house. My mind was burdened by many thoughts. I did not think I could meet him freely again, this caused me more distress than any other thoughts. It must indeed be a blessed thing to be a woman. The event that day would not have happened if I were a woman. For a long time I sat crying. It was very late when I went inside the house. I slept without eating that night.

My bed was in the front room of the house. The

window consisted of two planks but it did not have a proper latch to secure the planks, anybody could easily open it from outside. That night I did not care about latching the window before I went to bed. I must have dozed off for a while when I heard somebody softly calling my name. In my half-roused state I opened the window. Meitrabak was standing outside the window, crying. I had lost hope of seeing him again. In that sleep-deprived state, he was like an apparition to me. I climbed out of the window. His shirt was torn, there were marks on his face. I was scared that my family would be awake and so I took him outside the grounds of the house. We stood under the electric pole in the lane. I asked, 'What happened? How are you in this state?'

Meitrabak said, 'While running away from Ema, I was caught by Da Inaotomba (his cousin brother) at Lainingthou lane. He held me by my neck and dragged me to my house. As soon as we reached home, Baba asked me to breathe out to check if I had been drinking *yu*. Then he asked me with whom I went to drink *yu*. He beat me with firewood. They said that I could never go out with you. I fought with them and came here. I will never go there again.'

I could understand his anger, but he had made a decision at the height of his emotions. It would be futile to ask him to go home that night, I knew he would not. For that moment the only option seemed to be for him to stay at my house.

I knew this would only add to my problems. None of my friends had stayed at my house overnight in the past. Meitrabak would only make my fragile relationship with my family worse. Moreover, his relatives would surely come in search of him, leading to a major conflict at home. So I tried to persuade him, 'Meitrabak, you are very young.

Every parent would be upset if their children start drinking at a tender age like yours. Even my parents would react in the same way. So, it would be better for you to go home now. I will take you to your house.'

My words enraged him. 'You are also no different,' he shouted. He turned to leave which panicked me. I stopped him. I was willing to go anywhere with him, no matter what the consequences. I would not leave him alone, I would not rest in the comfort of my home when he had nowhere to go. I asked, 'Where should we go? We should not stay at my house. Your family will come in search of you.'

Meitrabak said, 'There is nobody at our house in Porompat. Let us go there.' He meant the old mud house that belonged to his parents.

I asked, 'But do you have any beds there?'

Meitrabak said, 'There are two beds there.'

I asked him, 'Is the house not locked?'

Meitrabak said, 'Yes, it is locked. But Indira, my cousin sister who lives next door, has the key, I will take the key from her.'

We went to Porompat that night. When Meitrbak opened the gate, the first thing I saw was a huge zinc-roofed *yumjao,* a large quarter usually used as a living room. There were rows of rooms attached to the *yumjao,* and the house opened out into a huge courtyard. A thick grove of bamboo plants surrounded the house. We lit a candle. The interior of the house was very big, the light from the candle could not light up the corners of the house. We lay down on one of the beds that did not have a net, mattress or pillows. I folded my arms and rested my head on them.

He fell asleep soon. I looked at his face the entire night in the dim light of the candle. Observing him sleeping was as though I was dreaming. I feared the dawn. I wanted to know what he was feeling even though his mind had wandered away from the real world in that dream state. I wanted him to stay with me all my life. I was lost in thought, wondering if one would experience a similar freedom on one's wedding night. I did not want anybody or anything to disturb the tranquillity all around me. It was as though I could challenge the world with him by my side. That night the hard wooden plank of the bed, which no one would consider worth lying on, was nothing less than a luxurious bed decorated with soft pillows and mattresses. The folded arm under my head never grew tired or ached. The nocturnal sounds of the insects charmed me like the song of a cuckoo serenading me.

The crowing of roosters nearby told me that dawn had broken, but I had not slept a second. I got up from the bed and sat on the floor. I could hear the sound of people talking in the street outside, and suddenly I grew anxious. I wondered how I would come out of the house. While I was absorbed in these thoughts, the members of both his family and mine arrived. From his side, his mother and father had come and from my side, my Ema, Ema Keina and Ebok Gani were there. It was intimidating to see all of them together. Ema only spoke one sentence, 'Let us go home.' I got up from the floor and followed Ema out of the house, without any arguments.

When we were outside, Ema scolded me, 'People are saying that you have been doing the worst things. You have to face your Baba for this.'

Ema Keina said, 'This place is a refuge for criminals, it is not a good place.'

Ema said, 'He has never stayed at anybody's house all his life. Now, since his friends are not good, he has started doing this also. I have been troubled since the time this child of mine grew up, Eche Keina.' She turned to me and said, 'Stop wearing make-up from now on. Are you not ashamed? People are talking about you. Everywhere I go people talk about you. I am very ashamed.'

Their complaints and scolding did not bother me, my mind was preoccupied with thoughts of how I could meet Meitrabak again. Ema continued to chastise me until we reached home. The moment he saw me, Baba said, 'You, black sheep, aren't you ashamed?' He was about to launch into a tirade of abuse, but Ema now intervened and said, 'It is enough. You do not have to say anything more to him.' She took me inside the house. Ema Keina tried to console Baba.

For the next three days, I did not leave the house, even though I wanted to. After this brief period of confinement, the first person I visited was Khoidong. According to Khoidong, Meitrabak was being responsible and obedient, he did not go out anywhere, and he regularly worked in the hotel. On the other hand, my homo friends spread false stories about the events of the day. They spread a rumour that I had taken away Meitrabak by force, they also said that Meitrabak's parents traced my whereabouts and beat me. The rumours shamed me deeply. Whenever I saw somebody in the street, it felt as though they were looking at me and talking derisively about me.

After a while, when the heat of the rumour mill cooled down a little, I again made Khoidong a messenger between Meitrabak and me. We started meeting again. This time our meetings were different We had cut down on *yu* drinking. Mostly, we roamed around the Kongpal area and came back home. Sometimes, Khoidong also joined us.

Around that time, my eldest sister bought a second-hand Kinetic Honda. I was forbidden from riding it, although she generously allowed her other siblings to do so. One day when I had gone to her house and found she was not at home, I took the key from her eldest daughter and went for a ride. It was the 25th of January. First I rode to Khoidong's house and from there we went to Meitrabak's house. Meitrabak and I went to Khuman to drink *yu*. He brought along some fried fish wrapped in paper. When we were returning from the vend, the headlight of the Honda fused. We got off and slowly pushed the bike along the Khuman road. At the Lamlong Keithel, Army personnel and Manipur commandos were checking drivers and pedestrians alike. We were also stopped. One Army officer asked me in Hindi where I was coming from. Out of fear I said that I had been to a birthday party. Next, a commando walked towards me and said, 'Hey, park your moped properly.' I pulled down the stand of the bike and parked it as instructed. He asked me if I had drunk *yu*, and I said I had drunk a bit. He shouted at me, 'Do you know what day is tomorrow?' I said it was the 26th of January. Then he asked me if we were the ones who had planted bombs at Singjamei. I said no. After asking me that ridiculous question, he flashed the torchlight into my face. Then he laughed and said mockingly, 'Oh, you homo!' In derisive tones, he said, 'Hey, homo, where did you go with the kid? Your company is going to ruin him.'

The commando turned towards Meitrabak and asked, 'Now, who are you? Why are you in the company of this homo? Don't you have any other friends? You are inviting bad consequences upon yourself. You must be wandering off to deserted places with this homo in this befuddled state.' Meitrabak replied that I was his friend. The commando hit him with his baton and asked him where he lived. From this checkpoint, Meitrabak's house was just a short distance away. Meitrabak replied that he was the son of the owner of Vivek hotel. On hearing this, the commando let him go. I was left alone. He inquired whose vehicle we were riding and asked me to produce the papers. I told him that the vehicle was my sister's. I showed him the papers and he checked the details. Then he asked for my driving licence and of course, I did not have one.

The commando asked me to lie on my stomach on the tarred concrete of the road. I pleaded with him not to make me do this, but he threatened me with dire consequences if I did not obey him, so I lay down as he had commanded me to do. He was wearing heavy military boots and as soon as I lay down, he put his foot on my back and repeatedly hit my legs with his baton. The repeated blows seemed to take away the pain and replace it with anger. I cried and shouted for help by calling out the names of the local Meira Paibis.

One of them happened to be my friend's mother. 'Sibu Mama, these Army men are going to shoot me, I am innocent. Help me.' I shouted these words over and over again. The commandos pulled me up and slapped me on the face. 'Do not shout,' they said. But I had gained courage by now, that night I did not want to stay submissive and mute, I did not feel any shame or fear. I had a feeling that the more I shouted the more chance I had of living.

My voice must have reached Sibu Mama. She arrived with a few elderly women to rescue me. They asked the commandos, 'Who are you torturing now? It is painful to hear the shrieking voices of the innocent. You are inflicting pain on the innocent everywhere you go. Release this person.'

The commandos replied, 'Ema, please go back. This is

not a big matter.' They were trying to get rid of the elderly women. In derisive tones, one commando said, 'This homo got drunk and started arguing with us, so we beat him. He does not have a licence, the vehicle has no headlight. Besides we have to implement security measures for 26th January.'

I replied, still crying, 'Sibu Mama, they are lying. They are beating me for no reason.' On hearing my anguished cries, Sibu Mama and the other women held up their *Meiras*—torches—and forcefully broke the cordon of the Army and the commandos. When Sibu Mama finally recognised me, she exclaimed, 'Are you not Santa? This is one of our children. He is my son's friend.' She helped me to stand up and wiped my tears. Then she turned to the commandos and said, 'He is innocent and an obedient child. I know him very well.' She scolded them again for troubling innocent people. As I walked behind Sibu Mama, after she successfully managed to deliver me from the tyrants, I looked back and shouted at them, 'Dogs, servants, illiterates, if you have the courage, kill me now.' One commando ran after me and hit my legs with his baton. I did not run. Sibu Mama held the commando's baton and stopped him, saying, 'That is enough.'

When I reached home, I found a crowd had gathered outside my house. I did not understand how the news that I had been beaten by the commandos had spread so quickly. Among the crowd was Ema. She rushed to me, asking if I had any serious injury. I said I didn't but began to cry once again. When we checked my sister's Kinetic Honda the following day, we found that the paint had flaked off in some parts. The police must have mishandled the vehicle. My sister scolded me severely, she made out that I was completely devoid of any sense. I vowed I would never ride her bike again. Her harsh remarks in the wake of the torture I had suffered at the hands of the Army and the commandos, made me start looking at my own family and everyone else as my enemy.

Soon after this incident happened, Ta Anday sent a message to Ema about a vacant position at Om Laboratory Clinic on RIIMS Road. The laboratory needed a lab technician, and I had the necessary qualifications. On Ema's insistence, I visited the clinic to enquire about the job, and they took me on. The clinic was owned by one Shiv Choron, and the presiding doctor at the clinic was called Mohen. Dr Mohen approved all the diagnostic tests conducted at the clinic. Two women also worked at the clinic—Priya and Thoibi. The clinic paid us twenty rupees per day, which they gave us at the end of the day. Apart from this, the management provided *singju* and *bora* snacks in the afternoon. The two women were very friendly towards me, but Shiv Choron and Dr Mohen were different. They had an unpleasant way of interacting with the lab staff.

It was the year 1996, and the Bheigyachandra Open Air Theatre (BOAT) was newly opened. The theatre regularly hosted music concerts. It also hosted various beauty pageants that were popular in Manipur at that time. On the first of November that year, a beauty pageant called Miss Kut was being held at Kangpokpi, Senapti District. Bob was the one who told me about this event. I wanted to take a day off so that I could go, but Dr Mohen was a very difficult man to talk to. So, I requested Priya to talk to him on my behalf. The doctor asked me, 'So, are you participating in the contest? But you are so ugly. Forget about a beauty contest, you are not even fit to act a female role in a Shumang Leela. Are not the Nupi Sabis of Shumang Leela beautiful? You look very skinny, your face is longer than my height.' In this insulting manner, he laughed off my case.

His cruel words humiliated me, it was impossible to keep my composure in that moment of shame. Sensing my embarrassment, Priya quietly said to me, 'Do not take it to heart. This is his usual style of interacting with people.' But I had never been humiliated in that fashion before. A little after Dr Mohen left, I also came home. From that day onwards, I stopped going to the laboratory.

Bob and I met at Lamlong. From Cheimeirong we took a bus to Kangpokpi. Most of the passengers on the bus were going to Kangpokpi to witness the Miss Kut pageant. It was apparent from their conversation that the pageant was a major attraction of the Chabang Kut festival. Some said that the festival that year would have tight security, last year miscreants had hurled stones at innocent people who had come to watch the pageant, and many were injured. They also said that it would be better to stay at Kangpokpi rather than return to Imphal late at night. I didn't pay any heed to what they were saying. My mind was fixed on the pageant.

Some people on the bus asked if I was Tom Sharma—the top fashion designer of that time who was also a homo— and if I was mentoring any contestants. The fact that people associated me with Tom made me happy. It made me come close to being popular.

The road was in a good condition only uptil Sekmai. From Motbung onwards, the constant jerks on the road and the din inside the bus drained my energy. I became annoyed and impatient.

It was very late when the bus reached Kangpokpi Bazar. Bob and I did not know where the beauty contest was going to be held. We followed the group of people who had been on the bus with us. A little distance off the Kangpokpi Bazar, there was a big community hall overlooking a football ground. The moment we reached the hall, a new sensation overtook me, I suddenly felt released from all constraints. The hall was crowded with men and women, mostly Meiteis. I was somehow emboldened to talk, I wanted to share a camaraderie with everyone, it did not matter whether I was acquainted with them or not.

There was no separate Green Room for the contestants to change their clothes, and some of them complained about this. Some others were practising the catwalk in a corner, they all wore high-heeled shoes. Each contestant was attended by a make-up artist. Tom Sharma was teaching the catwalk to a few contestants. He had a thin face and high cheekbones, his hair was long. The contestant for whom he had designed dresses and done the make-up was Chanam Lilabati. She was extremely beautiful—tall, good physique, and fair complexion. I was struck by her good looks. She treated Tom Sharma with great respect. Apart from Lilabati, everyone at the venue knew and acknowledged him. The way people respected him inspired me to be like him. I wanted to be a very important person, a person without whom people could not accomplish anything.

After a while, some locals entered the hall and asked all the non-participants to go outside. Bob and I came out and took our seats with the audience. The pageant started around 9 p.m. Most people in the audience, with the exception of the relatives and immediate family members of the contestants, were drunk. Bob opened his long, curly hair and let it fall on one side of his shoulder. A group of men was also standing beside us. They hooted at every contestant, and every word coming out of their mouths was foul. In fact, the entire ground where the audience was seated reverberated with indecent utterances. Bob and I also joined the crowd in hooting, but we did not utter any curse words, we were just making a noise. Bob and I looked at one another each time we hooted and laughed. Meanwhile, the group of men standing nearby approached us. One of them asked, 'Can we know you?' It was easy to conclude that they were attracted by Bob's looks. They asked if Bob's eyelashes were false, they also said that Bob was more beautiful than the contestants in the pageant. The men were also from Imphal. They said that we could drink with them. Bob laughed seductively and drawled, 'Okayyy.' The men said, 'Your laughter is so intoxicating.' But Bob just turned way from them in a disinterested manner.

Then they invited us to join them. Bob held me by my wrist and said, 'Come on, babe,' and we followed the men out of the audience.

At the far end of the field where the community hall was located, there was a parking lot for vehicles. We sat down on the ground in this parking lot. One of the men said to another, 'Bhai, go and get the thing in the vehicle.' By 'thing' he meant, *yu*. The others started gathering firewood to start a small bonfire. Meanwhile, the fellow who went to fetch the *yu* also returned. We lit the fire, and began drinking. As we slowly got drunk, all of us started talking in English, not caring in the least for correct grammar or pronunciation. Bob started singing songs from bands like Nazareth and Scorpion. Bob was very fond of Western heavy metal and rock music, he could sing very well too. The men had the same musical taste as Bob's. They had studied and stayed outside Manipur for many years. I also sang the song 'It Must Have Been Love' by Roxette. Unlike Bob, I was not good at singing but this song had stuck in my mind ever since I had seen *Pretty Woman*. Since that time, I had rehearsed the song many times.

The men generously praised Bob and me. They thought

that despite being homos, Bob and I were very educated and smart, they even said, 'You two have guts.' For every word of approval they uttered, we took one more shot of *yu*, and with every sip of *yu*, we spoke one more line of broken English. Then I started dancing the cabaret to the distant music coming from the community hall. It felt as though the entire audience had fixed its gaze on me, and I was more beautiful and talented than the contestants. I felt as though I was living in America. When we heard the contestants introducing themselves in English, we criticised those speaking incorrectly, shouting, 'Down, down.' The men repeated everything we said.

Then, amid the music and cheering, we heard the sound of fights breaking out. Some said that the local men had started the fight. This news broke up our gathering. The Meitei formed into different groups and gathered together in one place.

By the time the pageant concluded, it was one a.m. Those who had come from Imphal prepared to leave. Each group searched for its members. Utmost care was taken that no one was left behind. If anybody was missing, a search party was sent out, calling out the name of the missing person. As the intoxicating effect of the *yu* faded and Bob and I gradually came to our senses, we began to see the trouble we were in. We had neither a vehicle nor any acquaintances in that place. We looked for empty seats in every vehicle and finally came across a contestant who was with her family. The family had a car, and they were our only hope at that moment. They were not very welcoming, but the situation was becoming dangerous and so they reluctantly allowed us to get into their car. All the vehicles going to Imphal were escorted by the police. As everyone had feared, a vehicle in front was attacked. Everyone panicked and started driving fast. We reached Motbung in that state of panic. At last the danger was behind us and everyone was relieved.

―――――――――――

The morning after the pageant, I was preoccupied with thoughts of Tom Sharma. Tom occupied a privileged position at that time, and I wanted to be as influential as him. I wanted to be somebody with some worth, able to command respect from society. I needed to make a decision about the future course of my life. Tom constantly figured in my mind as the proverbial beacon of hope for what I could accomplish. I was fully convinced that meeting Tom would lead to success. He was not afraid of owning his identity in public, he wore feminine clothing and make-up openly, most of his friends were women. It was evident that he did not deceive himself about who he was. He did not hide behind the curtain of the norms of society, rather he walked ahead of the age-old customs and prejudices.

Everyone knew that Tom Sharma was a homo, yet he was welcomed and accepted wherever he went. In contrast to the respect conferred on Tom, my fellow homos, devoid of the confidence to own their identity and seeking refuge in a deceptive double life, chastised and discarded me. They were also ill-treated by society, their caution did not bring them the fame and respect Tom Sharma enjoyed. My friends' fear of their own, real self, discouraged me. On the contrary, thinking about Tom, the trajectory of his life, his confidence, gave me courage. I looked forward to a time in the future when I too could openly live as I wished. Here also the solution lay in meeting Tom, to learn how to be like him. Money, fame and talent did not discriminate between men and women, between those who were homos and those who were not. Talent leads to fame and fame brings money, and people follow the rich. I was no longer interested in being around those who did not see eye to eye with me, I wanted to cut away from their narrow and small-minded way of thinking.

My initial idea was to follow Tom and learn make-up and dress-making. In order to achieve this, I had to get acquainted with him by any means. I firmly believed that Tom and I could be very good friends.

My eagerness to meet him was matched by a complete lack of familiarity with him. Sometimes I went to the bazar in Bob's company in the hope of meeting Tom, but it seemed that he was not part of the nocturnal gathering of Bs at the bazar. Instead, I met a beautiful B my age called Chandrika at the bazar. Chandrika was from Khagempalli. We had never met before but since we were Bs we started acknowledging and talking to one another. When I told him my name, he said he had heard about me, and asked, 'So, you are Santa from Khurai?' I said I was the same Santa. He added, 'Every B in Manipur knows you. We heard that you are very smart and bold.' Chandrika came with another B called Sonipao who was from Moirang. Both of them were staying together at Imphal. Sonipao was beautiful and feminine even without make-up. The three of us decided to meet up again.

But sometimes luck finds its own way to you. One day I was sitting in the *mangol* of a Bamon family who lived behind our house, talking with the daughters of the family. The mother, whom I called Ema Yaima, was about to go the bazar to sell silk *phaneks*, woven on the loom the family owned. Suddenly she said, 'Tomba had taken a few *phaneks* from me. I do not know what has happened, he has not returned them.'

Ema Yaima's younger sister, Eche Ebeyaima, said, 'He said that he would be returning the *phaneks* today, or he would return them after the fashion show. They have a fashion show at the conclusion of the Yaosang Sports.'

Ema Yaima said, 'What to do with this child? The other day he came to hide from his brother, because his brother was trying to force him to cut his long hair.'

The last bit, about long hair, startled me. I was sure that they must be talking about Tom Sharma and asked Ema Yaima if that was who she was referring to.

Ema Yaima said, 'Yes, there is somebody like you at Kongba.'

I asked her many questions about Tom Sharma. Ema Yaima answered my questions in great detail, telling me all about him from his childhood days till the present time. After she left for the bazar, I carried on asking questions to Eche Ebeyaima. She asked, 'Do you want to be friends with him?' I told her that I had been thinking of meeting him for a long time. Eche Ebeyaima said, 'Go to his house. Tell him that you are our neighbour. You two will be a good match as friends. But he is not at home most of the time. He travels to many places for wedding make-up and fashion shows.' In addition to all this information, she gave me Tom Sharma's address.

I did not know much about the Kongba neighbourhood. I thought of borrowing my neighbour Eche Naobi's Luna, I was confident that she would help me since I had helped her many times in the past. Eche Naobi always sent me to convey her messages and letters to her boyfriend and gave me her Luna to get to her boyfriend's place. Moreover, she was very kind to me. That day too when I requested her to give me her Luna, she agreed willingly. I told her that I was going to Kongba, and she explained to me how to get there and what routes to take.

The first landmark I reached was a bridge, after crossing the bridge I asked the owner of a shop nearby for directions to Tom Sharma's house. The shopkeeper told me where it was, he knew Tom very well. Following his directions, I came to a small hotel. I went inside and said to the young woman in charge, 'May I ask something?' The woman was absorbed in her work and did not look at me, I saw only her back. Without turning round, she said, 'Yes, ask?'

I asked, 'Where is Tom Sharma's house?'

She turned to face me then, and exclaimed, 'It is you?' I thought that I had heard her voice somewhere before. It turned out that she was Eche Surbala, she used to stay at Ema Yaima's house for a while. Both of us recognised each other instantly and both of us were surprised by the unexpected nature of our meeting.

Eche Surbala said, 'Tomba is my relative.' I told her that it was the first time that I would be meeting him. She asked about her relatives in Khurai and I told her everyone was doing fine, and that it was Eche Ebeyaima who had given me Tom's address. Eche Surbala took me to Tom's room. Tom was sitting on his bed and working on some clothes with a pair of scissors. He was wearing a dress in a style that was very popular among the young girls of the time. He was one of the rare people who wore feminine clothing even at home.

Eche Surbala said, 'Tom, here is a friend who has come to visit you.'

Tom looked up from his work and asked, 'Who?'

Eche Surbala replied, 'This one. You must not have seen him, ever. He is Eche Yaima's neighbour.' Tom politely enquired why I had come to see him. I told him that I was just paying him a friendly visit, and I was curious to know him.

Before meeting him, I thought his fame would be accompanied by a superior attitude, but his conduct proved me wrong. He greeted me warmly. His voice was very soft, he was polite and unassuming. After we had talked for a while he said that he had heard my name before, which I thought was very fortunate and would work in my favour. He requested Eche Surbala to offer me tea and *bora*.

It was the first time I had been welcomed with such warmth and respct. Tom was completely different from other homos. He did not bitch or gossip about anybody. Without a hint of pride or envy, he complimented me on my skin, figure and hairstyle.

I said, 'Will you teach me how to apply make-up?'

He happily agreed but said that he did not take anyone as a student. He said that he would intimate me whenever he got a contract for make-up so that I could observe and learn. His kindness and sincere enthusiasm encouraged me even before I started the real work. He showed me the dresses he had designed for various contestants in beauty contests in the past. I was astounded by his talent and creativity—it was difficult to imagine how he arrived at those designs, and where he stitched the dresses! Tom even asked me to try on the dresses one by one. He also gave me tips on how to style my hair and apply make-up that could complement the shape of my face.

All the outfits were stylish and elegant but there was one that appealed to me in particular. It was a multicoloured top of orange and red, with beautiful butterfly sleeves, and a large floral print on the back. The top was paired with bell-bottom pants. While I was trying on this outfit, Eche Surbala came in with tea and *bora*. Both Tom and Eche Surbala agreed that I looked very good in the outfit. Hearing them praise me made me want to own the dress.

I was still wearing it when I sat down to have the tea and snacks. Tom invited me to eat the morning meal at his house, but I told him that we could eat together some other day, and moreover, I had already eaten the snacks. I could not ask Tom to give me the top and pants. But as I started changing into my own clothes, Tom asked me to keep the outfit. 'Santa, the dress suits you a lot. You better keep it for yourself.' Eche Surbala also said, 'Take it while Tom is giving it to you.'

I carefully folded the top and pants and wrapped them in a piece of paper. Both Eche Surbala and Tom accompanied me to the gate. I was very happy that day, joy filled me as I rode back on Eche Naobi's Luna. I could not wait to wear that outfit, for a moment I even thought that I would stop somewhere along the way and change into it. I could not stop smiling all through the ride back home.

Tom knew many beautiful girls from GP Women's College, he was also well-acquainted with many beauty pageant contestants. In fact he was their make-up artist, dress designer, and catwalk instructor. I closely observed Tom teaching the catwalk to these beautiful young women, and when I came home from these rehearsals, I would practice the walk. It seemed to me that I was a good learner, my friends in the neighbourhood told me that I could do the catwalk really well.

It could be said that I was entering a new phase, a new beginning in my life. But even in this new phase, there were things that tried to interfere with the direction I wanted my life to take. Oja Santi, a neighbour of ours, told Ema that Shija Clinic had a vacant post. She said that the owner of the clinic was her friend and she could help me to get a job at the clinic. Santi, who was a teacher, urged Ema that I should get a job in order to make use of my training as a laboratory technician. It was Ema's turn to urge me. I reluctantly went to Shija Clinic to give an interview. It turned out the interview was for the post of a receptionist not for a laboratory technician. A lady doctor conducted the interview, in English. She asked me if I could come to the clinic even during bandhs and strikes. I said that I could come on a bicycle and if I had an identity card from the clinic, it would be easier for me to travel during such times. Next, she said that I should cut my hair short and wear man's clothing as a requirement for the job profile. I replied, 'Ma'am, I respect you and your clinic but I cannot comply with your terms and conditions for the job.' She concluded the interview.

I was sure that was the end of it, but after a few days, Oja Santi came to my house to tell Ema that I was selected and I should join immediately. I did not join the clinic, and every time I met Oja Santi she chastised me for having missed such an opportunity. At home Ema never stopped scolding me for the same reason.

One day the domestic drama started early in the morning, even before I got out of bed. Baba started his lecture—I was a black sheep, he had wasted his money on my education. Ema too joined in scolding me as she swept the floor. As always, Baba's hurtful remarks infuriated me. I got up from the bed, grabbed a knife and ran towards him. Baba also ran towards me with a thick rod in his hand. People around us tried to separate us. In a short while, many people from the neighbourhood assembled at our *shumang*. Some people snatched the knife from my hand. I went inside the house and took out all my certificates and threw them in the *shumang*. I shouted, 'Look at these sheets of paper. You constantly insult me for these! Why did you pay for my education? I do not want these certificates now.'

I went to the kitchen to get the kerosene bottle, emptied the oil on the scattered sheets and set fire to them. Some people tried to collect the certificates and documents before the damage was done. But they stepped away once the fire caught all the sheets of paper scattered in every direction. Eche Mubi tried to douse the fire with a piece of cloth.

From that day onwards I started challenging Baba. That day I visited Tom. I did not tell him about the fight that morning. He was cleaning a pair of boots. A leather jacket was hanging in the sun. I asked him if he was going somewhere. He said that he was going to a beauty pageant, then he asked me to assist him in styling the contestant's hair. His offer made me very happy. I replied, 'Of course, should we go together from here?'

Tom replied, 'No. I will go from here now. You can go home and get ready. I will give you an entry card.'

I did not know what my task would be at the pageant, although Tom had said that it was styling the hair of a contestant. I sometimes styled Tom's hair but to style hair for pageant contestants was altogether a new task for me. I could not afford to make a mistake at such a huge event. Tom's offer and the entry card rescued me from the day's abyss. Immediately after reaching home, I took a bath. I borrowed a black leather jacket from one of our neighbours, Ta Ramananda. Then I boarded a bus that took me to the bazar, from there I took an auto to BOAT, the venue of the pageant. It was one of those large autos that carried five or six passengers.

Inside the auto, I felt like chatting with the passengers, but they did not talk. I had to initiate the conversation myself, and I started talking about the Miss Fabico pageant, where I was headed. When people asked who I was, I told them I was a student of Tom Sharma. I felt proud to be associated with Tom. Everyone knew him as a famous make-up artist of the time and they encouraged me to continue my pursuit. Even though I was wearing noticeable make-up, the co-passengers did not show any sign of disgust towards me. Maybe my association with Tom Sharma did the magic trick.

I reached the BOAT. There was a huge crowd at the gate of people eager to get in. Many people could not get tickets. The gatekeeper said that only those who had tickets and entry cards would be allowed inside the theatre. I proudly showed my entry card and told them, 'I am Tom Sharma's assistant.' I entered the theatre without any problem amid the din and crowd, and felt very superior to those losers struggling to get in. I looked for Tom in the Green Room. Tom was applying make-up on a contestant. I greeted him, 'Tom, I am here.'

Tom looked up and said, 'It is good that you have come, I thought maybe you would not.' When he had finished doing her make-up, Tom asked me to take care of the contestant's hair. I styled her hair in the manner of the contestants in the Miss World and Miss Universe pageants. The magazines I read kept me up to date on all the latest trends in beauty and fashion. The contestant's name was Melody Mutum. I was her proud hairstylist from the first to the last round. Beyond the purview of my job as a hairstylist, I coached her on how to answer the questions. She was also reading something from a paper in her hand. In the final round, she wore a short *potloi*, designed by Tom. Tom said that Melody would come in the top ten. Indeed, Melody was crowned the second runner-up.

Tom and I met Melody's mother outside the theatre. She spoke to us with great respect and invited us to visit her house and eat dinner with them someday. Tom gave

me some money that day, as a reward for my hard work.
I also met Bob and a few of his friends at the venue, they
were wearing bright, gaudy make-up. They were returning
from partying at Mahabali Khun, where local rice brew
was manufactured and sold. Mahabali Khun was a place
in Imphal that was mainly populated by tribal people, and
Meiteis went there to drink the local rice brew.

Bob and his friends were among the unfortunate ones
who had not been able to get entry tickets. I told Bob
about my achievement that night. Bob appeared genuinely
happy for me, 'That's you. I always knew that one day
you would do something like it.' Then he told his friends,
'Santa styled Melody Mutum's hair, you know Melody
Mutum is the second runner-up.' Bob and his party were
headed to the bazar, but I opted out of it. I was tired, I
was also too happy to go anywhere. I wanted to go home
immediately, I was eager to break the news of my success
to my family. While I was standing by the parking lot, I
saw a few boys from my locality who were preparing to
leave on their motorbikes. I called out to them and asked
if they were going home. One of them asked, 'Ta Santa,
you also came to watch the contest?'

I replied, 'No, we had a contestant.' They were impressed
by the fact that Melody Mutum was second runner-up and
I had styled her hair.They offered to drop me, but I told
them that I would be going with Melody's family. The
reality was that Melody and her family had already left the
venue, I just made up the story to show off my association
with one of the night's winners. But after doing this drama
for a bit, I accepted their offer.

At home, Ema asked why I had returned so late. I
told Ema where I was coming from. Ema said, 'We heard
that one person died after falling off the gallery at the

BOAT.' It was Ebok Ebemhal, an elderly woman in the neighbourhood, who had told them this news. Not bothered by Ema's concern I told her about my role in the beauty pageant. But Ema did not show any interest or excitement. She went to bed to sleep. That night I had a meal of cold rice that had become dry and hard in the winter cold, blanched mustard leaves and a *yongchak sinju* (smelly beans curry). But I did not feel cold at all, I ate the meal as though fresh hot food had been served to me. In fact, the meal tasted really good.

The next day I went to every house in the locality, with the morning's newspaper in my hand. I showed them Melody Mutum's picture in the paper, and gave them a detailed account of my role in her achievement, and my association with Tom. Everybody praised me. After this beauty pageant, people in my locality talked as though I was some kind of expert in make-up.

I began to read fashion articles in newspapers and magazines. I encouraged good-looking girls to participate in various beauty pageants held in Manipur. I found it easy to make their acquaintance. I would talk to them and convince them that they were beautiful and should take part in a beauty contest. I even asked my relatives if they had any good-looking friends. If I got to know of any beautiful girl, I told Tom about her, and if I had photos I showed them to Tom. In this manner, I entered into a positive phase of my life.

My sister, Eche Mubi, had her heart set on going to Madurai to study home science. This hope was planted in her by one of Oja Ibomcha's friends. Baba finally gave in to her pleading, but Ema was not willing to let her to go Madurai in the company of strangers. I was given the responsibility of taking Eche Mubi to Madurai for admission. Her friend Melu was also going, and Melu's younger brother, Boinao, was to be her escort. Once the decision was made, we started planning our journey. The train tickets were booked from MSRTC. It was a summer morning when we all left Imphal for Guwahati by a Blue Hill bus. We reached Guwahati the next morning and stayed one night in a hotel at Guwahati. On the third day we boarded the train to Chennai. The journey to Chennai took a couple of days.

We reached Chennai railway station around mid-noon. It was a hot day, and we were exhausted from the long journey and the harsh weather. We showed the college address to an auto driver, but he said that the college was very far from the station, and we would have to get there by bus. He was, however, willing to take us to the bus station. We didn't know that Madurai would be that far from Chennai. Indeed, it was a nine-hour journey by bus from Chennai. We bought tickets and got on the bus. I showed the conductor the piece of paper on which the college address was noted down. He looked at it and smiled, which indicated that he knew where it was. We took our seats and waited for the bus to start. A short while into the journey, I began to feel nauseated by the noise of the passengers and the stink of their sweat.

We reached our destination by evening. There was a small market but not many hotels. After a considerable search, we finally found a small, dilapidated hotel. There did not seem to be any better option than this. The next day we went to the college and completed the admission formalities. Next, we went to the hostel authorities to talk about getting hostel accommodation. The hostel in-charge told us that the admission process would only start after the vacations, and we should wait for a few days before applying. This was the normal process everywhere, but we had come a long way from Manipur and other than the hostel, my sister did not have any place to stay. The money my sister and I had was not enough to stay on in the hotel or rent accommodation elsewhere for any length of time. Our plan was to complete the admission process as soon as possible and return home immediately. We explained the problem to the hostel authorities. They said that they could arrange private accommodation for us until the hostel opened. We asked if the accommodation would be a rented place or another hostel. They said that they would arrange accommodation for us at the house of a Manipuri woman. They explained to us that the woman was married to a Madurai man who was one of the founding members of the college. We readily agreed, we were relieved that the woman was a Manipuri. One of the college gatekeepers took us to the house of the woman.

The woman, Annie, was born and brought up in Churachandpur. She must have been in her late forties or early fifties. She had a daughter my age, called Sonia. Sonia could not speak Manipuri. Eche Annie also had a son who was studying for his MBBS in Nepal. She said that she met her husband when she had come to Madurai to study theology. Her husband had been living in Nepal after the birth of Sonia, and had not visited Madurai even once since that time. Sonia was very disrespectful to her mother, but Eche Annie couldn't say anything to her daughter. One night, while Sonia was asleep, Eche Annie narrated the sad story of her life. She said that she had had to raise her children all by herself, her husband did not take part in bringing up his son and daughter. She told Eche Mubi and her friend, 'Don't get married to Mayang men. They have no sympathy for people. My husband has never returned, he never sent money for me and Sonia, his own daughter. When my son finally grew up, he was taken to Nepal to study for his MBBS. I have not heard anything from my son since that time.'

We had been staying at Eche Annie's house for ten days. We needed to move out soon or pay Eche Annie more money if we had to extend our stay. The extra money Eche Mubi and I had asked for from home had not yet arrived. Asking Eche Annie for a loan was out of the question, it would mean that we were insensitive to her situation. She was already under immense pressure trying to run a family all by herself. Sonia's ill-temper could also cause trouble for us and her mother. Having to cook and feed four of us must have already become a burden for her. I thought that if any Meitei was living nearby, I could try borrowing some money. Building my hopes on this lone possibility, I asked Eche Annie if she knew of any Meiteis in the locality.

Annie said, 'I know an engineering student called Chaoba. He lives very far from here. But he visits here once in a while.'

I took his address. She asked why I wanted to meet him.

I replied, 'Boinao and I have to return soon. We are running out of money. Eche Mubi's college admission is done, there is no use staying here any longer.'

Annie said, 'How are you going to ask for money from strangers?'

I replied, 'If he is a Meitei, there is no harm in asking. Besides, I will return the money soon.'

That night I told my companions about my conversation with Eche Annie. Boinao was not keen on accompanying me, in fact he did not encourage me to go there. I could not blame him, it was not a pleasant task to ask for money from strangers in a strange land! Eche Mubi also advised me not to go, she said, 'Our money order will reach us in two days.' I told her that I could go alone and she should not worry about it.

The next day, I borrowed Sonia's Ladybird bicycle, since I did not have money for the bus fare. After almost every 100 meters, I stopped to ask people on the roadside the location of the college. Most of them looked at me curiously but I ignored their stares. After riding for several hours I finally reached the place. There was a big signboard at the gate of the college. I rode inside the gate. One man told me where the administration section of the college was located. I went to the administration section and enquired after Chaoba. Everyone knew who I meant, it appeared that Chaoba was the only person who had a distinctly Manipuri look in the entire college. I told the man that I was from Manipur and I wanted to meet Chaoba.

Chaoba arrived quite soon, he must have been surprised by the sudden appearance of a Meitei. He was around my age, very fair and healthy-looking. He asked me politely who I was. I replied, 'My name is Santa, I am from Khurai. I came here for my sister's admission. I was just curious to know if there were any Manipuris around this place.'

He said, 'I am also from Khurai, Liarikyengbam Leikai.' This was a neighbourhood just across the Imphal river. I told him that I had a few friends from his neighbourhood. He had also studied at Don Bosco, in fact, he said that he knew me from school and I was his junior. After exchanging small talk and pleasantries with him, I explained the reason for my visit. Then, I requested him to lend me three thousand rupees. I told him that I would return the money soon, my sister Mubi and I were expecting a money order from home any day. Eche Mubi would return him the money as soon as she got it. I gave him Eche Annie's address and college details so that he could collect the money from her after I left Madurai. I also told him he could ask Eche Annie about us. After hearing all this, he agreed to lend me the money. My trip ultimately paid off.

It was evening by the time I reached Eche Annie's house. Eche Mubi asked, 'Where did you go?'

I replied, 'To look for Meiteis around this place.'

She asked, 'What for?'

I replied, 'About the thing I told you yesterday.'

Eche Mubi had been worried about my absence since the morning. She had been anxiously waiting for my return. Now she asked, 'Do you think you will get help in this strange land?' When I went to our room, I found Eche Melu and Boinao in a very worried state too. They had started thinking of how they could search for me. After a short while, Eche Annie came to our room, she was also very relieved to see me. That night, at dinner, I told everyone about how I met Chaoba and borrowed money from him.

The following day, we told Eche Annie that Boinao and I would be leaving. Everyone suggested that I should wait for a train reservation that could be arranged in two days' time. I assured them that I could manage without a reservation. The same night Boinao and I packed for the return journey to Manipur. Boinao agreed to travel with me by general compartment. We left for the railway station in the morning before breakfast.

Immediately after I reached home, my parents and I went to Oja Randhir's house to call Eche Annie's number, and inform Eche Mubi that I had reached home. She wanted to talk with Baba. She told him how I had managed to get money from a stranger and reach home. I had performed a remarkable feat that everyone could be proud of! Baba said in a noticeable tone of pride, 'Ah, Boi managed to borrow money!' At home he told everyone what Eche Mubi had told him. This story of my intelligent and brave handling of the situation at Madurai reached our neighbours through Ema. From whatever the elders in my neighbourhood told me, it appeared that Ema had really sung my praises. I became almost popular after my little victory in Madurai. Soon, exaggerated versions of the story began to do the rounds.

Indeed, my family recognised my efforts in Madurai, but they did not approve of my desire to wear make-up and women's clothing. The two sentiments presented two different sides of the picture. If I had to elicit words of praise from their mouth, I had to perform certain tasks that they themselves could not perform. I had to do the unthinkable. But I could not make this my longterm goal. I had my own dreams and aspirations that outweighed their fleeting and conditional praises. Contrary to my desire, they treated me and looked upon me as a man. This was the bone of contention between my family and me.

There is nothing certain about how people and society view us. What people say and think about us can elevate us one moment and drag us down the next.

I had a Nupa Maanba (trans man) aunt called Tondang. I called her Eney Tang. Eney Tang had been staying at her friend's house in Chaithabi Leirak for more than twenty years. I was a small kid when she went there to stay with her friend, Sanatombi. Sanatombi and Eney Tang were very hard-working. They used the piece of land my grandfather had given Eney Tang to plant paddy. They stored the harvest from the field at Sanatombi's house. Both of them ran a small shop too. They saved enough money to arrange a government job for Sanatombi, as a Hindi teacher.

One day Sanatombi and Eney Tang came to meet me. They wanted to discuss the prospect of Eney Tang going to Delhi to get a degree in a computer course. Ton Tonbi, a relative of my sister from her husband's side, was working in Delhi as a computer engineer. I thought it would be useful to consult Ton Tonbi about Eney Tang's prospects in Delhi. Eney Tang and Ton Tonbi talked on the phone. The latter said she would help in securing admission for Eney Tang.

I had got ten thousand rupees from a *marup*. This was a traditional way of saving money through forming a collective and mobilising members to contribute money and hold a lottery or divide the amount collected among the members. I used this money to accompany Eney Tang to Delhi. When we reached Delhi, we hired an auto rickshaw from the railway station to get to Ton Tonbi's house in Okhla. Her flat was not easy to locate, so we had to pay the auto driver extra money to take us to the exact address. Ton Tonbi welcomed us. She cooked for us but did not have time to eat with us. She packed her meal in a tiffin box and left for work. Eney Tang and I stayed at her place to rest and recover our energy after the long journey. The next day was Sunday and the three of us went sightseeing to the Qutab Minar. On the way, Ton Tonbi pointed out some institutes that offered computer courses.

The next morning Eney Tang and I visited a few of these institutes to enquire about the admission and the courses. At one institute, people at the reception desk stared at us while we were signing the register for the visitors—Eney Tang looked like a man in every way, she wore men's clothes and had short hair, and I looked like a woman. At one institute some people were really surprised when Eney Tang filled the female column. They asked if she was a woman. I boldly said yes, and they did not inquire further. On our way back to Ton Tonbi's place, we laughed and made fun of these people and the expressions on their faces.

On the way, I saw a beauty parlour with a sign in front that said it offered beautician's courses. We stopped and went inside to enquire about the courses. The course I wanted to study was too expensive for my resources. It would be very difficult for me to pay the entire fee. The cost of the basic course was five thousand rupees. This was the only one that I could afford with the ten thousand rupees I had with me.

The following Thursday, both Eney Tang and I got admission in our respective courses. A few days later, we rented a place to stay. I put aside enough money for my return journey and used the rest of it to buy food and groceries. My course was for a month. At the end of the month, I asked the owner of the parlour to issue a certificate that I had completed the course, but I was told that the certificate must be issued by the head of the institute, who was not there at that time. I left the task of collecting the certificate to Eney Tang whenever it was available and returned home. Eney Tang's course was for a year and hence she would stay on in Delhi after I left.

When I reached home, I heard that Sanatombi, Eney Tang's friend, had eloped with a man. I convinced Ebok not to tell Eney Tang about this. Undoubtedly, our relatives were very upset with Sanatombi's conduct, she had exploited Eney Tang's resources, trust and money. It was obvious that she had manipulated Eney Tang for her own ends. Ebok decided that she would never let Eney Tang meet Sanatombi again. However, Eney Tang did get to know about Sanatombi's elopement, though we did not know how the news reached her. Eney Tang came back to Manipur just before Sanatombi's wedding. She did not say a single word about Sanatombi or her own pain to anybody. She did not go to Sanatombi's wedding, she stayed at home from that time onwards.

And so time moved on with the sad stories of others and my own acts of defiance.

It was the year 1998. By now, my bold attitude and way of dressing was grabbing attention everywhere.

But I wanted to be known as someone who was sophisticated, I wanted to study further and be erudite and learned. I asked Sanamacha, a young homo from my neighbourhood, about getting admission to DM College of Arts where he was studying. I was told that I needed a duplicate mark sheet and certificate for the Class XII examinations. Without these documents, an admission form could not be issued. I met the principal of my alma mater, MBC School, and the council staff, and asked them to issue the duplicate certificates. It took a long time to get the required documents. Eventually, my hard work was rewarded—I was eligible for admission. With the help of Oja Raghumani,who worked in the sports department of DM College, an admission form was purchased. I sat for the entrance exam for the English Honours course and cleared it easily.

My style during those years was very radical—black nail

polish, two piercings on each side of the nose, five piercings on each ear, and transparent tops. I also started wearing a bra. This radical change in fashion had already started around the time I returned from Delhi. I had bought a bra in Delhi and started wearing it and now I did not feel comfortable without it. I wore a bra whenever I went out, it became a quintessential, soulful piece of clothing for me.

My style of dressing did make me the target of insults from the male students and also the teachers, but in DM College, I also made many new friends. One of my closest friends was Bonnie Gurumayum, who was previously crowned Miss Northeast, India. Bonnie's style was different. The most unique aspect of her look was curly ginger hair and beaded hair strands. One day a female relative of hers, called Kalpana, visited her in college. Kalpana was also very fashionable. She wore a pair of sunglasses that I liked a lot. She said that she would get a pair for me next time she visited Bonnie. But I never met her again.

My number of friends increased day by day. Whenever we were free, we sat together in the common room or beneath the big mango tree in the middle of the college ground. Linda, Elizabeth, and Josy were some of my close friends. In fact, almost everyone in the college knew me, even though I was not particularly friendly with all of them. I knew that many of them made fun of me and talked about me behind my back.

The boys especially teased me a lot. Some boys asked me to approach my female friends on their behalf. I interpreted this as a form of disrespect towards me. Every time they approached me to seek this favour, I replied, 'Why don't you date me? I will help you in passing exams very easily.' Some of them would reply, 'Enough, you homo *thigunlao*!' to which I responded by spitting at them.

One day I went to college wearing a loose top embroidered with *wangkhei,* traditional embroidery. There was a concrete path that cut through the college building, with blocks of classrooms on either side. As I walked down this path, all the boys in the surrounding blocks clapped at me and shouted in unison, 'Homo, homo.' I did not hear any women's voices in the din. As their voices grew louder, my footsteps slowed down. I was determined that if anybody as much as dared to come near me, I would confront them and bring them to the principal's notice. I reached the classroom, but instead of entering, I walked further in defiance of their mockery. When the boys saw that their efforts to shame me had failed, they grew tired of jeering and stopped clapping and hooting.

In B.A. Second Year, I wrote an article for the college magazine. The article was called 'Life is Like Living in Hell'. It was based on the unhappy incidents of my life. Sanamacha also read the article on my request. I showed the article to Oja Ebempishak, the head of the Department of English. She read the article and praised me. The article was approved by Oja Ebempishak and published in the college magazine.

At a college literary meet, my friends submitted my name for a dance performance. When he was announcing my performance, the anchor introduced me with very insulting words, 'Please welcome, the one and only homo of the college'. The words deeply hurt my feelings. However, I did not permit myself to be discouraged by the announcer and his ugly words. I told myself that I was in no way inferior to the announcer. Once on the stage, I took the microphone and started talking with tears in my eyes, 'Yes, I am a homo. But my real name, given by my parents, is Santa. I am a human like you all, I have the same feelings as you,

I get hurt, I feel love, I can cry, and nobody can beat me in any field.' The teachers sitting in the front row looked at me in surprise. Then I turned to the sound operator to play the song for my dance. When I was dancing, a few boys came forward and threw money at me. I collected the notes and pushed them under my top, inside my bra. I wanted to respond to their attempt to humiliate me in an equally insulting way.

When the college elections came around, my friends advised me to contest for the post of secretary of the girls' common room. I was never desirous of contesting the college election, or any election. But my friends told me that if all the women students in the college voted for me, I would definitely win. They even said that there were chances of me winning uncontested. All this talk and excitement about the college election reminded me of a story Baba told us when we were young, about an ugly incident relating to elections. The story led me to permanently hate elections. Baba said that elections were a form of addiction. Ministers and politicians did not care for their families and children. How would people who did not even love and care for their own family serve the multitude! Politicians were a most corrupt and selfish lot.

Whenever the boys who wanted to date my friends approached us, we made fun of them. There was one incident I will never forget from those days. This was when one of the girls, Elizabeth, gave a fitting response to the boys that tried to bully me. My friends, including Elizabeth, and I had gone to the college canteen. A group of boys said in hushed tones, addressing my friends, 'You girls are so pretty. Don't you feel embarrassed hanging out with a homo *thigunlao*?' All four of us heard what they said. Elizabeth flounced towards the boys and confronted them, 'Who are you calling homo? What do you mean by *thigunlao*? You must have seen and done things. That is how you came to know about it. You bastards!'

My friends and I discussed many issues about men, mostly men's sexist and risqué nature. Sometimes we decided that we would not take men seriously. I said, 'Losing a bottle of nail polish is sadder than breaking up with a man.' My friends reiterated this dialogue very often. Whenever they praised me, I said, 'I am the moonlight that happily beams through the night. However, how silvery it is, it cannot show you the ants crawling on the floor, no one can thread a needle under such moonlight.' They adored the lyrical and poetic words in which I expressed my feelings and emotions.

One day, towards the end of my second year of college, my friend Aruna's sister visited me. She said that a parlour at Chingmeirong was looking for a person to work there. Aruna's sister and I visited the parlour to meet the owner. The parlour was built on a plot owned by one Dr Loken. The parlour was called Memtombi, after its owner. A few days after meeting with the owner, I joined the parlour. Since beauty was my dream job, I did not skip even a day at the parlour. The parlour owner was a very smart person, she treated me as a friend and never said anything that could hurt me. In fact, she liked my work. I got paid every month. More than money, it was the contentment of doing work that I loved, that drew me to that parlour.

In 1999, news spread that there would be a beauty pageant titled All Manipur Nupi Sabi Beauty Contest. Local newspapers advertised the event for several days. The beauty pageant was going to be the first one of its kind for Nupi Sabis. The form for the contest was available at the office of the Democratic Youth Federation of India, located at Governor's Road. Without delay, Poison and I went to buy the form from the office. At the office we were told that a document certifying that you were eligible for participation in Shumang Leela was required, as proof of eligibility for buying the form. The beauty contest was mainly organized for Shumang Leela performers, but non-performers were also allowed to participate after getting a certificate from the Leela office. Poison and I immediately went to one of the Leela offices on Governor's Road to enquire about the certificates. The person at the Leela office told us that one certificate would cost Rs 200. I did not have two hundred rupees at that time, but my desperation to participate in the contest emboldened me to bargain hard. After bargaining for a long time, the price for one certificate was fixed at Rs 100. We bought the forms and returned home in a happy mood. The next day, we went to the Youth Federation office to submit the form. It was an auspicious beginning for which there should be no delay! In addition to Rs 100 for the certificate, I spent Rs 500 for the final submission form.

The whole of Manipur came to know about the event. One day when I was going to Lamlong, I was greeted by Echemsi, a neighbour. She said she wanted to talk with me, which made me curious. She asked, 'Are you participating in the Miss Nupi Sabi Contest?' Her interest in the beauty pageant was obvious. I replied happily, 'Eche, I am participating, I have submitted the form.'

She asked, 'Who is going to design your dress?' I replied that Tom would be designing my dress. Echemsi said, 'People say that he is very expensive. But his designs are very beautiful and popular. My friend also hired him for make-up and dress at her wedding.'

I replied, 'I know Tom well. I used to be an assistant to him before.'

Echemsi was impressed, 'That is very good. You know, Lairikyengbam Ebemma just completed a fashion designing course from Delhi. She is at home now. She will also be willing to design your dress.'

'Ebemma?' I asked in surprise. I knew Ebemma quite well, she was Echemsi's cousin sister. We had been at the same coaching institute at one time. I used to visit her home during those days, and whenever I visited, I drank black tea and ate puffed rice dressed with mustard oil, diced onion, chilli and salt. I liked the snack a lot. I thought that perhaps it may be better to get my dress designed by Ebemma.

The next day I went to Ebemma's house to talk about the dress. On seeing me, she called all our old friends in the neighbourhood. They said, 'Santa, long time. We heard that you have become very popular in Lamlong. Your fashion is very edgy.' We reminisced about the days at the coaching institute. Somebody said, 'Those were the good days of our lives.' After talking for a while, I told them that I would be participating in the forthcoming beauty pageant for Nupi Sabis. I added that I had come to ask Ebemma to design my dress for the event. They were very excited about my participation. They said they also wanted to buy tickets to the contest so they could come and watch me. They enquired about the other contestants, and if my homo friends would be participating. I replied, 'I do not know about others. But I am going to give my best, and enjoy myself a lot.' Ebemma agreed to design dresses for every round of the contest.

For the make-up, I talked with Poison. I firmly believed

that his make-up could make me look very beautiful, he would make me as beautiful as himself. For the hair, I borrowed a wig from a Leela Nupi Sabi. I went to Poison's house to try on the wig. Bob, Ronu and Khoidong told me that I looked like the heroine of the film *Double Revenge*.

Wherever I went, I heard people saying that the contest would be won by the Leela artist Sanaton. At home also Ema said, 'Do not participate in the contest, you look like a man. You look very ugly, it is embarrassing for me.'

The pageant was to be held on 20th November. Early in the morning, I collected my gown which was yellow in colour. A butterfly cut out of black cloth was secured on the back of the gown. I had already talked with Ta Amuba to take me to the venue in his van. Ta Amuba's family was very kind to me and his family took a keen interest in my participation in the contest. Around 10.30 a.m, Ta Amuba took me to Gandhi Memorial Hall, the venue of the contest, in his vehicle. He dropped me at the gate of the hall and returned home.

Inside the hall, everyone said that the event was going to be telecast on ISTV, the first local TV channel in Manipur. In the Green Room, I met Poison who was in the process of applying his own make-up. I sat beside him, waiting for him to finish. Poison was already wearing a beautiful dress. He was fully prepared. But I had not done anything. The contest was about to start, but I still had to get my hair and make-up done. For some reason not known to me, Poison was acting very indifferent to me, he did not honour his words to me, that he would help me with my make-up. I could never have imagined such a thing. I was relying on Poison to do my make-up so I had not asked anyone else.

A slow-burning anger built up in my head. I wanted to compete with him on the stage, I wanted to win and see him lose. But something had to be done about my hopeless condition. When I looked around, I saw Tom getting Sanaton ready in a corner. I went and sat beside him and started applying my make-up. Beside me, Bishesh, the recent international trans queen contestant, was being prepared by his mother, he was still very young. When I checked myself in the mirror, I looked very ugly—the urgency of the situation, my inexperience in applying make-up, and the hurt and anger I felt at Poison's betrayal completely ruined my mood. Tom helped me after finishing with Sanaton, but he was not able to fully concentrate on me.

Maya Chowdhury was the anchor of the event. She wore a green gown. The hall was packed with an enthusiastic audience, it was as though there was no one left on the streets of Imphal. Around one hundred contestants participated in the event. All the contestants walked on stage and introduced themselves. After the three introductory rounds, twenty contestants were selected. As the announcer kept calling one name after another in the Top 20, my legs were trembling in anticipation of my own name—I imagined myself standing on the stage with a microphone in my hand and answering every question lucidly. I was convinced that once I passed the question and answer round, I would be one among the three to be finally selected. Unfortunately, my name did not feature in the Top 20. Inside the Green Room, all the contestants who were not included accused the panel of corruption. Despite their anger, the contest continued. In the final round, Sanaton was declared the winner, Dinesh, the First Runner-up and Poison, the Second Runner-up. In the dance competition, Jenny was the winner.

When everything was over, my misery knew no bounds. My disappointment turned into rage against Poison's false assurance that he would do make-up for me, when in reality he had no intention of helping me. I was galled by the logic that if he had declined my request, I would have asked Tom in advance. Anger and embarrassment made me leave the place immediately after the winners were announced. I had a raging desire for another beauty contest to happen again, in the next contest I would definitely win a spot for myself.

At home, I got another dose of frustration from an unsupportive Ema. She had watched the live telecast of the contest on TV; in fact, everyone in my neighbourhood had watched the telecast. Initially, they were very excited when my name was announced. The elders said to my mother, 'Sanahanbi, watch this, you son is on stage now', which was accompanied by their laughter. Ema said that she was too embarrassed to even look at the TV screen. The embarrassment and the pain of watching her ugly son on stage made her extremely angry. She reiterated that she warned me not to participate in such contests, because I was so ugly.

The following day, I went to Ta Amuba's house. He said mockingly, 'We eagerly waited for you to walk on the stage. But your mouth pouted more and more with each round. Finally, you looked like an ape.' Ta Amuba laughed loudly at his own joke, joined by Eche Thoibi and his wife. I replied, 'It was not my fault. It was your TV set. You should consider changing your set.' Ta Amuba said, 'Yes, yes, you can keep on blaming my TV set, you really did look like an ape', and he laughed again.

Everyone said I looked ugly, but their unanimous comments did not discourage me. Rather, I resolutely decided to prepare for next year's event. I tamed my resentment towards Poison. From that time on, whenever I met him, I told him one thing, 'You were already last year's runner's up, so you cannot participate again. Next year you have to apply my make-up.' Poison said that he would surely fulfil his promise next time. It seemed to me that on hindsight he also regretted his behaviour a little bit.

Around the time of the beauty contest, Tamo Jugimohon from Thoidingjam was preparing to contest in the election. Kaka Tombi was a very active worker for Tamo Jugimohon. On the Kongpal side, Bihari was a strong contender, he also had very dedicated workers. Kaka Tombi said that I must gather all the homos in the constituency to vote for Tamo Jugimohon. He said that if all the homos in the constituency voted for Tamo Jugimohon, he would do anything we asked in return.

In the previous election, Tamo Jugimohon had lost to Bihari. Tamo Jugimohon was not a familiar figure to the voters in Khurai, he could not have got many votes from our locality. Kaka Tombi believed that if all the homos campaigned for Tamo Jugimohon, he would get more votes. When I told Bob and Taton Ramananda about Kaka Tombi's proposal, they said that we should ask for something in return for our support. They suggested we should ask for a friendly feast. I had a different suggestion— we could have the feast anytime, but we should first ask Kaka Tombi to arrange a *Thabal Chongba* for all the Bs. Both of them were very happy with my suggestion. Kaka Tombi readily agreed. As soon as the *thabal* was confirmed, the news spread like wildfire among Bs.

The day of the *Thabal Chongba* was fixed, and the venue was to be the Thoidingjam Laimarembi ground. Initially we wanted the venue to be another ground, but a person called Ngangbam Premchand argued in favour of a local ground nearby. He believed that it would be easier to prevent unfortunate stuations at a local ground. Thoidingjam Lairembi was a small ground, nevertheless our desire for the *Thabal Chongba* was too intense to be thwarted by an issue like the size of the ground. Bs from all corners of Manipur gathered at the ground that night. Some came by auto, while some came in their own vehicles.

When they arrived, every B looked manly. Almost every house in my neighbourhood was occupied by three or four Bs preparing themselves for the *Thabal Chongba*—make-up, putting on dresses, and such. All the manly-looking Bs transformed into beautiful-looking women after all these efforts. I had never seen such a huge gathering of Bs in my entire life. Apart from Bs, a huge crowd arrived at the Thoidingjam Lairembi to watch the *Thabal Chongba*. At one point, the gate of the ground had to be locked as more and more people flocked into the ground. It was the first *Thabal Chongba* for homos in Manipur.

The *thabal* was a big success, and the news reached Candidate Bihari. The following morning his workers came looking for us. His workers told Da Romen that Bihari wanted to have a talk with us. A few of us, Bob, Ronu, Manimohon, and I met at Da Romen's shop at Porompat. Together with Da Romen, we went to meet Bihari that same night. Bihari met us at his brother's house that was located behind his own house. Bihari said, 'This term, if you all work for me and help me win the election, I will arrange a huge *Thabal Chongba* for you.' After this meeting, we campaigned for both the candidates, Tamo Jugimohon and Bihari. Bihari won the election for that term. Honoring his word to us, he arranged a *Thabal Chongba* for homos at Duwa Train at Porompat, near his own house. That was the second *Thabal Chongba* for homos in Manipur.

After this second event, we started taking the initiative for the *Thabal Chongba* on our own. Bob and I were usually the ones to initiate the arrangements. Others were not keen on managing this task. We took care of the money collection. Money was not the only thing needed for organising a *Thabal Chongba* event. We needed to talk with important people to get permission for the event. Bob and I went to different places to meet these people on his Honda Sleek. After the third *thabal*, Bob and I decided we would not arrange any more of them, we had had enough of the hard work. That year, the local club arranged the *Thabal Chongba* at Aka Train ground. On the day of the *Thabal Chongba*, the ground was cordoned off with GI sheets, galvanized iron sheets, from all directions. The *Thabal Chongba* was made an exclusive event—only homos were allowed free entry, all others had to buy a ticket to enter. The club must have earned a fair amount of money—the number of people admitted inside the fence was countless, the ground was so overcrowded, there was hardly any space for even securely planting two feet.

I was not happy with the day's event. I told the homos, 'They are using us to earn money. It embarrasses me that we are happily consenting to this.' I had also consumed a good amount of *yu* that night. I continued, 'Homos cannot speak for themselves even when they are being treated in the most denigrating manner. We cannot even think and act for our own welfare and happiness. Is there no other person, apart from Bob and I, amongst you to arrange your *Thabal Chongba*? Would you not have any *Thabal Chongba* if Bob and I died?'

I fought with many Bs and some women who had come to watch the *Thabal Chongba*. I left the ground while the event was still in progress. Anger and the effects of the *yu* made me careless about walking on the damaged concrete road in high heels. I reached Jawaharlal Nehru Hospital. All the hotels around the area sold *yu*. I entered the first one I came to. In that hotel many Bs who had come to participate in the *Thabal Chongba* were drinking *yu* and talking. They greeted me and asked, 'Santa, why are you not arranging the *thabal* this year?' to which I replied, 'Could you not arrange it instead of waiting for me?' They did not ask me any more questions. On my part, I did not stop scolding them, but they did not show any signs of anger or offence at my ranting. I said, 'Are we zoo animals? Why do we let people push us inside that iron wall? And they charged money for entry. Why are we not saying anything against this?' My words awakened them, they suddenly got angry, they even said that in the future they would not allow anybody to interfere in the affairs of homo *Thabal Chongbas*.

In due time, the *Thabal Chongba* for homos became a regular affair. Every Yaosang, it was organised at Khurai ground. Eventually, Bs started organising the *thabals* in their own localities, beyond Khurai.

This was the time when the Social Awareness Service Organization (SASO) was actively working on an HIV prevention program called Men Having Sex With Men or MSM. Awareness on HIV/AIDS was being imparted everywhere by the SASO staff. The general public came to see us as diseased persons.

On the night of 31st December, 1999, Sarat, a staff member at SASO, arranged a party for us at the Khuman Youth hostel. On that occasion, the SASO staff and Sarat talked about HIV/AIDS and the importance of using condoms among Bs. We stayed the night at the same hostel, and performed songs, dances and other items.

After this party, SASO organised HIV awareness programs for Bs at its office. HIV tests were also regularly conducted. SASO payed the expenses for Bs to come to the office for this purpose. Many reports about the high incidence of HIV among Bs were published in newspapers. Ignorant people perceived us in a very negative light. People everywhere started saying that homos were spreading HIV in Manipur. Previously, people called us homo in a derogatory manner, now they added disease to our identity, they started looking upon us as the virus that carries HIV. It was as though people did not want to be near us. Whenever I reached home late, family members would start saying things they had never said before, like, 'Reform your conduct, otherwise you will bring disease to the family.'

There were times I thought I was a carrier of the disease. Many times I doubted myself. The doubt weighed down on me, I lost my confidence. A great gap was being created between me on the one side and society and family on the other side. I got myself tested for HIV many times, the number of my reports could have filled an entire register. In due course even the mention of HIV created an upheaval in me. I hated the word and did not ever want to mention it in conversations.

HIV was the greatest of all the hurdles and disappointments I faced till that point. This pushed me in a new direction, and led me to questions that were never raised before. I became aware of the oppression around me and the need to fight it. It was important to show to the world that I was not a bad person and homos were not the spreaders of the disease. In every forum I spoke about how transgenders were singled out in every dialogue about

HIV. I questioned the annual data produced by the Manipur State AIDS Control Society, and why the prevalence rate of HIV among transgenders had never gone down but kept increasing. I questioned where the Society had got these numbers, and what work did they do? If their program was successful in sensitising the population and creating awareness and prevention, then surely these numbers would decrease?

The All Manipur Nupi Sabi Beauty Contest was held for the second time in the year 2000. But some obstacles presented themselves in my path again. It was as though there was no rice in the pot when you are famished! I had been waiting an entire year to buy the form for the contest. But just when the sale of the forms began, a violent protest erupted after the news that the Army had shot some innocent people at a bus stand at Malom, an incident which is still remembered as the Malom massacre. The Army had made some ordinary civilians stand in a line, and fired their rifles at them. News about the unfortunate incident reached every corner of Manipur. Because of the tense situation the sale of the forms for the contest had to be halted. A woman called Irom Sharmila decided to go on a fast as a protest against the Malom tragedy. The police took Sharmila first to her relatives' houses and then to the Meira Paibi Shang, but they refused to take her in. (These are small sheds which the Meira Paibis in that locality use to conduct their affairs, and as a shelter at night. There are shangs in every locality.) The police then took her to the house of Ngambam Pabitro, since they were Sharmila's relatives. Meanwhile, the Meira Paibis had begun to respond to the tragedy. One night, Meira Paibis called out people from every household by hitting the electric poles with stones, to produce a sound—this was their traditional way of calling out people whenever there was a crisis. Hearing the sound, Ema and Ebok also ran outside the house.

I was not very concerned with Sharmila or the shooting of the civilians. I wanted to kill those Army personnel who had done it, because they had created this crisis and prevented the Miss Nupi Sabi Contest from happening on time.

After the tension died down a little, the sale of the forms resumed. The event was being organised by DYFI, the same organisation that had organised it the previous year. I again approached Poison to do my make-up, I also requested a Leela Nupi Sabi, Arun, for help. Sanaton gave me the dress for the event. Compared to the previous contest, the audience was much smaller. The winner was Sonipao, the first runner-up was Bisesh and the second runner-up was me. Each of us was given an envelope, and a crown made of copper and decorated with multi-coloured stones was placed on our heads. I was curious about the prize that must be inside the envelope. But my excitement at coming third was greater than the desire to know the contents of the envelope. My fellow contestants and the audience praised me for my answers to the judges. One judge asked me, 'Were you fully confident that you would win the contest when you decided to participate?'

I replied, 'My dear judge, who would appear in an exam with a doubtful attitude and a disposition towards failure? I was fully confident that I would win a place in this contest, and that was how I arrived on the stage.' Loud clapping from all directions of the open-air theatre of BOAT greeted my response.

When I opened the envelope at home, there was only a white paper, neatly folded. I opened it and read the word 'Sorry'. I did not fret about the fact that there was no prize money inside it. My achievement was enough.

The next morning, I checked the newspapers in the hope that they would have carried pictures and stories of the beauty contest, in which I was crowned second runner-up. But no newspaper reported even a few lines about the event, it was as though it had never happened. This incensed me, and now I began to feel angry about the empty envelope that did not contain any prize money. I interpreted the entire chain of events as utter disrespect to the winners, an open betrayal of homos. The organisers had exploited us for their own gains. I decided I would confront the DYFI, they must give reasons for the empty envelope.

A few days after the pageant I went to the DYFI office to talk them. But the office had disappeared. I asked the people at the Shumang Leela offices if the office had shifted somewhere else but they said they had no information. I felt like a victim, I thought that one day I would organise a Miss Nupi Sabi contest for homos with the pomp and glamour, respect and recognition they deserved.

In those years, a fair called Winter Mela was held every year at Yaiskul Athletic Club (YAC) ground. As a part of the fair, seven Bs were invited to dance at the venue. These seven Bs were not ordinary, little-known persons, they were all winners of beauty contests and dance competitions. The dance item was cast as a charity show to be performed every day for the entire duration of the fair. Tom was the manager of the dance shows, he named the group 'Seven Sisters'.

The dance performances by the Seven Sisters attracted more people than any other item at the fair.

I heard from a few B acquaintances of mine that the members of the Seven Sisters earned a fair amount of money from these dance shows. This made me think about my own impoverished condition, and what I could do to increase my earnings. I decided to use my training and skill in beauty treatment. I went to the houses of those that needed the services I could offer—facials and shaping of eyebrows were an important part of one's beauty routine, and there were many who could afford to pay for them.

I did not have anybody to help me or collaborate with me. At that time herbal products were very popular in Manipur. In my training, I had learnt that fresh fruits were very useful for a facial, and so I used ripe papaya and oranges as key ingredients in the facials I gave. I began earning a modest amount of money, which was sufficient for my needs at that point of time. My clients advised me to set up my own parlour. The truth was, I did not have money to open a parlour. My maximum saving was six thousand rupees, an amount I had got from the *marup* or financial collective I had joined with Eney Langlen. I wanted to open a parlour but this amount was not enough.

There was an empty room on the top floor of Boy's house at Lamlong. Boy was a friend of mine, and the house belonged to his parents. The room had been unoccupied for a while. I knew that if I asked, Boy would let me use it, but the dilpaditated state it was in discouraged me. A parlour had to look glamourous and stylish if it were to attract clients. Instead, I was interested in a room on an upper floor of Da Ido's building, which was next to Boy's house. This building was in a good condition and located at a strategic place. Once again, I did not have enough money to realise my dreams, the amount of the deposit was way beyond my means.

I introduced the matter of opening a parlour to my family. Predictably, they refused to listen to me, or show an iota of interest in my idea. Baba flatly said that my idea was an impossible one. I did not pursue the matter further. No matter what they said, I was convinced that a parlour could be a regular source of income for me. My only aim was to find a practical way to achieve this, without getting affected by the negativities engulfing me.

I was calculating various possibilities in my mind when I remembered Jenny—he was my friend and we were from the same place. I could ask Jenny to contribute money to open a parlour. A beauty parlour would be a steadier occupation than dancing at fairs. Fairs happened only once a year, while a parlour was a daily profession. So, I went to the YAC ground mela, where Jenny was one of the dancers, to meet him.

Jenny was a little surprised to see me. Although we knew one another, we were not very close at that point of time. He asked, 'Santa, where are you going?'

I replied, 'I have come here, to meet you.'

Jenny replied, 'Why, what happened?'

I replied, 'Nothing much. I want to discuss a matter with you.'

Sensing Jenny's curiousity, I continued, 'I want to discuss if it would be possible for us to jointly open a parlour.'

Jenny replied, 'Who will come to a parlour for makeup? Listen now, select a song for our performance tonight, and teach me some dance steps, too.' Jenny knew from before that I was a good dancer; I had taught him how to dance to the song 'Bada Dukha Deyna' from the Hindi film *Ram Lakhan,* for which he won an award at the beauty contest.

On that day I chose 'Aap Jaisa Koi Meri Zindagi' from the Hindi movie *Qurbani* and choreographed it for him. I was a little confused by Jenny's casual response to my proposal. I returned home immediately after teaching him the dance steps.

I thought day and night about opening my own parlour, but no one was willing to help me realise my dream. Then one day Jenny visited me and started discussing how we could open a parlour. I did not know what had made him change his mind.

Jenny said, 'Nupi, will a parlour be useful? I don't have any training, you know.'

I replied, 'Why won't it be useful? I have training, I'll teach you everything.'

Jenny told me that he had already paid for a training session in make-up at a parlour in Nagampal.

I said, 'You can go there and at the same time we can have our own parlour.'

Then Jenny asked how much money we would need, and where would the parlour be located.

I replied, 'We don't have a lot of money right now. We can use the old equipment I have, and you can buy a carpet and two mirrors.'

Jenny asked, 'How much will that approximately cost?'

I replied, 'It could cost approximately 3,000 rupees. Let us buy the things tomorrow.'

Then Jenny told me, 'Nupi, my brother has invested some money for me for the post of peon in the electricity department. I am waitng to know if I have got the job.'

I replied, 'Meanwhile, you can open the parlour.'

Jenny replied, 'Yes. When the job result is declared, and if I succeed in getting it, you can continue with the parlour.'

Thus in the days between the opening of the parlour

and the last days of the fair, I took Jenny with me as my assistant on my visits to various homes where I had got bookings for haircuts and facials. We shared the money earned from these home visits.

One day we had an appointment at three houses near Popular High School at Khurai Konsam Leikai. One of our clients was a young married woman. While I was cutting her hair, her husband suddenly arrived and started abusing me, 'You homo, bastard! How can you touch a woman's body?' Then he pulled his wife's hair, beat her, and dragged her away. Shocked by this scene, Jenny and I began to pack our things and were about to leave, but the other women present consoled us, 'Do not listen to that man. He is crazy, do not get upset by his behaviour.' A few among them angrily opined that the woman should not have been informed at all about the appointment. After a few moments of tension, Jenny and I continued with our work, chatting and laughing in the company of our clients.

Jenny and I informed one another of any booking for a facial or haircut or make-up that we separately received. Soon we began to receive bookings from outside the Khurai locality. Tom was already very popular for make-up and dress design. Simultaneously, Jenny and I were also becoming popular as beauticians. We continued visiting our clients at their homes, we became totally absorbed in our work. It could be said that we did not even have enough time to rest and socialise with our friends. If we happened to visit two different places separately, we shared the money equally. We would meet at night or the next day and divide the proceeds between us.

After the Winter Mela concluded, the Seven Sisters continued to be hired to dance on different occasions at many places. Out of my close association with Jenny, who was a founding member, I also became a member of the band. Bunty, Chandrika, Jenny, Sonipao, Naobi, Naocha (from Lamlong) and I became the new line up for the band. Jenny and I were the leading members. I was the anchor, conductor, and choreographer; I was also in charge of finance and managing all the bookings.

The Seven Sisters became extremely popular at that time. On many festive occasions, we replaced the Leela troupe. The organisers would often offer us lots of *yu* at the time of paying the fees, so that they could cheat us. So, Jenny never drank a drop of *yu* before the payment.

After the Winter Mela, I built a new narrative around the name 'Seven Sisters', originally given by Tom. When I was young, Eney Hanbi told me a *phungawari*—a folktale—called Khonjom Nupi, and I based the narrative of Seven Sisters on this tale. Before each dance performance,when I went on the stage, I retold this tale to the audience. Relating homos to the tale, I said, 'Homos are very beautiful. But like the Khonjom Nupi, we cannot enter into conjugal life with men. Countless people are gathered here to witness our beauty. We are the living Khonjom Nupi of this land.' This prologue formed the introduction to our dance.

In June 2001, all the beauty parlour work and Seven Sisters' shows came to an end. The reason was the demand by the Manipuri Nagas for their own homeland. A movement was initiated against the Indian Government protesting the conceding of Manipuri land to the Nagas. There were Meira rallies in every locality every night. I participated in many such rallies in the company of Sangeeta, a married woman in my neighbourhood. One night people in our neighbourhood organised a rally. Ema and I were together in that rally. Meira Paibis from every corner gathered at Lamlong Keithel, from where we proceeded towards Porompat. I wanted to walk in front and pour out all the frustrations inside me. That night a few homos also joined the rally at Lamlong, I told them we should walk together at the head of the rally. A few young men standing on the side of the street joined the rally and walked in the same direction as ours. The Meira Paibis chastised the boys, 'Men cannot participate in the Meira rally.' The group of young men replied, 'Are homos allowed? Are they not men?' Sangeeta gave a fitting reply to their impudent remarks, 'Yes, they can participate, they are friends.' Sangeeta's words emboldened me, and I shouted at the top of my voice, 'Manipur *gi saktam kaiba yarro* (long live Manipur).' I was willing to lay down my life and face every hurdle and danger. The sound of gunfire filled the air from every direction. One could see the faces of the persons walking beside us as they were illuminated by the sparks of light from the distant gunfire.

Halfway down the Porompat road, the Manipuri commandos and the Army began firing teargas at us. We did not stop, we continued to march on. From different directions, people started hurling stones at the Army and commandos, who started beating us and firing teargas. More forces came in. Some began running away to escape the platoons of paramilitary forces that were deployed to quell the agitation. At the Lamlong diversion, more Army troops came in. Ema and I reached home with great difficulty. At home, Baba scolded us for joining the rally. We did not reply to him, to avoid further provoking him.

It was the afternoon of 18 June. I was talking with Eche Manitombi when, suddenly, a countless number of people from Khurai Konsam came swarming down the road in front of our house, it was as though a beehive had been disturbed and the bees had taken flight in every direction. This was followed by the loud sound of the clanging of the electric pole by the Meira Paibis. Ema said, 'This has reached Khurai, now it is war.' The slogan of the movement, 'Manipur *gi saktam kaiba yarro*,' could be heard from every direction. Men and women from every household in our neighbourhood came out and joined the protesting crowd. I also joined the mass of people. This time I was somewhere in the middle rows of the protestors.

At Minuthong, the rallies were dispersed by the Manipuri commandos and the Army. They were present everywhere in those troubled years. They would charge indiscriminately at the protestors, a large number of whom were women. The cries of women filled the air, and people ran for their lives to escape the attacks by the armed forces. A few friends and I escaped through the Khuman locality. Such violent attacks and lathi charges took place wherever there was a rally. After a short while, the melee on the road would disperse and the road would bear a lonely and deserted look.

The Manipuri commandos and the Indian Army beat Manipuris like animals. Army platoons were posted outside the gate of every house. Nobody was seen on the streets. News of people dying at the hands of the Army became a staple tragedy of the time. The number of deaths increased every day. Every once in a while, we could hear the sound of people crying and weeping in the street, some innocent person must have been killed. The evening edition of the newspaper often declared the number of people killed by military bullets.

One evening, news came that some people from Konsam Leikai were killed in the firing. I wanted to know the details of the atrocity. I went to Jenny's house by taking a safer route through the *shumangs* of the houses of the neighbourhood. Jenny was very surprised to see me, he asked me how I reached his house amid the hell unleashed everywhere. I explained how I had got there. He said, laughing, 'You are so fearless, it seems like you are not afraid of death at all.' On seeing me, Jenny's mother said, 'Lamlong lai, how did you reach here? You will die! Go back as soon as possible. Soldiers have surrounded this place.'

I replied, 'I am not afraid of them.' Jenny and I went inside his room and talked. The people killed in the firing were from the house behind his. That day we did not talk about dance or parlour. We only talked about the future of Manipur. We talked about the relationship among the various communities and ethnic groups in Manipur. When it was time for me leave his house, he came with me all the way to Chaithabi Leirak, a small lane that ran at the back of his house. Soldiers were being posted even in the interiors of the neighbourhoods at that time. Seeing the sodiers present in every crevice of the neighbourhood, I thought I would not be able to reach home. But if I did not reach home that day, I would surely be trapped for almost a month in Jenny's house. The curfew was not going to be relaxed very soon, I had to reach home by any means before the curfew became tighter.

The Army personnel did not check the women in the streets. So I devised a plan to get out of the situation—I took a *phanek* from Jenny's sister and wore it, I took a *khudei* too and covered my head with it. In this female ensemble I was able to escape the Army and the curfew.

The gloomy political condition in Manipur escalated. Curfews, rallies, police firing had brought our lives to a standstill. I could not visit my friends. In every household, people talked about the tragedy that would engulf Manipur in the event of losing its integrity and freedom. I was very sensitive to the talk about losing freedom, it filled me with indignation. It made me very sad to think about the situation inflicting my own land. There was a growing desire in me to know more about Manipur, I wanted to trace the origin of the suffering in Manipur.

One early morning, before dawn, Ema came to my bed quietly and whispered, 'Ebungo, be alert. The soldiers are in the street.'

I replied, 'So what? Let them be.' Baba also woke up and sat on the bed, inside the mosquito net. That day, people in our neighbourhood gathered in groups outside their houses, they talked about the political situation of Manipur that was creating Army presence even in the early hours of the morning. Every household was on alert. Everyone said that the sons in the family should not be allowed to leave the house. Ema strictly advised me not to go out for even as short a distance as the gate.

Despite the utmost circumspection, the Army had arrested one of the boys from Ta Amuba's house. The women in the locality decided to meet to protest against the arrest and discuss the possible course of action to get the boy released. Ema also hurriedly left the house to be a part of the gathering on the road. Immediately after Ema left, I also hurried toward the gate to ascertain what the matter was. I went further to Oken's, whose house was by the roadside, and talked with him. I came to know from Oken that the women gathered on the road had decided to build a Meira Paibi Shang in front of the Thoidingjam Lairembi. The purpose of the shang was for Meira Paibis to gather every night to look after the neighbourhood.

During those days, there were soldiers stationed outside our house every night, our gate had become an Army checkpost. One night, the locality was darker than before because of a power cut. After I had had my meal, I was going to Enama Tampha's shop to eat *kwa*. Suddenly the light of a torch was directed straight into my face from behind the thick, dark shady leaves of the taro plants on the roadside. Startled by the sudden flash of light, I started running. Before I could reach home, the soldiers and the Manipur commandos overtook me, pushed me with gun butts, and started beating m. They did not allow me to utter a single word. I cried out in pain. Just when they were about to push me inside their vehicle, Oken's grandmother, Ebok Ashangbi, arrived at the scene and rescued me. I should thank my luck, that could have been the end of me. When I reached home, Ema chastised me, 'Why did you have to go out? Why did you act so fearless? You are in this condition because of your rebellious attitude.' After comforting me for a while, she left for the Meira Paibi Shang.

The next day, Khumukcham Ebecha visited us and enquired about my misadventure the previous night, 'Santa, how did it happen to you?'

I replied, 'I only went out to buy *kwa*. Then they started beating me.'

Ebemcha said, 'We could hear you crying, we were inside the shop. We did not come out for fear that they might start beating Taton (her eldest brother), too.'

With the gradual relaxation of curfew, I started taking make-up appointments again. The Seven Sisters resumed their dance shows too. Curfews were relaxed, but commando and Army postings on the streets in the name of maintaining law and order also increased. Once we were returning after a dance performance at Kakching. Our vehicle was stopped at the Kakching Lamkhai checkpost by commandos. They must have been struck by the make-up and dresses we were wearing. They asked, 'Where are you coming from?'

I replied, 'We are returning after a dance programme.'

One commando exclaimed, 'What kind of dance! You know the situation is very tense these days!' He asked us to step out of the vehicle and stand in a row, and then he asked us to dance. We stood still, as though none of us had heard what was demanded of us. Another commando said, 'Start dancing,' and with this he raised his baton to beat us.

Just at that moment, Jenny cried in a loud, shaky voice, 'B Naos (junior Bs), start dancing.' Saying this, she broke into some dance steps. Seeing Jenny's antics, the rest of us covered our mouths with our palms and began to giggle. Jenny's little dance seemed to have satisfied the commandos and they let us go.

By 2002, my financial condition was a little better. Jenny and I decided to share the costs and set up a parlour. However, we still did not have sufficient money to pay the deposit for renting a space. We had a discussion, and I suggested that we could start by using the room in the front part of my house, while we saved money to rent a bigger room at Lamlong later. Jenny readily agreed.

With the money we had jointly raised till then, Jenny and I went to the market. We bought a carpet, two mirrors, a blue plastic chair, and a small wardrobe. At every shop we went to, Jenny and I did our bit of promotion for the parlour; we said, we are buying stuff for the beauty parlour we are setting up at Khurai Chandam Leirak, at Santa Khurai's residence. We piled the furniture we bought onto a rickshaw, and carried everything into the room intended for the parlour. When Jenny and I were shifting the furniture into the room, Baba asked, 'What is all this for?' I replied that we were setting up a beauty parlour. My reply made him very angry, 'You never invested your time in useful endeavours all these years. You are still wasting everything.'

On hearing Baba's words, Jenny said, 'Nupi, I am anxious now. Is this going to work?' I replied, 'Do not worry. When this turns out successful in the future, they are going to change their words and accept that they were wrong.'

With the help of a carpenter from our locality, the wardrobe and the mirrors were fixed on the wall. When everything was in place, Jenny and I sat down to think of a name for our parlour. Jenny trusted me with the task. We named the parlour Sanjen—a combination of our names. We went to Buddhi Art at Lamlong, to get a signboard bearing the name 'Sanjen Beauty Parlour'. We put up the signboard at the entrance of the Chandam Leirak. Over a period of time, we were able to procure most of the things needed in a parlour.

Baba continued to criticise me and my work. Sometimes, he would say, 'I found hair in my food. We all are going to die someday from such recklessness.' But Ema supported me.

I was beset by one thought—who was there who was willing to see what my purpose in life was, and the path I was treading? If I became a famous and well-respected person, my family would also surely become respectable. I believed that my success would also bring trust and respect to my community. Regardless of my hopes and feelings for others, it would be ignorant of me to expect help from anyone, I could not even ask for change of one hundred rupees from the people in my surrounding.

In the beginning, we did not have customers. Not many people knew about the parlour, and besides the situation in Manipur was always ripe with tension and violence. Slowly we got a few clients, and then more clients followed. Recognition was slow but it undoubtedly came. We fixed the charge for our services in this way:

Haircut

Men—Rs 20

Women—Rs 30

Eyebrow threading—Rs 10

Facial—Rs 200

There were also times when our clients requested us to visit at their homes. At such times, both Jenny and I went together. In this manner, we were able to conduct our business in both ways—home and parlour. With the gradual success of my business, I was able to give money to my mother. I was also able to join a new *marup*. I bought gold rings for Ema. Ema was able to see and feel my success. But in the changing landscape of my life, Baba's happiness, was absent. I had my own money, I freely wore women's clothing at home. Ema had ceased to protest against my choice of dressing. But, in the midst of all this, Baba said one day, 'There is no place for you in this house. You will not have any share in my property.' I never forgot these words uttered by my father. In fact, I was not interested in any piece of land Baba may have intended to leave in my name. Rather, I wanted him to leave all the land in the name of my younger siblings, I wanted to buy my own property with my own earnings. I did not feud with my siblings on the issues of land and inheritance. I wanted to live in harmony and constructive dialogue with everyone in my surrounding. Unfortunately, my family could not appreciate my thoughts and needs. In moments of joy and sadness, in moments of discussion about family affairs and money, I could not participate, I was not considered a part of this family process.

Meanwhile, our clients kept increasing and we began to establish contacts with a few influential people. We were hired for bridal make-up for both the bride and the bridegroom. We were also hired to do the make-up for models in beauty contests and Man Hunts—a beauty contest for men. Alongside the parlour, we also tried to make the Seven Sisters more professional—getting printed recipts for our fees and announcing of our shows in the newspaper. The Seven Sisters became more popular, and more dignified as a group. The members also began to wear make-up openly in public. Jenny had changed in the manner she wore make-up, she was becoming more open like me. The hatred and disgust with which people looked upon me when I walked in the street in the clothes I desired and the make-up I loved had reduced by a noticeable degree.

Around the time Jenny and I were becoming popular, an interesting development happened. The screening of Hindi language films was totally banned in Manipur. The barber shops run by Mayangs were banned and shut down. The background music for the Seven Sisters performances was replaced by the Manipuri language songs. Attempts were being made to replace the usage of Bengali script with the Meitei Mayek script. Every public signboard had to carry the signs in the Meitei Mayek script above the other languages. All these bans finally led to the wave of digital video albums in Manipur. More men started visiting our parlour for haircuts, since the barber shops had drastically reduced in number after the shutting down of Mayang shops.

Romesh, a model I had worked with for Man Hunt, secured the title of Most Photogenic. Right after this event, Romesh was approached by Kaka Muhindro from KAMS, a digital video production company, to act in a song by Ranbir Thouna. I also approached Romesh to be his make-up artist free of charge, my only request was that he would bear the cost of buying the make-up products. Kaka Muhindro and Romesh agreed. I had one more request which was that the name of the make-up artists was included in the credits of the video. This was also acceptable to Muhindro, and the name Sanjen appeared in the credits. I would have proudly watched the music video featuring Sanjen, but our family did not have a television set at that time.

Our second assignment was for an album called 'Tattana hangingi mapao' starring Kaiku and Prameshori. After the second venture, Sanjen's popularity soared. We got one order after another to do the make-up for album artistes, followed by orders for wedding make-up. The fees for a wedding was Rs 1000, and for an album, Rs 5000. We bargained hard for the fees for album make-up.

One day while I was watching television at Ta Amuba's house, the music video called 'Nungsibadi howbata ngairi' was showing on the television. Initially I was engaged for the make-up of this team, but I let Jenny continue with the assignment alone, the reason being my contract with another team. I pointed out to Ta Amuba that I was the original make-up artist for the song. But in the credit section of the music video, it was written 'Makeup by Jenny Khurai' instead of Sanjen. I was shocked to see it, it was hard to believe that Jenny had doublecrossed me. Anger and disappointment followed. The next day when she came to the parlour, I angrily confronted her. I said if she was so eager to work independently, she could do so. I could manage the album and wedding assignments on my own.

From that day on, Jenny did not come to the parlour. After a few days, a woman in my neighbourhood told me that Jenny would be opening a parlour. Jenny himself had said this to the woman. Shortly afterwards, Jenny and his elder sister came to my house. They proposed that Jenny and I must equally divide all the furniture and equipment in the parlour. I agreed. I took the carpet and the mirrors. Thus Jenny and I finally parted ways.

Jenny opened his own independent parlour at Lamlong and I continued to work at the parlour at home. Many young men sought me out to prepare them for Man Hunt, in addition to my popularity as a make-up artist for music albums. I was on good terms with Kaiku, Gokul and Romesh. My popularity increased and I had established contacts that would further my position in the business. I had lots of male friends at that time. These were not romantic or sexual relationships, but very close friendships.

People told me that drinking *yu* while working on make-up was not dignified behaviour, *yu* was not a sophisticated thing to consume in the professional space. So, I replaced *yu* with Spasmo-Proxyvon tablets. Spasmo-Proxyvon was a very strong painkiller—now banned because of its side effects and consumption abuse—but then it was freely available. It had the effect of making me feel very calm, active and positive. I stored boxes of these tablets in my room.

One evening, around 5 p.m. when I came home from work, Ema told me that Romen had visited me. She said that he was very eager to meet me. Ema looked anxious and advised me to visit him soon. I changed into fresh clothes and went to his paan dukan located outside JNIMS hospital. He was not wearing any make-up, nor had he shaved. He was wearing a red T-shirt. He was very happy to see me, we were meeting after a long time. He still called me 'Ebungo'. We sat together inside the paan dukan. He said he needed to talk with me on an important matter, and he wanted to hide the matter from his elder sister, Memcha. I was intrigued by the secrecy he contrived to maintain. I went out to see if Eche Memcha was around. She was nowhere to be seen, and so I came back and told Romen he could open his heart to me. I sat down beside him.

He cautiously touched my hand and said, 'Ebungo, let me tell you something, but you must not tell anyone.' I assured him that I would keep the matter secret from everyone. He held out his forearm and showed me the marks on his hand and then similar marks on his legs. I told him that the marks were not particularly noticeable. But he insisted that they were very deep, prominent marks. His anxiety and unusual manner that day made me think that there could be something very wrong with him. In order to convince me of the seriousness of the situation, he pulled his skin and showed me the red marks left when the skin was released. I told him that this was natural, especially with fair skin. I even pulled my own skin to show him that there was nothing to be worried about. But the red marks did not appear on my skin. Seeing that my skin was intact, he said, 'Do you see, nothing happens on your skin?'

I told him that there was nothing serious and he should consult a doctor to resolve the matter. He did not listen to my suggestion, instead it appeared that he wanted to tell me something more. He continued, 'It is said that Addy (his ex partner) used to use drugs. One woman from Kakwa, Addy's neighbour, told me about this, she also told me that Addy is sick now. People now say that Addy must be HIV positive. I am really concerned. What if the doctors tell me I am also positive?' Whenever Romen had anything of importance to share with people, he would talk non-stop, without being distracted by any other subject. So, I tried to take his mind off his problem by talking about other things, mainly anecdotes from the sets of the video albums, new techniques of make-up, and such-like. I told him I wanted to drink *yu* and eat fried chicken. He said, 'You can eat and drink. But I will not drink.'

Romen continued talking about his doubts even when he was frying the chicken. 'Ebungo, where should I go for the test? SASO or JNIMS?' he asked. It seemed that he was sometimes talking to himself. Consumed by the tension, his conversation was often distracted. He was also worried that other homos would come to know about his condition. His fear had taken such deep roots in his head that he did not even allow his nephews to come near him anymore. Meanwhile, I slowly sipped the *yu*. I firmly told him that he was not showing any signs of being HIV positive. I even said that there was no need for testing. 'You must not worry about this matter anymore,' I said firmly.

I did not know what new thoughts had come to his mind, he finally drank a glass of *yu* and then another glass and another. Ultimately, both of us got drunk. He started crying. Just then Eche Memcha came and asked what the matter was. I told Eche that he was just talking about Addy, and that had made him start crying. Then he turned to Eche Memcha, 'You must not leave me alone for a second. It would be better if I die and then you will live peacefully.' After sitting with him for sometime, I returned home.

When I reached home, Ghoben, a friend of mine was waiting for me outside the gate of our house. He asked me if I had any heegok, a codeword for Spasmo-Proxyvon tablets. I had only four tablets at that time. Four would not do, because he had not had any that day. He needed to buy a few more, so both of us headed to Thoubalkhong to buy enough supply of heegok.

The interiors of Thoubalkhong were very dark. We rode his bike inside a dimly lit lane and parked outside a shop. Ghoben asked me to wait outside by his bike. There were some men standing around in the lane. My attire, a halter top and a pair of bell-bottom pants, worried me. That kind of outfit usually attracted unwanted gaze from the onlookers. While I was building up imaginary fears in my mind, Ghoben returned. He started taking out some of the tablets but I urged him that we should first leave the place. At the very moment that we were starting the engine, the group of men came near us and asked us to stop. Rather than stopping, Ghoben speeded up his bike. As we sped away, they shouted behind us, 'This immoral couple is running away. Stop them!' Without looking back we rode till the bank of the Iril river. Once we were at a safe distance, we were able to calm down. Ghoben and I considered ourselves very lucky to have escaped. The effect of the SP tablets and the bike incident somehow truncated my worries about Romen.

Shortly after Jenny and I parted ways, the Seven Sisters also broke. The members began to invest in make-up and parlour ventures. Every new development seemed to be aligned with the consequences of the banning of the Hindi language films.

In 2003, I had a contract for make-up with one of the contestants in the beauty contest at GP Women's College. The girl was called Maya. She was the winner in the contest. She also participated in the Miss Manipur Contest the same year, and she insisted that I should prepare her for the contest. Unfortunately, the contest was cancelled due to some disagreements. The 2004 Miss Manipur Contest was organised by UMTC, and Maya won the second runner-up title. Maya's father was very happy with the result. He sponsored a Shumang Leela, that was performed at a ground near her house at Top Khongnangmakhong. I was felicitated at the beginning of the Shumang Leela.

Four days after my felicitation at Top, I heard the news of Romen's death. Ema broke the news to me. I asked her how he had died. Ema said he took his life by hanging himself at his house. My relatives did not seem to be saddened by Romen's death. Ema had a different concern, she directed her worries at me, 'Homos are immoral. This is the cause of their death. You are also becoming very thin. You also be careful.'

I was angered by Ema's unfeeling words at a moment that was very tragic for me. 'What bloody harm have homos done to anyone?' I said. While I was arguing with Ema, Kaiku came to take me to a shooting site, I was working as a make-up artist for him. I told Kaiku, 'Kaiku, please drop me at Porompat first. One of my relatives has died. You can carry my make-up kit to the shooting site. I will come a bit later.' Just as Kaiku and I were about to leave, the guy that usually brought SP tablets for me arrived to deliver my tablets. I asked Kaiku to drive ahead and wait for me there. I took the tablets from the guy without attracting Kaiku's notice.

When I reached Porompat, Romen's cremation had

already started. First, I went to his room and popped a few SP tablets and then I came out to the cremation site. The burning logs of wood assured me that he would not return again, I would never see him again. I cried a lot. After a short while the effect of the drug lifted all the pain and worries. I stopped crying. I asked one of his nephews to drive me to the shooting site.

I had become successful. My busy schedule took me to many shooting sites. I could no longer meet my close friends daily, in fact I became completely unaware of the events of their lives. A distance was inadvertently created between us. Sometimes I heard stories of their tribulations, but I was living a different life from theirs. While I earned money and become popular among people, their life had turned more dire than before. They were without a job, they drank more *yu* than before, and they had become older. Even when we met on the roadside, they avoided me. Their condition saddened me a lot.

One morning, I heard some people in my neighbourhood talking about somebody's suicide at Lamlong. The person had hanged himself from a big mango tree at Lainingthou ground. The deceased person was a homo and he killed himself because of a break up, they said. I was shocked when I learned the person's name—it was Maibi Macha. My friend had died, killed himself. Even at this painful moment, in which a person took his own life, people made the ugliest and the most unsympathetic comments! Why? because it was not just a man or woman that died, it was a homo. They said his life had been futile, nobody looked upon him with kindness, nobody was willing to mourn his death. I did not attend his cremation. It was my busy make-up schedule that kept me away from the final ritual. Later I met Ronu and enquired about Maibi Macha's death.

Ronu said Maibi Macha in fact had a very loving boyfriend and his death could not have been on account of a bad relationship. In fact it was the third time that he had tried to kill himself. How people perceived his death was just a fabrication. Love did not kill Maibi Macha.

At that time, the fact of my homo friends' deaths did not sadden me for long. Drugs and a busy schedule prevented me from missing their presence in my life. The money earned from working was good enough to rent a room for running a parlour. I had all the reasons under the sun to shift my parlour to the Lamlong Bazar. I had saved enough money, and some of my clients had reservations visiting me at my current location, my home. Besides my house was a little far off the road. A parlour had to be visible to everyone. At Lamlong Bazar, I found a room above the Puthem Printing Press. There were a few problems with the new space, it did not have a washroom, and the stairs leading to the room were in a very bad condition. The room itself was very small. However, that room was still better than my home. After repairing the room in a few months, I shifted my parlour to Lamlong Bazar.

But now my fortunes took a turn for the worse. My business began to rapidly decline. My drug abuse was taking its toll—there were changes in my physical appearance and Jenny too had started spreading false stories to people to damage my image. I was not able to give money to my family. In these circumstance, it was impossible to add new and attractive equipment to my parlour.

Jenny's parlour, located just across the road, was gaining popularity among the people. In fact, Jenny had become very successful. He was occupying an undisputed position in the market of the Manipuri digital film business. Many younger people were trained under him. In contrast, my condition was deteriorating. The youngsters who got trained under me also left my parlour immediately after the training. Most of them joined Jenny's parlour after leaving mine. Of course, people always follow the high and mighty. At home, I was questioned where I kept the money earned from the parlour and why I was not helping the family. Such questions were hurled at me on a daily basis. In order to avoid these questions, I did not eat meals at home. I began to eat my morning and night meals at a hotel at Lamlong Bazar.

I had become a drug addict, the drug being SP tablets. In addition to SP tablets, I had become a heavy drinker. Sometimes I took ganja, too. My worsening drug addiction was followed by a proportionate decline in my parlour business. There was no client left to visit my parlour. I spent my time inside the parlour reading Osho books, writing stories and poems.

My life had become very lonely. Wherever I turned, I did not see anybody that could be called my own people. The ratio of Jenny's and my earnings per day must be 1:5, Jenny earned five times the amount I earned in a day. I took refuge in the wisdom that others were reaping the harvest of their talent and hard work. Jenny could afford luxury—he bought a mobile phone and a car. Much like in the early days of my life, I was friendless, nobody came to meet me, except on the occasions when they needed to hear my opinions. Instead of harbouring resentment against them for coming to me only in times of their own needs, I was happy to see them and welcomed them with food and drink.

My health deteriorated. Other homos spread the rumour that I had AIDS. This rumour itself prevented people from visiting my parlour. Ema, who was visibly upset by my condition, often observed, 'What happened to you? You are still very young. Do not get discouraged, keep trying.' Ema's loving advice could not comfort me, on the contrary her advice angered me, and I took out my anger on her.

Two old chairs were the sole furniture left in my parlour. The cosmetic suppliers also did not show any interest in doing further business with me. They had a logic for withdrawing their investment from my parlour—since my business was declining, I would not be able to pay their money on time. They were right in sealing me off.

Despite all these troubling circumstances, there were a few people who trusted me and believed in the expertise of my hands. They stood by my side. However, nobody had a haircut on a daily basis. Make-up could never be compared with hunger. The disappearance of my name from the Manipuri film fraternity was a nail in the coffin. Nobody wanted to hire me or visit my parlour. But I kept on trying.

I stayed alone inside the parlour on those long days, without work, without clients. My mind was blank. The only therapy for my situation was reading Osho books and writing stories from my memory. I asked myself—what was the purpose of living? The world had turned so indifferent towards me. During my prosperous days, I never lacked for company; now that my prosperity had left me, everyone left me. All discontent and despondent thinking converged on one point—everything negative that had inflicted my life was because of the fact that I was a homo. In my weaker moments, I wanted to die. In moments of extreme pain, I wished to climb to a hilltop and cry out my pain—who was I? Parallel to the declining business, I was also losing my self-respect. Besides, our *engkhol*—our homestead—was being sold piece by piece, as Baba did not have enough money, and I was no longer contributing to the household. A considerable part of the property had been sold. Only the land in the immediate precincts of the house was left in our possession. Even in this state of poverty, Baba did not listen to anyone else other than my Eche and Ema. Whenever I said that we should not sell our *engkhol*, they argued with me. I was not allowed to take part in any decision-making in the family.

Eche never stopped consulting a certain old man in our neighbourhood. Whenever she consulted with him, a part of our *engkhol* was sure to be sold. One day when that old man visited our house, I threatened that he could not step inside our house. My tantrum worked and that fortunately prevented us from parting with our own *shumang*.

Right from early in the morning, creditors came to collect money from Eche Mubi. Eche Mubi had got into a relationship with a man from Kakching Khunou and he had cheated her in a business venture. Money was the only topic of their conversation. When I had asked for financial help from the family to open a parlour, Baba declined saying that there was no money in the family. However, he had the family *engkhol* to sell piece by piece, to pay of Eche Mubi's financial debt. The circumstances unfolding in my personal life and the grievous situation in my family made me distraught. What would befall my family in future? I did not think about myself because I was not going be married, but what about the future of my two younger brothers! My long-cherished dream for sex reassignment surgery was also fading away. But I had to live for others, I would not let others face the same suffering as mine. This commitment to the welfare of others was a life-sustaining medicine for my existence.

In 2008, many drug addicts in my neighbourhood died one by one. This helped me to make a decision to change my ways. The value of life began to dawn on me. I took a stand to quit drugs. I began to realise that my dependency on drugs had finally led to a form of abuse that had ruined my life to a great extent. My body and mind had become weak, drugs had deprived me of the slightest will to work. The SP tablets, initially used as light distraction, had taken hold of my life. This was no longer a harmless indulgence, it was becoming my weakness and ruination. This was a supreme form of bondage.

I thought of rehabilitation, it held out a new hope for me. But I was weighed down by another concern. If I were to go to the rehab centre, all other homos might get discredited on my account. I thought of another way to reorient myself in healthy ways. I consulted with Bobby who ran a pharmacy at Lamlong. He gave me tablets for sleeping, a vitamin syrup and a few other tablets for building body stamina. Following Bobby's advice, I gave up all the friends with whom I took drugs. I tried to eat my meals as early as possible and did not touch the SP tablets. On the second day of this self-monitored de-addiction, I was in severe pain. I had never experienced such pain in my life before. For four nights I clenched my teeth in the pillow. The only sound I heard was my own moaning. Diarrhoea and high fever worsened the pain my body felt. I was confined in my room for a week. I did not let anyone enter my sick room, only Ema could come and see me. For three nights, I woke up in the dead of the night, when everyone else was asleep, and walked around the *shumang* again and again. I thought this exercise would override my pain.

As a part of my new struggle to save my life, I left behind my old company. Even when they visited me, I hid inside the house. My behaviour must have appeared suspicious to my homo friends and acquaintances, they thought that I was still taking drugs. Only time, when I changed myself into a better human being, would tell them my struggle to transform my troublesome life. Meanwhile they continued to gossip about me. However, Sonia, a young homo friend who came from Moirang and had opened a beauty parlour at Chingmeirong Khongnag Ani Karak, was the only friend who didn't leave me alone. He was very happy to know that I had quit drugs. Sonia had always been a person who admired and appreciated my skills and talents. He would visit me after closing his parlour and shared stories and jokes that would make me laugh. He had a very good sense of humour and a comic way of interacting with people. He said he would take me to a maiba, to conduct devotional activities for me to get me out of my pain. Sonia was one among those people who I considered responsible for changing my life.

After successfully quitting drugs, I started writing articles. While some articles could be completed and published, some remained incomplete. I wrote stories related to my life. The Osho books helped me to conduct my daily life without tension, in addition to broadening my consciousness. My life improved after quitting drugs.

In 2010, Jotilal, who was previously a regular client of mine, visited my parlour. He always praised and encouraged me in whatever I did. Often after listening to my story, he used to tell me, 'Human beings are equal. Nobody is above another. One should not look down upon another.' He was a great believer in my talent and ability as a human being,

'Leishabi,'—he called me by this name—'it is your right. Never get discouraged. A person as talented as you should not get discouraged.' He was the only person who could engage in sane conversation over a glass of *yu*. At the time that he visited me, Jotilal was working with Da Babloo, who was a forerunner in the human rights movement in Manipur.

The day he visited me, I assumed that he was coming for a haircut. I duly prepared to give him a haircut. Smilingly, he said, 'Leishabi, I have not come for a haircut. I have come here to give you an invitation.' I asked if the invitation was for a dance show. He laughed aloud and said, 'Leishabi, your ideas and thoughts are one-tracked. Do I look like I am interested in dance and songs only? I have come here with an invitation to quench the rage inside you.'

The invitation was from Babloo. The mention of Da Babloo's name intrigued me. I thought very highly of Da Babloo, he came across as a kind-hearted man who was sensitive to the plight of others. I had actually thought of visiting him in moments of pain and suffering. The fact that he was known as Human Rights Babloo also influenced my impression of him. To know that a person of his standing wished to see me was a matter of privilege for me, as though I had actually touched heaven with the sleight of my hand.

I asked, 'How did he know of me?' Jotilal said that Da Babloo had seen one of my articles in the newspaper. I was disbelieving, but Jotilal said that it was really the case, 'It is true. I also told him that I know you in person.' Then he handed me the invitation card. I opened the envelope to see what was printed on the invitation, but I did not understand anything, except the information that there was going to be a big workshop on human rights, sponsored by one United Nations Human Rights Organisation.

I asked, 'What is United Nations? I will not able to say anything at the workshop.'

Jotilal said, 'You know who you are. So talk on those lines, and also learn to listen to what others say.'

I said, 'I don't have money to attend the workshop.'

He said, 'The organiser will bear all the expenses for you.'

Jotilal left after informing me about the time and venue of the workshop.

On Tuesday, the following week, I went to Da Babloo's house. I was very happy to see him, and very anxious at the same time. A few senior men were also present. We sat around a table. He asked if I knew about Section 377. I said I knew about it. I answered, 'Carnal intercourse.' He asked me what were the critical effects of Sec 377 in Manipur. Next, he asked me to narrate the story of my life. I narrated the difficult struggle of my life to everyone sitting around the table.

A few days after this meeting with Da Babloo, a meeting was organised as a part of the two-day program at NEHU University in Shillong. A team went to join the program. Da Babloo was the leader of the team. I was also a part of the team. At one of the lunches, Erengbam Arun, a senior journalist from Manipur, told me a story. He told me that during the times of the kings, feminine men were called *pheidas*. He also said that Bir Tikendarjit Park was a meeting place of the *pheidas*, and hence the place was called *pheidabung*.

I shared a room with Eche Nandu at Shillong. After coming back from the program I asked Eche Nandu about many English words. These were the words people used at the program. The program enlightened my understanding in many ways.

From that day onwards, I moved forward toward freedom. After some time I was made the Secretary of AMaNA (All Manipur Nupi Maanbi Association). I also worked with SAATHII (Solidarity and Action Against HIV Infection in India). I began to invest all my time and energy in the new path that I was increasingly very attracted to. I could not continue my parlour business. I started joining many human rights conferences and events. An awareness movement that was aimed against the usage of derogatory terms, such as Nupi Sabi/homo/B/*ngamarak shamarak* was becoming active in the Nupi Maanbi/homo community around that time. The term 'Nupi Maanbi' was increasingly being used, as the term 'Nupi Sabi' implied an impersonation for the sake of festivity. People often called us Nupi Sabis and did not believe in our womanhood. We are unlike the Nupi Sabis who act the role of women in leelas. It is important to let the society know that we are different and we have an identity that is not Nupi Sabi. The claim of Nupi Maanbis was to prove that homos, Bs, are the people to whom the male gender is assigned at birth but who are feminine in their innate or natural gender and expression. Nupi Maanbis need to be recognised as a different category of women. This has been my vocation ever since that day.

Epilogue

In 2010, it was as though everything happened all at once. I returned to Imphal from the Northeast Regional Consultation on the 2nd Universal Periodic Review. The consultation was followed by the formation of a state level coalition body of civil society organisations. The apex body was given the nomenclature of the Civil Society Coalition on Human Rights in Manipur and United Nations (CSCHR).

Meanwhile I was invited by the founder members of the All Manipur Nupi Maanbi Association (AMaNA) to attend the Annual General Body Meeting on 3rd October. The meeting was held at the SAATHI (Solidarity and Action Against HIV Infection in India) office in New Checkon, Singh Publicity Building. The agenda was to reshuffle the executive members of AMaNA and appoint new members. AMaNA was a state level apex body, and SAATHII was a national level organisation that served as AMaNA's parent body. More than thirty feminine males or Nupi Maanbis, participated in the election. However I was the only person wearing women's clothing. The others were all in men's clothing, looking very neat and tidy. A few of them had long hair but covered it with a cap. They were all from east and west Imphal, and we all knew each other.

The members had to select three individuals to stand for the position of Secretary of AMaNA. I was one of the chosen three. It was a very fair process and it was community oriented and this gave me the confidence to take part in the election. But I was completely ignorant about the rules and responsibilities of the organisation. I made up my mind that I would learn everything from the senior members in case I won. When all the votes were counted, I had got the maximum number, and was appointed Secretary.

That was a landmark moment for me. It was the moment when I felt like I had a responsibility from now on to protect and support the people of my own kind. This was when my life as an activist truly began. It was also a moment of pride and recognition of my existence by my own community.

That evening I threw a party at Ningol's vend which was located at Khurai Awang Kongpal. Most of the members attended the party. Bob and Ronu were also there. Dr Debabrata Roy, the convenor of the CSCHR at that time, also joined the party. Everyone was very excited about me taking up the secretarial position. Since Dr Roy was a senior activist and also a very community friendly person, I asked him to tell me what would be expected of me as Secretary. He told me I should be very good at managing people and know how to delegate work to the other members and he also said that integrity and transparency are the core values of a good secretary. The party went on till late at night. Dr Roy dropped me home in his blue car.

It was a time when there were frequent meetings and events conducted by the CSCHR. AMaNA was also a member of the coalition. These meetings and programs did help me to learn a lot about human rights issues that I had not known before. Through the CSCHR programs, I got the opportunity to go along with other senior activists and in this way I learnt the process of carrying out fact-finding missions, understanding victims and how to deal with different human rights situations. That was a time when I explored and studied issues that were internalised due to certain political reasons in the state. It helped me to understand how gender, vulnerability and marginalisation are related to the political instability in a state.

AMaNA's association with CSCHR has shaped my understanding of identity politics, oppression, geo politics and armed conflict. CSCHR provided a friendly space to me and allowed me to get involved in various UN procedures like the Universal Periodic Review and the Shadow Report. The Shadow Report was a United Nations initiative that allowed NGOs to supplement or present alternative information to reports that governments are required to submit under human rights treatise. AMaNA had been actively involved in many UN procedures and submitted reports to be incorporated in the collective UN reports.

One of the joys of my association with people at CSCHR was that they started addressing me by female names. Dr Debabrata call me Maipakpi, and it was Paonam Thoibi, a clinical psychologist who used to work at Dr Roy's trauma and healing section, who first addressed me as Echema—sister—publicly. The first time I heard her calling me this, I was in shock, because being called by a feminine form of address in public had not happened to me before. I thought it was just a joke but when someone addressed me as 'Dada' she rebuked them. Not only Thoibi, Eche Nandu, who was also a member of CSCHR, called me Abemma, girl. I loved being called by those names; it encouraged me to open up the woman that had been buried for a long time. The respectful tone they used when they called me by those names developed an emotional connection between us. Paonam Thoibi became one of my favourite sisters throughout my journey and Nandu was like a pillar of strength. These women never say 'no' to me, instead they always encourage me to take my own path.

After my election as Secretary, I started going to the AMaNA office. AMaNA shared office space with SAATHII, which provided support to AMaNA through training programs on community building, organisational development and other topics related to LGBTQI+ rights, gender and sexuality. I had bought a laptop but didn't know how to operate it. Reena, Savana, and Randhoni, who is now Associate Director, SAATHII Imphal, taught me how to use it. All these opportunities and collaborative efforts liberated me to become a voice for my community and people of Manipur.

As I got more involved in my work with AMaNA and CSHR, I was not able to go to my beauty parlour regularly. This was a time when beauty parlours run by Nupi Maanbis had become very popular in Khurai Lamlong bazar and other parts of Imphal and outside Imphal. Their business was booming. But my earnings had stopped completely, I was jobless. At that time, I didn't get any salary from AMaNA or SAATHII. My growing commitment to AMaNA and SAATHII and my desire to participate in the meetings and protests, pushed me to willingly face the financial challenges. Often, I didn't have the auto fare to go to the office or attend the programs. A young Nupi Maanbi called Naomi or Beauty Laishram which was her chosen name, also had a parlour at Khurai Lamlong bazar. Naomi addressed me as Da Santa, and was always very generous and loving towards me. She would give me Rs 20, 50, or sometimes even Rs 100 which I used for my travel expenses. Most people thought that because I held the position of Secretary in the organisation, I must be earning a huge amount of money. Naomi was the only one with whom I shared my truth and she has supported me until now in many ways, including my mental and emotional breakdowns.

I also used to get a sum of Rs 100 or 200 as my travel allowance for participating in the programs held by CSO and SAATHII. That was how I was somehow able to manage my auto fare from home to the SAATHII office and around Imphal. But I was extremely poor compared to my earlier life when I had regular earnings from my beauty parlour. I had to change my style of dressing drastically because of this financial crisis. I bought the cheapest cloth from second-hand markets to make my dresses. I had a white kurti with green embroidery around the neck which I wore at all big functions. I had bought it for Rs 30. That white kurti became my hallmark. But the beauty of the situation was that though I was poor in my outward appearance, my inner being was full of potential, courage and the spirit to sacrifice for the needs of others.

After associating with SAATHII, my awareness of gender and sexuality increased considerably. SAATHII used to conduct workshops regularly with the People Living with HIV (PLHIV) community. As an office bearer of AMaNA, I got the chance to participate in many SAATHII programs and events. During that time AMaNA was supported by American Jewish World Service through a project called Empower. One of AMaNA's founder members was working as a consultant in that project. His task was to take care of AMaNA's organisational development and he used to get a consultancy fee from SAATHII. Hence many of the programs were conducted under the banner of AMaNA and SAATHII and my active participation in those programs was compulsory. SAATHII and AMaNA also began conducting frequent Training of the Trainers (ToT) workshops in Imphal.

These programs introduced me to human gender and sexuality and I got to learn about various English terminologies like preferred gender pronoun (he, him and she, her), binary, non binary, non conforming, non normative and transgender in particular. For a very long time my understanding of transgender was a person like myself, a person assigned the male gender at birth but having feminine subjectivity and expression. The term trans man—that is, a person assigned the female gender at birth but having a male identity—was not known to me. The English gender pronoun was also very confusing for me while writing reports and other documents because Manipuri is a gender neutral language. In Manipuri, we don't have a gender pronoun, one common term—Ma— is used for both men and women. We identify men and women through their names, which are either masculine or feminine. I finally understood that if a transgender is a male aspiring to be a woman, then 'she' is the appropriate gender pronoun to use. This is how I started using 'she' for transgenders like myself.

In community spaces and gatherings, and in radio talk shows and local TV discussions, I started introducing the term 'transgender'. Gradually this term began to be widely used by the community members and also the rest of the people. Now, people who called us 'homo' began to be considered uncivilised and uneducated. The term 'transgender' became the acceptable term.

Through SAATHII's HIV intervention program, I was introduced to Manipur AIDS Control Society (MSACS). As a part of AMaNA advocacy activities and ties with MSACS, we received financial support to organise a Miss Transgender Beauty Contest. That was the first time I wrote a complete proposal with the help of Randhoni Lairiyengbam. She is a mentor and like a sister to me, a strong and dedicated woman who never discourages me from achieving what I want to do. With all the support around me I felt as if I had finally found the true people in my life. The beauty contest was upgraded to Northeast level from 2012 onwards and participants from different Northeast states contested in the pageant. That helped to spread AMaNA's name and visibility across Northeast India and expanded the transgender network in the region.

In 2012, SAATHII received funds from UNDF (United Nations Development Fund) and implemented a project called Agency for Socio Legal Protection (ASLP) for the Most at Risk Population (MARPs) community. Most at Risk Population includes Men Having Sex with Men (MSM), Transgender, Injecting Drug User (IDUs) and Female Sex Worker (FSW). It was a two-year pilot project. I worked as a consultant in this project. The project was led by Savana Yumnam and I got Rs 3,000 as my monthly consultancy fee, I received the total amount for three months every quarter. That was my first earning in my career as an activist. Randhoni suggested that I should save a certain amount from this money as a corpus fund for AMaNA development. I agreed to her suggestion and gave her Rs 3,000 each quarter from the Rs 9,000 that I received. She put that amount in a separate envelope and kept it in her official custody. When the project was officially closed after two years, she took out the brown envelope from a steel almirah and handed it over to me. The next day, I went with an executive member of AMaNA to the Manipur Women's Cooperative Society Bank and deposited Rs 30,000 which was a long-pending amount that we had to pay to get AMaNA legally registered. AMaNA got its legal certificate of registration on 8th October, 2012.

Side by side, I was also appointed as a Community Advisory Board member under SAATHII's Pehchan project. It was an unpaid position carrying big responsibilities like monitoring the project and steering it to make it more effective and community friendly. That project allowed me to associate with SAATHII's staff based in Kolkata and my network started expanding outside the state.

From time to time AMaNA started getting small grants from foreign funders through SAATHII. In the process I got to know Dr Ramakrishnan (Ramki), Vice President, SAATHII, and Pawan Dhall, Founder, Varta Trust. Both of them were very wise and noble persons. More than colleagues, they were like friends and Dr Ramki in particular was a father figure to me. He supported me in so many aspects in my life starting from family and relationship issues to how to apply for grants.

These were times when the Sec 377 movement was intense across the nation and there were many programs to mobilise and educate the LGBTQI+ community to strengthen the movement. However when I looked at the Manipur scenario, it was quite irrelevant to actually do advocacy with the state to support the movement. In Manipur no transgender has ever had a case lodged against him or her under Sec 377, which applies to same sex sexual conduct or relationships. The problems that transgenders face in Manipur are always related to transphobic and transgender hate attacks. In our interactions with the transgender community members, they shared stories of being shunned by their families, social bullying and atrocities by the police and central forces. There were also several violations meted out to transgenders by civilian men and social and cultural organisations, the so-called moral brigade. These cases could not be dealt with under the existing laws as the laws favour heterosexual people only. If we demand justice as citizens of the country, the nature of violence meted out to us doesn't come under the ambit of the existing law. The law demands evidence to prove and validate the violence or the crisis and in most cases, it is difficult for us to provide such evidence, when the person or persons inflicting the violence are members of the police or armed forces, and if they are civilians, no one will come out in our support. These cases cannot be argued under Sec 377 which applies only to sexual conduct. The nature of the violence faced by transgender people in the many different states of the Northeast is completely based on gender expression, not sexuality. It is more like a masculinity project to claim social authority by heterosexual men. In such cases there is no fair avenue to start a discourse around gender and sexuality. If such conversations did happen, people were unable to digest the subject of the discourse.

The other reality is Manipur is a highly militarized zone with excessive forces from both the state and the Centre. In such a situation, it is more risky to scale up awareness around Sec 377 because there are higher possibilities to use Sec 377 and torture the community. Hence the issues faced by the transgender community in Manipur are quite complex and multi-dimensional.

On the other hand the transgender and queer national movement which followed a national standard framework as under PAN India (Presence Across Nations) created tensions within the LGBTQI+ community and spaces. The LGBTQI+ is a diverse community which cannot be homogenised. For instance, in the common perception, especially in north India, hijras represent transgenders, and many marginalised communities are overshadowed by the hijra cultural identity and hence fail to get proper recognition and representation in national and international forums. Northeast queer and trans people have remarkably low representation in the national movement. Hence in any decision-making processes related to queer and transgender rights, Northeast realities have been completely annihilated. And I also experienced that within the transgender and queer community, there has always been a numbers game where the majority gets more privileges and the minority struggle for recognition from the same community and also from the state.

For instance, the 2014 Supreme Court NALSA (National Legal Services Authority) judgement is considered as the most progressive judgement in the history of gender equality. This was the judgement that led to the recognition of transgender people as the 'third gender' and stated that the fundamental rights granted to all citizens under the Constitution of India, would be equally applicable to them. It also said that transgenders would have the right to choose their own identity as male or female. However, the judgement failed to mention Nupi Maanbi (trans women), Nupa Maanba (trans men) and other native terms of the Northeast in the judgement. This is one example among many other untold realities that I being a transgender person from Manipur faced when trying to advocate for a more democratic and secular transgender and queer movement.

The way that Northeast transgender people are marginalised is also clearly seen within the transgender and queer space itself. The disparities in language, and the barriers created by our socio cultural background and geographical location, often make me feel left out and cornered in various big forums. There were times when I would be sitting like a statue and many Hindi and English-speaking people dominated the spaces and suppressed my confidence because of their attitude. For me it took time to understand a sentence whereas people from mainland India always have a well-organised community support system in those spaces like translators and interpreters. They always share common narratives and my story is sidelined because I come from a completely different linguistic and cultural belt that is difficult to accommodate in their understanding of gender, sexuality, law and violence. Hence when the meetings end the recommendations and decisions have always been dominated by the voices of the majority.

The conversation around equality at the national level included family, marriage and intimacy. The roots of the discussion were mostly based on personal experiences of the mainland realities. Hence my understanding was quite different from the rest of the people. Even though I tried to share the socio cultural aspects of Manipur, other mainland Indians were not able to understand or appreciate it. My participation in those spaces made me question what is a transgender and queer safe space, what should it be and how should it function. The whole idea of 'equity, inclusion and diversity' is a beautifully crafted concept to decorate the dictionary. In reality it is a fine cosmetic that covers the power and control that the privileged have over underprivileged people for the sake of showing off their fake humanity.

These painful realities opened my eyes to look at things critically. In my experience there are many divisions in the trans and queer movement in India, and sabotage happens based on caste, racial identity and socio political privileges. In my view, the movement has somehow failed to find a democratic way of liberating marginalised communities, like the trans and queer people of the Northeast.

In the course of my journey to understand marginalisation from my own experiences, I found that my gender identity and expression is just a fragment of my overall identity. My native (Northeast) identity and culture was the main reason why I was not welcomed in many transgender and queer spaces outside the Northeast region. And I concluded that the political realities related to my racial identity was one reason why my presence was not always respected in those spaces. The conflict also lies between the native understanding of gender and transness and the international standard of gender equality awareness. In the national trans and queer movement, the mainstream issues dominated and colonised the gender realities of the Northeast and Manipur in particular.

My work at the state level was again another challenge. I used to look after the Churanchandpur and Senapati districts. These are districts dominated by hill tribes. Senapati is a Kuki and Naga inhabited area and at the time of community reaching out, I was not able to go and meet either Kukis or Nagas. I always feared that if the Kuki people saw me meeting Nagas, I would get attacked and vice versa. On the other hand these districts are Christian dominated areas, where the trans people are not able to come out in family and society. Hence most of them have come down to Imphal and work in Meitei Nupi Maanbi-run beauty parlours. Staying in Imphal provided them a sense of freedom and safety to live in the way they wanted to.

The other factor that made it difficult to reach out to the hill community was that the tribal society is controlled by armed militant groups. The experience has inspired me to write a piece based on a true story of a transgender person from Senapati. I titled it 'The distant dream'. The story was about her dream to live openly as a woman. Her story ended with insult and torture. She was publicly paraded and her head was shaved. Since then she has become an alcoholic and is now mentally impaired. In my last visit she didn't recognise me. However due to various political reasons, the story has not been published.

Meanwhile I kept trying to scale up awareness of Nupi Maanbis at the local, domestic and international level. I wanted to do research and document stories of people in both the written and the visual medium. I felt that if my representation and leadership was not counted at the national level, then I was not delivering justice to the Nupi Maanbis, who are historically margnisalised, misrepresented and oppressed. The challenges were humungous. I didn't have the resources to take up the research, especially manpower and finance. I started reaching out to people who were willing to support me in the venture. In 2014 I met a photographer, a man from Imphal. I approached him and requested him for support in my first Nupa Maibi project. The project was to make a documentary movie on the transgender shamans. The man had all the equipment and I provided the research and ideas. That was how we collaborated and came out with the documentary movie *The Unheard Voice*. It was screened at a few queer film festivals but the man cheated me and dragged me into a legal dispute. He had stolen the copyrights from me and he later on edited the documentary and got a national award.

I did not lose hope because that film was like sharing just a tiny piece of my knowledge, even though I was not able to claim it as mine. That man would not have been able to produce such a film without me, and in fact it was the first and last documentary he made.

In 2014, there was a program in Thailand to which I was invited. I didn't have a passport, but I had to go to Guwahati for a program, and in that trip, I went to the regional passport office to get my passport. My documents kept being passed from one counter to another. The passport officers sitting at the counters would look at the documents and then look at me. The reason was that I was applying for a female passport. The way that the staff kept staring at me made me feel really uncomfortable. I asked at one counter who was the head of the department, and the man pointed me to a room at the back of the hall. I went in there and showed my documents. The lady officer checked my documents and then she looked up at me and asked me if I was a woman. The question was embarrassing as there were other people in the room who were all looking at me. I felt nervous and ashamed but I didn't lose my courage and replied, yes, I am a woman.

Then the lady officer asked, why do you have shaving marks on your face? I started explaining about transgender expression and so on, but she was not convinced. Then I produced the Supreme Court NALSA judgement documents and showed her the self-determination section that gave trans people the right to choose their own identity as male or female. But she was not concerned about the judgement. Instead she asked me to produce a Sex Reassignment Surgery certificate. The arguments went on like this for almost two hours. Eventually the lady suggested that she could help me if I ticked the transgender column in the forms. I didn't want to do this but travelling to Guwahati from Imphal meant a lot of effort and money. And I had to travel to Thailand in time for the program. So unwillingly I accepted her suggestion and applied for a transgender passport.

Shaming and insult were always a regular experience for me. I took every insult as a new learning, every rejection as a strength. That day's insult helped me to understand the gap between the ground reality and the laws passed by the courts. Such incidents shaped and sharpened my tactics of advocacy and activism.

Around this time, I met Anindya Hajra from Kolkata. Anindya was leading a Netherland funded project that aimed to form a South Asia regional organisation for the LGBTQI+ community. I was appointed as a steering committee member for Northeast India. Through that project I started travelling outside the country and learnt the human rights documentation process. It also provided me a deeper understanding about the intersectionality of LGBTQI+ identities. I was very keen to learn new things and improve my knowledge about international human rights laws like the Yokgyakarta principle. (This principle says that the preamble of the Universal Declaration of Human Rights issued on 10th December 1948 by the United Nations should be applied to the LGBTQI+ community to advance and promote our rights.)

Time flies like an arrow. I did not even realise how much time had passed since I became actively involved in the transgender movement. Apart from SAATHII's consultancy job, I took AMaNA to another level of advocacy. I started advocating for a transgender inclusive policy and program in different states of the Northeast, reinforcing the implementation of the Supreme Court NALSA judgement in Meghalaya, Assam, Nagaland, Mizoram and Arunachal Pradesh. Since 2014, I started organising sensitisation and awareness events with the support and guidance of AMaNA and SAATHII. I had frequent meetings with various government stakeholders in the different states of the Northeast. In 2014 Empowering Trans Ability (ETA) was formed under the banner of AMaNA and SAATHII. Soon it was legally registered and became a formal group for bisexual women, trans men and women, and lesbians.

In 2015 a transgender sister from Australia connected with me on Facebook. Her name was Karen D Konyak and she was a linguist expert. She told me that she wanted to do research on Nupa Maibis. I committed to support her and she came to Manipur and stayed at my home for six months. I helped her to meet with traditional scholars and Nupa Maibis. I also helped her in the process of translating the archive language used by the Nupa Maibis into modern Manipuri language. The modern Manipuri language was again translated into English. It was a labour of love.

This was also the time that I started my hormone replacement therapy (HRT). I talked to Karen about the cost of having sex reassignment surgery, and the roadblock I faced of not having the money. She suggested that she could do a crowd funding on my behalf in Australia. Karen assured me that if we did not collect the amount required during her stay, then she would contribute the rest from her own pocket. The amount I needed was Rs 5 lakh.

Six months went by with a lot of happiness and joy. Till

the last month of Karen's stay, the fund had not reached five lakhs. Then, on 6th December, which was my birthday, I went to office while Karen was at home working. When I reached office she phoned me and told me to check my bank account. I hurriedly went down and checked my account at the ATM. An amount of five lakhs had been transferred to my account. That surprise took my breath away, at the same time I was very emotional. When I returned home, I asked Karen to drink Sekmai, a local brew, with me. We sat in the courtyard happily laughing, full of hope and joy and drank together. After few days Karen left Manipur. We still communicate through Facebook and WhatsApp.

In the cultural revivalism movement in Manipur, Nupi Maanbis are constantly targeted. The community is blamed and shamed by different militant groups and cultural organisations who claim to preserve and protect the Meitei Sanamahi religion. In December 2017, a Nupi Maanbi held a birthday celebration in Lamlai, a village to the north of Imphal East District. She organised a local concert to mark her birthday. In the concert some Nupi Maanbis were dancing in the rain. The scene was video recorded by some unknown men and posted on Facebook the next day. It went viral and on the same day a press note was released by one of these militant groups stating that Nupi Maanbis should not be seen in public wearing female clothing. It further stated that if the community ignored the warning they would receive severe punishment. The news shook the entire Nupi Maanbi community across the state. They came to me seeking help. We had a series of meetings and discussed how to respond to that statement.

The community meeting was followed by another meeting with CSCHR senior activists. The final resolution we came up with was to respond through a press release condemning the statement by the militant group. After the press release was sent out, I got a death threat from the organisation. I would get a threat call every night, warning me to step down from my position as Secretary. I was also threatened not to be seen in public.

After a few days, they left two bullets at the entrance of my house. Every night was a nightmare for me, I was angry, fearful and depressed. Before this, members of the community would visit me but after I got the death threat, they stopped coming. I thought of leaving Manipur but then I thought, why should I leave when I have done nothing wrong. Everyday I used to call Randhoni, Dr Ramki and Biswa Bhushan Pattaniak of SAATHII. Talking to them helped me to calm down and escape from the trauma for some time.

Eche Nandu, Thoibi and Sonia Nepram would call me frequently and console me. Sonia Nepram used to visit me regularly and told me not to lose hope and courage. At the same time, many heterosexual women began protesting against the moral policing by the so-called cultural organisations. Many women's groups started calling for a sit-in protest against the misogynist acts of these organisations. In their protests, my issue was also addressed, and that was how eventually the situation was brought under control. But it led me to a severe mental breakdown and clinical depression. I started taking sleeping pills regularly and talking to Paonam Thoibi who is a clinical psychologist. Time went on, and more responsibilities came my way. I had to start working again—people like me cannot afford to be depressed, not just because of our responsibilities to the community, but for economic reasons. I had to support myself and other family members who were dependent on me. By this time, I was working as a consultant under SAATHII and getting a consultancy fee. At last I had a regular income and I could not afford to lose it.

In 2018 I decided to have my sex reassignment surgery. The road to becoming a woman had been a long one—first HRT, then breast augmentation and bottom sculpting. The penile inversion surgery was the final step.

At that time, I was in a live-in relationship with Riyaz ud din Khan, a heterosexual man from Lakhimpur in Assam. I had met him at a hotel in Dimapur while I was working in Nagaland. After we had known each other for a few months, both of us committed to the relationship. Riyaz came with me to Imphal in 2017 and we lived together in a small room in the front part of my family house in Khurai. But my family members did not approve of the relationship and so we moved out after a few months. Riyaz first took me to his village where we had a nikah ceremony. It was a very conservative Muslim society and I was always afraid of a transphobic attack. But Riyaz guided me and made sure I didn't come to any harm. He told me to always cover my head and neck. It was a challenge to tone down my voice and sound more feminine. But he told his family that my voice was hoarse because I had caught a cold on the long journey.

In the beginning, my journey with Riyaz was like a fairytale. We stayed at his house for three days and then returned to Imphal. When we came back, we rented a room at Pangal Leirak, a neighbourhood that lay to the east of my family house.

Riyaz knew that I had planned to have the surgery and that I would be leaving soon. The dilemma was how he was going to stay in Imphal without me. Riyaz could not speak Manipuri and moreover, everyone tagged him as '*homo gi mawa*', homo's husband. Luckily, he did not know the meaning of 'homo'. Then Riyaz got a contract for building construction work in Mao, on the Manipur-Nagaland border. It worked to our advantage and we both came to a mutual understanding that he would go to Mao, while I went for my surgery.

I had started making enquiries at hospitals and clinics outside Manipur, to find out where I could get good medical care at the most reasonable cost. In the process, I reached out to non Manipuri community friends from other states. Gee Semmalar, a transgender brother from Bangalore, helped me to connect with a transgender doctor, Dr Sameera who worked at the Mahatma Gandhi Medical College and Research Institute, Pondicherry. After corresponding with her, I went to Pondicherry via Bangalore. I travelled alone to Pondicherry by night bus, with just a suitcase with a few clothes, some cash and my debit card. The money I had was very limited and I had to stay in the city for quite a long time. Hence I sought help from Father Thomas, a member of the National Council of Churches of India (NCCI), who provided me a shelter for my stay. NCCI also donated a sum of money to support my surgery.

The caretaker of the shelter was an elderly woman. The entire family lived in a small hut-like house just next to the main building. The lady had a daughter, a small baby girl who had just started learning to walk. I was not able to communicate with them because of the language barrier. Even so, within that short period of time, we grew very attached to one another. I called the elderly woman

'Amma'. The baby girl wanted to be with me all the time and followed me everywhere. Amma asked me a lot of questions, which I was unable to understand. But I could follow that she was asking me where I was from, who were my people, what food did I eat. I tried my level best to answer her, but I was not sure if she understood me clearly. But I had a good time with the family and thanks to them I didn't feel alone.

From here, I had to go to the hospital for my pre-medical check up and examination. Dr Sameera advised me to contact Sheetal, a transgender woman who took care of all the SRS related formalities. I visited her chamber and completed all the formalities with her help. Sheetal asked me who had come with me. She was shocked when I told her I had come alone. I had thought that the nurses in the hospital would take care of me, but Sheetal informed me that I needed someone of my own too, as the nurses could not be by my side twenty-four hours. She told me not to worry and that she would arrange for two of her 'chelas' to take care of me.

Two days later, I was admitted to the hospital and had to undergo a daily examination for five days. On the seventh day, my surgery was done and my penis was removed. A vaginal canal was constructed from this. My genital parts were kept bandaged for ten days. On the tenth day the surgeon remove the bandage and a tube of soft rubber that had been inserted in the neo vaginal canal. After removing the bandage, the surgeon smiled and asked me, 'Are you happy, how do you feel?' I didn't respond to him, because I felt so light, it was like a huge mountain had been removed from inside me.

I failed to provide an answer to the surgeon because I was struggling to find the appropriate words to express my deepest feelings. It was the most peaceful and satisfying moment for me. I felt that the woman that had been buried inside me was alive and open like a tender flower.

Sheetal's four daughters took care of me while I was in the hospital. They called themselves Thiru Nangai—Tamil for trans women. They would take turns to spend the day and night with me. They would touch my feet and call me Amma, which allowed me to connect with them from the core of my heart. I realised then that language need not be a barrier if there is genuine respect for one another. I used to speak in English and those girls spoke Tamil, but our medium of communication was a sense of humour, trust, love and belongingness.

Luckily, I didn't have any complications after the surgery and was able to return to Manipur in a few days. Before I returned, I had communicated with Riyaz and planned how to take care of the post surgery procedures. We both decided to live with Borish, my eldest sister's son. My sister and her husband had left behind three children when they passed away—Borish and his two sisters, Anjali and Papli. I had looked after all three children financially until the two girls got married, and I regarded Borish as my adopted son. Borish and his sisters had supported my relationship with Riyaz. So on returning from Pondicherry, I went directly to Borish's house. It was an old ruined building with no proper amenities, on the eastern side of the national highway to Ukhrul, quite close to my family's house. Originally, it had been a big property, but one-third of the land had been sold to pay off debts.

At that time, I also had a project to be completed with a grant from the Sandbox Collective, Bangalore. With this grant, I made a documentary film, *NAWA—Spirit of Atey*. The story was based on a true story of a thirteen-year-old non-conforming child. The film was screened on various platforms and also bagged the best non-fiction award in the 2019-20 Northeast regional film festival held in Nagaland. I would like to acknowledge the people who supported me in that venture.

Every rainy season in Borish's house was a nightmare. The filthy drainage water would enter the rooms and we had to clear out the water many times in a day. The house stank of sewage and maggots. Riyaz was working as a labourer at a construction site. He told me that if I had any money, he could build a house for us. But my bank account was down to zero. Hence I started looking for options to get some financial support to build a small house in the courtyard of the ruined building. My first attempt was to apply for government housing because I had earlier spoken to Rangita Bali Waikhom, Deputy Commissioner, Imphal East, to provide housing under this scheme to a transgender. I submitted two applications, one for my friend Ningol, and one for me. The applications were approved and we received an amount of Rs 1.5 lakh each which would be paid to us in three instalments. Later I applied for a loan from Axis Bank, which was rejected because of my low income. Then Ramki suggested that I should get in touch with Harish Iyer, a Mumbai based gay activist who chaired the inclusion and diversity section in Axis Bank in Mumbai. He communicated with other Axis Bank staff in Mumbai and pushed the state branch to approve my application. But when the sanction came, the amount was too low, it was below Rs 1 lakh.

With that money Riyaz along with two local women labourers started the construction. As the money was not enough to build a house, I had to reach out to many friends and organisations. Ramki, Rashima Kwatra, Thoujal

Khuman, NCCI and Enamsi, a neighbour sister, all gave me money to complete the house.

My challenges during those days were not only the financial constraints but also the physical abuse that Riyaz had started inflicting on me. He started coming under a lot of negative influence from the neighbourhood. He was instigated by the people around that I was using him to build the house, and would throw him out once the building was completed. The other issue was that I was not able to give birth to a baby, even after the surgery and HRT. All this made Riyaz behave badly with me every day. I came to a point that I decided to leave Riyaz and just continue to live in the old building. My dreams to spend my life with the person I loved were completely destroyed by these negative influences. I told Riyaz to return to Assam several times and even blocked his contacts. But each time he would come back after two or three days and continue the construction. My mental state was such that I loved Riyaz but I also wanted him to go away from my life. I recognised the sacrifices he had made in marrying me, and his efforts to construct the house. But his atrocities on me were beyond tolerance.

The story of violence and hatred never ends, it is like a food for me. I feel like I die every day and I am born every day. A positive development makes me feel alive and each time there is an incidence of violence against me or my community, it pushes me to despair.

In 2019, on the night of 21st December, around 9.30 p.m., Riyaz and Borish went out to buy groceries. They came running back, looking terrified, and hid in the kitchen. I asked what had happened, and Borish told me our house was surrounded by police, and they were asking for me by name. I went out and saw a platoon of policemen in the courtyard. They were all men, and one of them asked me, 'Are you Santa?' I said yes, and they said they had got a complaint from the Chief Minister about something I had posted on Facebook against him. At first I did not understand what he meant, but one of them took out his mobile and showed me the post. I realised I had posted it the day before when I was in office. I described the Chief Minister as 'son of slave'. The post was related to his recommendation to the Center to extend AFSPA for six months in Manipur.

The reason I criticised the demand for extending AFSPA was because there had been no great good that Manipuris had received from the central forces that controlled our lives, only violence and loss of freedom. What the people of Manipur had received from them was civil unrest. The control had taken away people's freedom and bred anger and anxiety. Daily killings, curfew, arrests and rapes had become the norm in Manipur. In a society where there is violence, progress is slower. If AFSPA really protected the land and people of Manipur, then it would not be so regressive and violent. I believe that if people are allowed to live freely and without fear, then there will be less violence, and more progress. But the policemen did not listen to me. They forced me to make a public apology and delete the post. I counter-charged them for not having any woman officer with them when they came to my house. I again posted this incident on Facebook and the next day many journalists reached out to me and wrote about it.

I always yearned to have a peaceful life. But the struggle never ends, I continue to walk on a thorny road. Many a time I have felt isolated and lonely because I think critically and my thought process has always been very deep and serious. I recognise and appreciate the fact that

I am different. I have always been different because of my dedication to bring about an equal society and I am glad to have the ability to sacrifice my happiness and time for others.

Hence inspite of those trials and tribulations, I never thought of giving up raising my voice for the Northeast transgender and queer community. There was a need to respond to the unfounded claim of the cultural organisations that transgenders were not acceptable in Manipur society. I researched deeply into the subject to explore the native perspective of gender. My research revealed that in the erstwhile Manipuri society, there was acceptance of gender plurality. Nupi Maanbis, Nupi Saabis, Nupi Maibis and Nupa Maibis, all were accepted. The research was supported by the Astreae Lesbian Foundation and published by SAATHII and AMaNA, as a book titled *Pheida: Gender at Periphery*. The book was a turning point in the transgender movement in Manipur. It was distributed to stakeholders at different levels and also used at storytelling sessions within the community spaces at the district level. That book stood as factual evidence to counter the claim of the cultural organisations who claimed to uphold Meitei traditions. I also talked about the book on the local TV channel. A young scholar, Wangam Somorjit, helped me to upload the PDF on Google.

In 2012 February, I got a call from a Nupi Maanbi doctor, Beyonce Laishram. She worked at a private hospital, Shija Clinic, located at Langol in Imphal West. She said two other Nupi Maanbis had approached her at the hospital and told her that they were not being allowed to donate blood. It was an emergency, as their aunt was admitted in the hospital and needed blood. She went with them to the blood bank section and asked the doctor why the two Nupi Maanbis were barred from donating blood. The doctor, a woman, said in an insulting tone, 'You people cannot donate blood.' She produced the NACO guideline that stated this fact.

Beyonce called me and related the whole incident. She also shared the shame and disrespect she had encountered at the blood bank. Later, she WhatsApped me the NACO guideline.

I went through the guideline and it was clearly mentioned that MSM, Transgenders and Sex Workers are permanently banned from donating blood. The guideline shocked me. I called Jayna Kothari at the Centre for Policy and Research (CLPR) in Bangalore. I told her the story and discussed what could be done. I requested Jayna to help me file a writ petition in the Supreme Court.

Since that day we have had a series of discussions and have filed a case challenging the guideline. Unfortunately there has been only one hearing so far. However I still have hope and a positive feeling that one day the Supreme Court will hear the voice of the community and get the existing guideline knocked down. There will be a fair process in the blood donation guidelines whereby all people will be allowed to donate blood irrespective of their gender, sexual and professional identity and thus open doors to save the lives of others when we can.

Meanwhile COVID-19 broke out and along with the virus came the fear of transmission and death. The Nupi Maanbi community has always been the marginalised section of the population and has struggled with a lot of difficulties, with or without COVID. With the outbreak the community was further pushed back and isolated. Social distancing rendered many jobless wherever the work involved physical proximity. The Nupi Maanbi-run beauty parlours shut down, in an environment which has never been conducive to our growth, and many did not have the skill or resources to support themselves through the pandemic. There was mental upheaval in the form of anxiety, extreme sadness, the sense of loss and grieving.

Many of them reached out to me for support. The prolonged lockdown severely affected the community economy, but the state remained deaf and silent. Though the state failed to take care of them, it was my responsibility to take care of my own community. Hence I started reaching out to a few funders and sent emails to them. Some of them did come forward with funds but there was another difficulty. The recent Foreign Currency Regulation Act (FCRA) didn't allow transfer of money from overseas organisations to AMaNA's account. In case any local organisation was ready to act as a fiscal sponsor then I had to produce three different quotations from three different vendors having GST registration!

There was a complete lockdown and curfew in the state. Therefore it was not possible to get three different quotations from three different vendors. All the Marwari vendors were shut and they were the only community that had GST registration and proper documents. They dominated and controlled all the business in Imphal city. Only a few local smaller shops were open. These shops didn't have proper documents. The shops were also facing supply shortage due to the massive shutdown of Marwari vendors. I managed to connect with a Marwari guy from Paona Bazar and through his support, I was able to procure dry rations for the community. The funders transferred the money directly to the vendor's account and they then gave me the dry rations.

My neighbours and family members and a few Nupi Maanbis living nearby helped to pack the food kits. It was a time of curfew and so I was unable to reach the community members outside Imphal. I took support from the Chairperson, Manipur State Commission for Women. A Transgender Grievance Cell had been opened under the commission. She helped me with a flagpole vehicle and driver. That was how Bonita and I travelled to different districts of Manipur and conducted a mobile food distribution to the Nupi Maanbi and Nupa Maanba community. The Imphal community collected their food from my house. Throughout the COVID period, I was engaged in food distribution for Nupi Maanbi, Nupa Maanba and also to a few neighbours around my place and a few areas in Imphal West. Borish and I made home visits to deliver food to some community members who were sick and unable to come to my house or the food collection points.

We did get some support from NGOs in mainland India. The insensitivity that I saw in them, however, was that they rejected my request for funds for Ngari, fermented fish, which is a basic part of our daily diet. The Manipuris can live without edible oil but cannot survive without Ngari. The NGOs told me that if I wanted funds for food, I could replace Ngari with some other foodstuffs like flour and chickpeas. However, we eat rice, not flour. I realised that even in a time of crisis, a minority community, irrespective of gender and sexual identity, gets pushed into compromising their needs for the sake of survival.

Meanwhile, I had also applied for some fellowship programs and was selected by two of them. One was sponsored by the Asia Pacific Trans Network (APTN) and the other was sponsored by Rainbow Advocacy Program

(RAP), supported by RFSL, the Swedish Federation for Lesbian, Gay, Bisexual, Transgender, Queer and Intersex Rights, for which I was selected Fellow for 2021-22. Both the fellowships were intensive but it was a big opportunity to learn in depth about the UN system and mechanism. Through the second fellowship, RAP, I was allowed to deliver a statement on water and sanitation, representing the LGBTQI+ community from fourteen countries of the Global East and South. It was followed by another statement delivered on Rights of Indigenous People sponsored by ILGA (International Lesbian, Gay, Bisexual, Trans and Intersex Organisation).

Both the statements were delivered online. Hence there were non-stop rehearsals and brainstorming with various groups. The work helped me to free myself from the depressing COVID situation. It was a really fun community space where people from different countries shared their experience. It made me realise that the world is very small but at the same time very disconnected. That made me feel that such fellowships are important to make people get connected and understand the world through interaction.

The same year, the first South Asian queer anthology, *The World That Belongs To Us*, was published by HarperCollins. I contributed two poems, 'My Father', and 'Nupi Maanbi Thabal'. I got an email from the editor that my copy would be posted to me. A few days later, the postman delivered the copy of the anthology. I was overwhelmed with excitement and emotion. I asked the publishers to send me ten copies instead of my fee for the poems, and they did so.

Riyaz's violence against me continued. After a few years, the house was also completed, and the three of us moved in. I gave Riyaz a small room to the north side of the house. I hoped to help him open a small shop there.

Soon after, in winter, I was invited to Shimla for the UNMESHA International Literature Festival, an annual event held by the Sahitya Akademi. But as soon as I got there, I started getting calls from the neighbours back home, telling me that Riyaz was drunk and out of control. I also found that there were many standees where the photographs of all the trans and queer participants were displayed. Only my photograph was missing. When I approached the organisers, they paid no attention. I had been so excited when I was invited to the festival which was an opportunity for me to participate on such a big platform, but I could not enjoy even a moment of it.

When I got home, I found that Riyaz was drunk along with some other men from the neighbourhood, and the house was in shambles. It was then that I took the final decision to leave Riyaz. I had not had a peaceful moment in the new house. I thought, I cannot compromise my well-being for such a toxic relationship. I made a complaint to the Imphal East Women's police station. A Nupa Maanba (trans man), came with me to the police station. The next day, the police came and picked up Riyaz from the house. I completed all the formalities, and Riyaz was sent back to his hometown.

Yes, he has gone from my life and I am a free bird now. But the memories remain and come back to haunt me—the tender moments, our struggles together, the conversations. It is always easy to say 'time heals' but for how long can one carry the unseen pain of losing a love. It is a part of my life, I can pretend that everything is okay, but something triggers those memories every now and then. At times, I accept the pain as the beauty of transgender love because the relationship I had shared with Riyaz had nurtured my hopes for a happy married life. Very few transgender persons across the world are lucky enough to have a respectable relationship and married life. I also question why, when a transgender loves a person, it is similar to inviting violence, why does our love story always have a tragic ending?

In January 2023, the book, *Gaining Full Citizenship of Manipuri Indigenous Transgender* was published under the banner of AMaNA and SAATHII. In March, I went to Geneva as part of the RAP cohort. It was a physical meeting as a follow up to the online program. As Fellows of the RAP program, we were given intensive training and also educated on how to advocate for the LGBTQI+ community at the UN level. We were taken to the UN Palais des Nations, the UN office at Geneva, and shown every detail of the building. We were given the opportunity to meet the ambassadors from different countries and mock sessions were held with them to demonstrate and understand how the UN system worked. We were allowed to choose in what capacity we would take part in these mock sessions—as moderators, special reporters and so on. It was a practical session that helped us to learn and understand the UN procedures. The direct interaction made me feel empowered and inspired me to do more for the rights of queer and transgender people at the international level. It was ambitious, but I knew that with perseverance, hard work and confidence, it could be achieved.

I returned from Geneva and participated in the Delhi Sahitya Academy Literature Festival. After that I went to Jindal Global University along with Thoujal Khuman, a Nupa Maanba. Then I returned to Imphal and resumed office work.

After returning to Imphal, I had met a very calm, gentle and softspoken young transgender man, who always stood by my side in all I did. I began to have a close emotional attachment with him, it was difficult to express the kind of feeling I had for him. However, when I came back from Jindal University, my feelings for him grew deeper. I was in a dilemma—how could I fall in love with a trans man, was it possible and if so, what kind of relationship would it be? These questions kept buzzing in my head, I felt like I was drowning in my love for him, this unrequited crush. Then I decided to accept the feeling of loving him in whatever way, and stop myself from trying to reason it out. This is life, and love comes in different forms and every form is beautiful and should be cherished. It was a completely new experience to feel so deeply for someone that was not a conventional way of dating or romance. It was beyond friendship or a romantic and physical relationship, it was more a thirst to live life together and grow old together. Since then, I enjoy his company, and we engage in conversations about politics and issues that are completely non romantic. Yet every word is romantic to me. I have never expected anything from him and our relationship is free from demands and obligations.

I set him free doesn't mean, I am strong enough to
*   let him go*
I don't yearn the way I used to but I am sad inside
I laugh but the pain is deeper
I am more hurt now because I am more aware

*I am just controlling my mind not to make my heart
    cry anymore*
I don't want to make the last cry for a last lover
*I still love hearing him calling me Eche, sister, though
    sadness fills my heart*

The third of May 2023 gave a big blow to the peace
and integrity of Manipur. It was around 3.30 p.m. that
Facebook was flooded with the visual posts of houses
burning in Churachandpur district. In one post I saw a
middle-aged woman carrying one child on her back and two
children holding her hands and running for life. Behind her
fires were ablaze like a scene from a Hollywood war movie.
A voice was heard from the background calling *'Meitei echil
enao sa lakko, Meitei gi khun Kuki na tumna mei tharey,'*
meaning, *'Come Meitei brothers and sisters, Kukis have
burnt Meitei houses to the ground.'*

When I saw the woman and the children, I was in
shock. I went completely blank, trying to understand what
I was seeing. Meanwhile all the colleagues in the office
were telling one another to pack up and go home. I could
not move because I was overwhelmed by so many thoughts
and mixed emotions. One thing was very clear to me that
moment, that it was not people's houses that were burning,
Manipur was burning, Manipur that is home to so many
indigenous communities. Along with the houses, it was the
trust, belongingness and peace what were being destroyed.

In a while the internet was completely shut down and
people were not able to access further information. The
same evening there was largescale firing of guns, tear gas
and rubber bullets in different areas of Imphal and outside

Imphal. In the days that followed, Kuki houses in Imphal area were burnt by Meitei people.

My main worry in this situation was about the Kuki transgenders who lived in Imphal. Many of them worked at beauty parlours run by Meitei Nupi Maanbis. The other concern was the trans economy, which was just beginning to recover from the COVID 19 disaster. And I was deeply worried about Borish, who was working as a chef at Ellora Hotel, a three-star hotel at Moreh on the Myanmar border. Moreh is a Kuki-dominated area and the news reports all said that Meitei houses were burnt by the Kukis in the first two days of the conflict.

Since 3rd May, the burning of houses and killing of people by both communities continues. More than 70,000 people have been displaced and are taking shelter in 350-plus relief camps sponsored by the local communities. There has been not a single initiative coming from the government in terms of providing daily basic requirements to the inmates. The anger of both the communities, Kuki and Meitei, has grown so high and reached its zenith so that 'home' and 'peace' have lost their meaning. The silence of the state and central government has also intensified the anger and escalated violence.

The idea of home has been completely destroyed by the ongoing communal strife. The very idea of peace is poisoned, corrupted and polluted by the tensions of the people. And people in power are throwing tantrums against both the communities under the garb of restoring peace. Hence the victims and the innocent civilians of Manipur are left to deal with the situation alone. Maybe people have different ways of understanding home, peace and conflict. However, being a Nupi Maanbi activist my perspective towards these values comes from lifelong experiences, collective efforts, understanding, trust and belongingness. In our transgender society and culture these are the capitals that we have invested through solidarity, support and networking. The conflict has led many to leave their hometown and move to other big cities of mainland India. And a few of the transgenders who live at the relief camps expressed feelings of discomfort, loneliness and lack of privacy. The dilemma that many of us are going through while trying to adapt to a new environment which is considered to be a safe space needs to be looked at critically. The tension between the host (the relief camp organisers) and the guest (the Nupi Maanbi survivors), the socio cultural disparity between transgenders and heterosexual people which gives a lack of belongingness and understanding, is not taken into account.

My reflection on the ongoing conflict from my personal experiences is not from transgender specific narratives but the overall perspective on the devastation, which I wish to share with both the domestic and international audience who are the survivors and victims of such conflicts. The painful experiences had inspired me to document my reflection around this conflict. The degree of the pain might differ according to the nature of violence encountered by different people. But expressing the real pain through storytelling is one way to regain human hopes. It is a hope that will lead a way to rediscover the trust and belongingness that are washed away by anger and political influences. This is a call to humankind to reconnect and reunite humanity as a family and society. My desire is to present the invisible narratives of women, children and transgenders who suffer the most during such crises. Further to reestablish the very idea of home in a larger political context because this is a fundamental element in restoring peace.

To take a break from the traumatic situation, I left

Manipur and came to Thailand. But I was restless, thinking of my hometown and my dear people. Then I received a message on Facebook Messenger from Borish and my niece Jessia. They informed me that the police had visited my house. Some time back, in September 2023, I had called out the Social Welfare Department for the mismanagement of the transgender funds and program in a Facebook post. On account of this post, the department had sent the police to my house to enquire about my whereabouts and to arrest me. Hearing the news I was alarmed and started posting it on social media. Then many queer and transgender friends from different parts of the country and outside the country reached out to me. They supported me and shared my posts on their social media accounts. I returned to Imphal to face this new battle.

I got legal support from Rohin Bhatt who is a lawyer practicing in the Supreme Court. He helped me file a case in the court to quash the police summons. The good news came on 18th October when the Supreme Court ruled that no inquiry should be done. It also stated that no further cases should be registered against me in regard to the social media post. The court's judgement read, 'No further cases should be registered against the petitioner on the basis of posts made by her.'

So another battle has been won. And I live to fight another day.

Acknowledgements

I would like to thank:
Dipu Ningthoukhongjam for helping me in recollecting the dates and events and fact-checking; Dr L. Ramakrishnan, Vice President, SAATHII, for always being by my side as a father figure; Pawan Dhall, Founder, Varta Trust, for encouraging me to write; Sonia Nepram and Paonam Thoibi for lifting up my spirits whenever I felt completely low and hopeless; and Rubani Yumkhaibam for her tireless efforts to translate this work and make it a much better story.

I would also like to thank my publishers, Speaking Tiger, and my editor, Renuka Chatterjee.

FERN ROAD BOY
Angshu Dasgupta

When he was little, Orko thought that he was going to grow up to be exactly like his mother. After she disappears, he struggles with the realisation that he is a boy, and boys grow up to be men. He prays to Ma Lokhi to turn him into a girl, like his friend Urmi, but his wish is not granted. Then his father signs him up for football camp, and it is there that things begin to go horribly wrong...

Set in 1980s' Calcutta, *Fern Road Boy* is an extraordinary debut—a tender, moving and immersive story of a young boy's journey through conflict and confusion to self-realization and strength.